ALSO BY STEPHEN BATES

The Poisonous Solicitor
Royalty Inc.
Penny Loaves and Butter Cheap: Britain In 1846
The Poisoner
A Church at War
God's Own Country
1815: Regency Britain in the year of Waterloo
The Photographer's Boy
Asquith

First published in Great Britain in 2022

by Old Street Publishing Ltd
Notaries House, Exeter EX1 1AJ

www.oldstreetpublishing.co.uk

ISBN 978-1-910400-88-3
Ebook ISBN 978-1-910400-89-0

10 9 8 7 6 5 4 3 2 1

A CIP catalogue record for this title is available from
the British Library.

Printed and bound in Great Britain.

THE
SHORTEST HISTORY
of the
CROWN

Stephen Bates

*For Owen Edward Hurd,
my first grandson,
born 27th August 2019 and
Lyra Alice Hurd, my first
granddaughter, born 4th
January 2022*

CONTENTS

CONTENTS

INTRODUCTION

A Common Thread

For at least 1,500 years, since the mists swirling around the Dark Ages began to clear, the British Isles have had monarchical rulers. This book is concerned with the most famous and enduring of these: the kings and queens who governed England, and who came to preside over Wales, Scotland and, for centuries, over Ireland too.

The study of kings and queens may be unfashionable these days, but it is central to this country's history. For hundreds of years they were the central figures of the nation: the focus of its politics and society, consecrated by God, endorsed (or not) by the nobility, the arbiters of its arts and culture, the makers of its laws, the directors of its government and the leaders in its wars. If you go back far enough, their names are often virtually the only ones to survive from their times, recorded on their coinage, extolled in the chronicles. We know far more about their lives than those of the vast majority of their subjects.

This book seeks to answer questions about how and why the monarchy in these islands has endured and evolved, becoming one of the most popular and unifying institutions in 21st-century Britain. As twilight gathers around the long reign of Elizabeth II, questions about the monarchy, its character and survival will inevitably recur.

Monarchs Worldwide

Of the world's 195 countries, 42 are still monarchies, but the British monarchy remains the most famous, perhaps even in those countries with kings and queens of their own. As a legacy of empire, the British monarch is head of state to 15 countries beyond the United Kingdom, from Australia, New Zealand and Canada to a string of island states across the Caribbean and the Pacific. Yet despite its longevity, the British monarchy is not the oldest in the world.

Monarchical forms of government date back beyond the Christian era. If we date England's monarchy from Athelstan (924–939 AD), who brought almost the whole nation under his rule, then five countries claim older roots: Japan (660 BC), Cambodia (68 AD), Oman (751 AD), Morocco (788 AD) and Norway (872 AD), although dating monarchies is often problematic. Japan's first ruler, Jimmu, is acknowledged to be mythological, as is the foundation date of its monarchy. In Norway, meanwhile, Harold Fairhair established the basis of a unified kingdom in 872 AD, but on his death, it reverted to a patchwork of fiefdoms.

Although the executive powers and influence of its kings and queens have changed and diminished over the ages, in the past millennium England has been without a monarch for only eleven years and four months, during the Interregnum of Oliver Cromwell, which followed the deposition and beheading of Charles I in the mid-17th century. The Scots, Welsh and Irish had their own kings until their absorption into a British state – and Ireland only became a republic after gaining independence in the early 20th century. The history of these islands can be written through the tensions between their constituent parts. Over seven centuries, from the reign of King Canute in the mid-11th century to the defeat of Bonnie Prince Charlie in 1746, only three monarchs escaped conflict with the Scots. In addition, monarchs had to contend with other sources of power and influence within the kingdom: with regional power brokers and barons, with the Church, then with Parliament and more recently with a largely unaccountable media.

The British monarchy has survived and thrived due to its flexibility, its eventual willingness to share and then cede executive power, and also because, for most of its existence, it has presided over a relatively stable, homogeneous society. Britain is a relatively small, narrow island with long-established transport routes and no insuperable geographic barriers: its mountains are low, its rivers navigable. Surrounded by turbulent seas, it has also been insulated from invasion. Shakespeare was right about that: 'This sceptred isle... this fortress built by Nature... against infection and the hand of war.'

For several centuries now, Britons have had a common language, a shared culture, a chiefly Christian identity and belief system, an enduring social framework, based first on land and latterly also on wealth, a common law and judicial framework (except in Scotland) and a stable political system. Unlike France, Germany or Russia, Britain has experienced neither the trauma of total defeat in war, nor of violent revolution.

The British monarchy has mirrored this stability. In the 200 years between the death of Richard the Lionheart in 1199 and the overthrow of Richard II in 1399, there were only six kings (two of whom were deposed and replaced without undermining the monarchical system). And in the two centuries since the death of George III, there have been just eight monarchs (with one, Edward VIII, lasting less than a year) including 63 years for Queen Victoria and longer for Elizabeth II. Even in the turbulent Middle Ages, Henry III, who succeeded at the age of nine, managed 56 years on the throne, and the otherworldly Henry VI ruled for nearly 40 years before finally being overthrown during the Wars of the Roses.

There have been good monarchs, bad monarchs, tyrannical monarchs, weak monarchs, mad monarchs, young monarchs, old monarchs, negligent monarchs, diligent monarchs, monarchs who have attempted, largely without success, to break the constitutional settlement, monarchs who have changed the religious order, monarchs who have attempted to usurp Parliament, monarchs who have been politically partisan, monarchs who have tried to annexe power, and monarchs who have been rapacious for money. But more than 330 years have passed since a monarch was ousted, more than 300 since one vetoed legislation and 180 years since one tried to change the government.

The 'Jubilympics Mug' of 2012, year of the Diamond Jubilee and the London Olympics.

Even as their powers and influence have waned, their image has become and remained ubiquitous, stamped on everything from coins to novelty mugs and tea-towels. Monarchs have had their heads depicted on the coinage for well over a thousand years. The royal coat of arms hangs above every courtroom with its admonitory motto: '*Dieu et Mon Droit*' – 'God and my right'; a host of officials from bishops to police officers and members of the Armed Forces swear loyalty to the sovereign and what she represents.

Each county has a royal representative in its lord lieutenant, just as the Anglo-Saxons had their ealdormen. Cabinet ministers inaugurated into the ancient office of the Privy Council, dating back at least 800 years, become the monarch's private advisors on matters of state, smartly-dressed men and women kissing the sovereign's hand and swearing an oath of loyalty just as their predecessors did in the medieval court. At one time Scotland and Ireland had their own privy councils, but Scotland's was abolished in 1707 following the Act of Union and Ireland's in 1922 after independence (the Great Council of all the peers of the realm has not been summoned since 1640). The words of the oath were only made public for the first time in 1998, but they are resonant with history:

> to be a true and faithful Servant unto the Queen's Majesty... [to] not know or understand of any manner of thing to be attempted, done, or spoken against Her Majesty's Person, Honour, Crown, or Dignity Royal... You will to your uttermost bear Faith and Allegiance unto the Queen's Majesty; and will assist and defend all Jurisdictions, Pre-eminences, and Authorities, granted to Her Majesty, and annexed to the Crown by Acts of Parliament, or otherwise, against all Foreign Princes, Persons, Prelates, States, or Potentates. And generally in all things you will do as a faithful and true Servant ought to do to Her Majesty. So help you God.

Across the world, dynasties have come and gone: the Bourbons of France, the Romanovs of Russia – too intransigent and extravagant – the Hohenzollerns of Germany, the Hapsburgs of Austria-Hungary, the Ottomans in Turkey – defeated in war – and the Qing in China – too reactionary. Despite a change of surname, however, the House of Windsor has sailed on, still one of the most respected, least challenged and best-known institutions in the country. It has achieved this by making modest concessions and strategic retreats, through a combination of good works, diligence and – usually – respectability, by staying attuned to the public mood, and, not least, by regular displays of ceremony and pageantry. In this it has followed the practice of kings and queens since time immemorial: showing themselves to their subjects – once curing scrofula by touch, latterly opening hospitals – and ensuring the succession of their heirs.

Queen Anne curing the young Samuel Johnson by touch

The monarchy and the Church have always been and continue to be inextricably bound together. Ever since the arrival of Augustine and his monks in Canterbury in 597, kings and queens have sought divine legitimacy and benediction, not just to ensure their personal salvation, but God's blessing on their reign. This has not prevented monarchs from falling out with the Church and its leaders: most famously, importantly and lastingly after Henry VIII sought the Pope's permission to divorce his first wife. Henry VIII may have got his way, but other kings have come off worse by challenging the Church's authority, as both Henry II and his son John discovered. Nevertheless, religion has served as an important bastion for the monarchy.

The old Whig interpretation of history – that, in Macaulay's famous words, 'the history of England is emphatically the history of progress' – is rightly no longer in fashion, but it has relevance to the evolution of the monarchy. Through power struggles with the nobility, with Church and Parliament, through constitutional settlements and relentless media scrutiny, the modern monarchy has emerged: reduced in its might and influence, but not in prestige. The line of succession may seem a tenuous one, but the story of how England – and Britain – got from there to here has a common thread of continuity.

CHAPTER 1

ANGLES, SAXONS, VIKINGS, CHIEFTAINS AND WARLORDS

Warrior-Chiefs to Crowned Kings

> I will be a gracious lord and a faithful observer of God's rights and just secular law.
>
> King Canute's Letter to the People of England, ca.1019

In the 650 years following the end of the Roman occupation of southern Britain early in the fifth century, a pattern of monarchical government developed. Warlords united, sometimes by agreement, sometimes by warfare, sometimes by marriage, first into regional statelet kingdoms, then gradually, from the reign of Athelstan in the 10th century, into a single English realm, the better to see off invaders and consolidate power. An embryonic administration developed, founded on local magnates giving conditional allegiance to the king and supplying him with troops and resources. If he was wise, he sought their advice and issued pledges of good government and law codes to regulate the behaviour of himself and his subjects.

With the last Roman garrison gone, and the Britons experiencing repeated raids from Germanic tribes, an appeal for help was sent to the Emperor Honorius. He responded by telling them to see to their own defences. How they did so in the coming century and a half remains obscure, as Saxons, Jutes and Angles crossed the English Channel and North Sea from northern Germany. If a native Briton King Arthur ever lived and fought against the invaders, it would have been during this period.

The best we have are archaeological remains, inscriptions and fragmentary, often unreliable texts written much later. Writing around 540, the Welsh (or Scottish, Irish, Cornish or Breton) monk Gildas bitterly denounced the barbarians forcing the Britons to move ever westwards, vigorously condemned the weak and brutal leadership of the British kings, and bewailed the shortcomings of the Church: 'What I have to deplore with tearful complaint is a general loss of good, a heaping up of bad'. His text *De Excidio Britanniae* (*On the Ruin of Britain*) was meant as a sermon, warning current rulers to repent. Despite its chronological inaccuracies and general lack of precision, it represents all the surviving contemporary written text that we have.

The Northumbrian monk Bede, writing nearly 200 years later and drawing some of his information from Gildas, mentions a king called Vortigern, who, rather than being invaded by Angles and Saxons, invited them over, to help repel Irish robber bands. These new arrivals were different: they stayed and settled, spreading across Kent into Wessex and from East Anglia to the Midlands.

Like their counterparts on the Continent, they were led by chieftains or kings: men who offered military leadership, protection and cohesion. Display – what these days might be called 'bling' – was an important way of demonstrating the power and influence these men wielded, both in life and afterwards.

Kingly Graves

The burial mounds of Sutton Hoo near Woodbridge on the Suffolk coast, first thoroughly excavated by archaeologists in the 1930s include the remains of a ship, alongside a great quantity of armour, metal work, engraved buckles, coins and ornamental items imported from continental Europe and the eastern Mediterranean. The ship burial was perhaps the tomb of King Raedwald, who died ca. 624 after a reign of 25 years, though no body has been found.

A similar but slightly earlier burial site at Prittlewell, near Southend was discovered in 2003, next to an Aldi supermarket. It may once have contained the remains of a member of the East Saxon royal family: possibly King Saeberht, who died in 616, or one of his relatives. The grave shows signs that the occupant was hedging his bets, spiritually speaking: small gold foil crosses, possibly once affixed over his eyes, within a coffin that, in line with pagan burial customs, included his most valued possessions.

The Sutton Hoo helmet was made from solid iron, covered in thin sheets of bronze into which assorted zoomorphic designs were impressed. It would have given substantial protection to its wearer, but the level of craftsmanship suggests that it had a symbolic function, more akin to a sovereign's crown than a soldier's kit.

Raedwald of Sutton Hoo was a contemporary of Aethelberht, the king of Kent, the local ruler who greeted the Italian monk Augustine and his colleagues sent by Pope Gregory on a conversion mission in 597. Their arrival at Canterbury cannot have come as a surprise to Aethelberht: he was married to a Merovingian – French – princess whose father, the king of Paris, had only permitted the marriage on condition that she was allowed to practice her Christian faith. She had even brought her own bishop along as chaplain. Pope Gregory himself wrote of 'a certain king of Kent', and Aethelberht clearly had links and influence across England as far north as the Humber, as well as on the Continent. This influence enabled Augustine to meet some regional Briton bishops at a gathering in the west of England.

The King converted to Christianity and according to Bede 10,000 of his subjects followed suit (clearly not an exact estimate, as he was writing over a century later). There were reversions to paganism by Raedwald and by Aethelberht's son Eadbald, but over the course of the seventh century, Christianity spread across the country. Missionaries set up monasteries and churches, rudimentary dioceses were established. Augustine became the first archbishop of Canterbury and kings glimpsed advantages in the new faith. Not only did it give them hope of eternal salvation, but it provided earthly legitimacy: their reigns were blessed and authenticated by God's chosen representatives. As Offa proclaimed in the eighth century: 'I Offa, by the divine controlling grace, king of the Mercians.' Dissidents and challengers – mere men – would think twice about confronting a monarch consecrated by God.

Kings could also use Church appointments to consolidate power. Offa wanted an Archbishop for Lichfield, in Mercia, rather than submitting to rule from the distant Archbishopric of Canterbury, in territory controlled by his enemies, and he lobbied successfully for this when Vatican representatives arrived at his court in 786. More generally, the Church provided learned men who could write and record events – often doing so in such a way as to flatter and lionize their royal patrons. With access to wider civilisations and customs, they could also help to frame laws, thus promoting obedience and stability. Towns started to coalesce around churches like Canterbury, York and Winchester, bringing craftsmen, shopkeepers and trade. A framework for communal living and commerce was gradually emerging.

A degree of religious uniformity had been established in 664 at the Synod of Whitby – presided over by the Northumbrian king Oswiu – which resolved the divisions between the Roman church and the Irish missionaries who had converted the north. The gathering brought Celtic practice into line with Rome, and with all singing from the same hymn sheet, the Church became a unifying force within England itself.

Strict hereditary principles did not apply to the choice of kings during this period. Although the new ruler was likely to come from the kin of his predecessor, it was not necessarily the eldest child who succeeded. Kings could nominate their successors, but their choice was not always accepted. The decision was taken by the leading nobles and churchmen, who assessed all the male descendants, including illegitimate sons such as Athelstan and William the Conqueror.

Ghosts Best Forgotten: Illegitimate Royalty

There have been royal bastards throughout history, although even back in 786, papal legates visiting the court of King Offa of Mercia decreed that to be legitimate, no king should be begotten through adultery or incest. That did not stop many English kings thereafter from fathering extra-marital offspring with their mistresses. The record holder is probably Henry I with 25, though Charles II ran him close with 20 ('Come hither you little bastard and speak to your father,' being one of his better-known quotes) while William IV had ten with his mistress, the actress Dorothea Jordan. Many were openly acknowledged or easily identifiable through the 'Fitz' attached to the front of their surnames and an identifying *bend sinister* (a leftward-leaning diagonal stripe) on their coat of arms. Few caused trouble to the succession, apart from Charles II's oldest, the Duke of Monmouth, executed in 1685 after attempting to usurp his uncle, James II (who had 13 illegitimate children of his own). Illegitimacy rates dropped steeply after William IV. Queen Victoria did not approve of 'ghosts best forgotten', though her son and heir Edward VII may have fathered at least one.

If two claimants had similar standing, the kingdom might be split, but generally a single, strong ruler was chosen from among the *athelings* – males of the Royal Family. Nor was it only kings who were powerful: their wives could be too, albeit behind the throne. Women such as King Alfred's daughter, Aethelflaed, Emma of Normandy and later William the Conqueror's wife Matilda were influential: William left Matilda in charge of affairs in Normandy when he invaded England. Royal marriages were increasingly strategic affairs, about expanding power bases and forging alliances as well as producing heirs – and they would be for centuries to come. The offspring of Elizabeth II were the first whose marital choices were not limited to the powerful county families of Britain or the royal houses of Europe.

By the end of the seventh century, local warlords were coalescing behind larger regional chiefs. England was still split between different tribes and kingdoms: Kent and Sussex occupied by the south Saxons, Wessex by the west Saxons, East Anglia by the east Saxons, Mercia by the middle Angles and north of the Humber (as the name suggests) was Northumbria – itself made up of the kingdoms of Deira (modern Yorkshire) and Bernicia, across the Scottish borders. Meanwhile, smaller local tribes, such as the Hwicce in Worcestershire, the Magonsaete in the Welsh borders and the Gewisse in the upper Thames valley were gradually being subsumed into the larger statelets, which were themselves constantly barging against each other.

TRIBES OF C7TH ENGLAND

GODODDIN

BERNICIA

RHEGED

DEIRA

ELMET

LINDSAY

GWYNNEDD

MERCIA

M. ANGLIA

E. ANGLIA

POWYS

MAGONSÆTE

HWICCE

DYFED

E. SEAXE

CANTIACI

W. SEAXE

S. SEAXE

DUMNONIA

MERCIA   Anglo-Saxon

POWYS   Celtic

King Offa (757–796)

> A certain vigorous king who terrified the neighbouring kings.
>
> Asser of Sherborne, 893

Prominent in this emerging patchwork of regional kingdoms was Mercia, a band of central England stretching from London to the Humber. For most of the eighth century it was ruled by just two men. Aethelbald's 41-year reign was succeeded by that of King Offa, who spent the years from 757 to 796 subduing local rulers and reducing their status to *ealdormen* – embryonic earls – who owed their lands, titles and loyalty to him. Offa also brought peace and employment: commanding thousands of men to build Offa's Dyke, a protective earthwork along the Welsh border, eight feet high and running for some sixty miles between the rivers Dee and Wye. The main towns of Mercia, like Hereford and Tamworth, were also fortified during Offa's reign.

Coins bearing Offa's image have been found across the Continent, indicating that commerce was flourishing. There was even a minor trade war with the great European ruler Charlemagne, after Offa grew too presumptuous in proposing reciprocal marriages for their children. Charlemagne addressed Offa in letters as 'dearest brother', but he also made the status difference clear: he was 'King of the Franks and Lombards and Patrician of the Romans'; Offa was just 'King of the Mercians'.

Attracted by the wealth of these Saxon kingdoms, marauders from Norway appeared – the first in 789, according to the *Anglo-Saxon Chronicle*. By the 830s, occasional plundering down the east coast had turned into annual incursions, after which Norwegian Vikings began settling down the west side of the British Isles in Ireland, Scotland, Wales and Cornwall.

In the 860s, Danish Vikings followed, as interested in conquest – in particular of England's plentiful good farmland – as in plunder. By 870 they had taken York, destroyed the kingdoms of East Anglia and Northumbria, and ruled over a great swathe of eastern England. The following year they camped at Reading, ready to take on Wessex, hitherto out of the firing line and thus – unlike East Anglia and Mercia – not yet overrun.

King Alfred the Great (849–899)

> I know nothing worse of a man than he should not know.
> Asser's *Life of King Alfred*, ca. 893

Lives were short in ninth-century Wessex, but even so Alfred the Great probably had low expectations of becoming king. It took three brothers to die in eleven years before the crown passed to the 22-year-old prince in 871, by which time the Danes were pushing ever westwards into his kingdom, which stretched from the Thames Valley into the West Country. The young King was forced to pay them off that spring, and he would be fighting intermittent attacks for the next quarter-century. The best-remembered of these, in 878, drove him into the Somerset marshes around Athelney.

Cakes or Fakes

According to legend, the fugitive king was sheltering in a swineherd's cottage near Athelney, and had been told to keep an eye on some bread rolls baking on the fire. Understandably distracted, he allowed them to burn and was scolded by the peasant's wife, who didn't know who he was. Alfred allegedly accepted the rebuke with humility – a rare and desirable trait in monarchs – and perhaps this is the authentic core of the story. The rest is almost certainly fiction: it went unrecorded for 200 years, until a chronicler dropped it into a biography of Alfred's Cornish contemporary, St Neot. It was subsequently repeated in an updated 16th-century version of Asser's *Life of King Alfred*, and a suspiciously similar legend also crops up in a 13th-century Viking saga.

King Alfred burns the cakes

Alfred didn't need legends to humanise him. He had a devoted contemporary biographer in the Welsh monk Asser, and his biography is the first to give a clear picture of a real, human king. Asser's original manuscript was destroyed by fire in 1731, so the work only survives in transcription, but it depicts a well-educated man – possibly groomed for an ecclesiastical career, since he was the youngest of four sons – who had met the Pope in Rome as a child, visiting the Carolingian king en route. Alfred was deeply devout and his own writings echo his many struggles, not just with his monarchical responsibilities, but with reconciling his faith with lust and personal conscience. He is the only English king known to have written a book before Henry VIII, 700 years later.

Alfred emerged from his exile on Athelney later in 878, mounting guerrilla attacks on the Danish army. After gathering local troops, he defeated the Vikings at Edington on the Wiltshire downs: one of English history's first great recorded victories. In the subsequent peace agreement, the Danish king Guthrum converted to Christianity (with Alfred as his godfather) and his army retreated to East Anglia. The victory persuaded the Vikings to lay off Wessex temporarily and convinced the Mercian king Aethelred to recognise Alfred as his overlord. Alfred's eldest daughter Aethelflaed married Aethelred, and Alfred entrusted him with the control of London. With the two kingdoms so powerfully enmeshed, Alfred began styling himself 'King of the Anglo-Saxons'.

The First Great Book

Our knowledge of the period comes primarily from the *Anglo-Saxon Chronicle*, a record stretching from the departure of the Romans to the establishment of Norman rule, which was updated annually by monks until the middle of the 12th century. It was begun at Alfred's instruction, perhaps by Bishop Asser, and certainly for propaganda purposes, to celebrate the King and his reign. Collating earlier monkish annals from the seventh century, it began by describing all the English, Christian, *Angelcynn* people who had submitted to Alfred's rule by 886. The *Chronicle* is remarkable for its authenticity and duration, but also for being composed almost entirely in dialects of Anglo-Saxon English, at a time when most records were in Latin. It has rightly been described by the historian G.C. Donald as 'the first national continuous history of a western nation in its own language... the first great book in English prose.'

By the mid-ninth century, the Danish raiders were settling across eastern England, farming, trading and inter-marrying with the local Anglo-Saxon population. The whole area east of the line running diagonally across England from the Mersey to the Thames – later known as the Danelaw – lived under Viking laws and customs. English kings would negotiate with this resident Viking presence warily, and sometimes bloodily.

Sea Conquerors

The Vikings have had a bad press from history, not least because their story was only reported by their enemies. It was Christian monks who could write, and they were the very people who suffered when their churches and monasteries were attacked by the pagan invaders. With no widespread written culture of their own, the Vikings remain a shadowy presence, glimpsed in the place names where they settled – the *-bys* and *-thorpes* marking their villages throughout northern and eastern England – and in what we can infer from the artefacts they left behind. They were skilled craftsmen, they traded across Europe into Central Asia, and their ships sailed as far west as Newfoundland. These expeditions no doubt brought vital intelligence back about the resources on offer, and the ease of getting hold of them. The Christian chroniclers vilify them as heathens, desecrators and violent pirates, but once they had conquered, many settled down and intermarried with locals to become farmers and traders.

Meanwhile back in Scandinavia, rival dynasties were emerging, as individual warlords accumulated wealth, influence and followers, then jockeyed with each other for more. Over time, institutions designed to promote stability among these squabbling elites were formed: for instance, the *Althing* in Iceland, the world's oldest functioning parliament, which was founded in 930 and gathered annually.

It is not hard to see how Alfred gained the allegiance of Wessex and Mercia. Victorious in battle, he was evidently an able defender of his subjects, and he was perceived to be a just king, whose rule promoted peace. In the 870s, he initiated a reform of the coinage, establishing its design, weight and value – and hence reliability – at mints across Wessex and in London. These coins were also circulated and accepted in Mercia.

In military terms, Alfred may not have been quite as great as the propaganda suggests. All those vessels named after the 'father of the Royal Navy' belied was not, in fact, the first Saxon king to prepare a fleet and see off the Vikings at sea. The *Chronicle* describes a King Aethelstan of Kent defeating a Viking force off the coast at Sandwich in 851. Similarly, the network of fortresses, constructed to ensure no settlement (*burh*) was more than 20 miles from protection, built on pre-existing structures and saw its most important development during the reign of Alfred's son, Edward the Elder. Alfred contributed significantly to the nation's defences, though, establishing a standing army made up of peasant levies (*fyrds*), half of which were battle-ready at any one time. This reduced the possibility of all the troops melting away at harvest-time and enabled the King to train and keep men in the field for longer. In 893, this new fighting machine faced down the Danes at various spots across England, forcing them to scatter east and west.

The levy system also ensured the patrol and upkeep of the fortresses: four men were assigned to every 16 feet of rampart and one man was to be supplied from each *hide* – the Anglo-Saxon measure of the amount of land needed to support a family, reckoned at 30 acres. These reforms laid the ground for a more permanent defence system: a considerable feat of organisation for an early medieval monarch.

Alfred also issued a new legal code, derived in part from the previous laws of Wessex and Mercia, but more importantly drawing on Christian doctrine – citing Moses and the Church Fathers to legitimise both his rule and the laws themselves. This was a significant step for English monarchy: submission to laws derived from Scripture implied submission to the Church, and this in turn gave the Church power it could use against monarchs.

Alfred's laws were not ground-breaking – for the most part, they tried to limit the blood feuds that had riven Anglo-Saxon society prior to his rule, and to protect the weak from oppression – but his code pointedly began by stating, 'It is most needful that every man most warily keep his oath and his *wed* (pledge).' It expressed a notion of a society bound at all levels by a contract of loyalty: masters and servants, peasants and lords, kings and subjects.

Alfred's administrative changes could not have worked without literacy, and few kings ever placed more emphasis on learning. Alfred wrote in 894 that not a single cleric in Wessex understood the Latin used in daily worship, or could translate a letter from Latin into English. He recruited scholars, monks and clerics to do just that. Asser – one of those scholars – says Alfred threatened to sack officials who 'neglected the study and application of wisdom,' adding that almost all his ealdormen and thegns 'who were illiterate... applied themselves in an amazing way to learning how to read, preferring to learn this discipline than... relinquish their offices.' The King translated some religious books himself, such as Boethius's *The Consolation of Philosophy*, and commissioned scholars to translate other 'works men most needed to know'. All this would have been an achievement for any monarch. That such ambitious reforms were carried out under continuing threat of invasion, by a king whose health was never sound (he may have suffered from Crohn's Disease), was remarkable. Unsurprisingly Alfred has been revered as a national hero down the generations: resilient and humble in adversity, resolute and victorious in battle, humane and innovative in reform and administration; the founder of navies and the homely burner of cakes. In 1740, almost 900 years after he lived, the song 'Rule Britannia' was composed for a masque to celebrate Alfred's heroism.

Yet no one called Alfred 'the Great' in his own lifetime, nor for seven centuries afterwards.* His tag may have had more to do with the political and religious upheavals of the mid-16th century. Since Alfred had written religious works directly in his native English, the Protestant writers of Tudor times presented the Anglo-Saxon King's words as 'pure' and untainted by Latin, and hence foreign (Roman/Popish) influence, and dubbed him 'the Great' in recognition.

Alfred died, aged about fifty, on 26th October 899. His great wealth, estimated at 2,000 silver pounds, not to mention the fact that his various estates were split among his five children,

---

* As Barbara Yorke of (appropriately enough) King Alfred's College, Winchester points out.

did not make for an easy transition. His son, known to history as Edward the Elder, faced a prolonged challenge from his cousin Aethelwold – the son of Alfred's older brother, the former King Aethelred – to secure the throne. Aethelwold persuaded the East Anglian Danes to join him in war on Wessex and Mercia, before being killed at the Battle of the Holme in 903.

Aethelwold's death enabled Edward to spend the rest of his 25-year reign focussed on other challenges, namely reinforcing the union between Wessex and Mercia and, like his father, fighting off Danish attacks. By the time of his own death in 924, Edward had married three times and probably had 18 children. The division of the kingdom between his two eldest sons, Athelstan and Aelfweard, did not last long. Within a fortnight Aelfweard's death had made Athelstan king of Wessex and Mercia.

Athelstan, First King of England (927–939)

> King of the English, elevated by the right hand of the Almighty, which is Christ, to the throne of the whole Kingdom of Britain.
>
> Church charter of 934

Athelstan grew his territory through a mixture of dynastic union and astute manoeuvre. His sister was married to Sihtric, the ruler of York, and when he died in 927, Athelstan annexed the city in a bloodless coup, proceeding to take all of Northumbria.

Thus did Athelstan become the first King of all England (except Cumbria). His coinage was duly inscribed *Rex Totius Britanniae*, a title no previous ruler had claimed, and his royal charters began to call him *Imperator*. From this position of strength, he gained the submission of the Scottish and Welsh kings. As the *Anglo-Saxon Chronicle* states for 927:

> In this year fiery rays of light appeared in the northern sky... King Athelstan annexed the kingdom of Northumbria. He brought into submission all the kings in this island: first Hywel, king of the west Welsh, and Constantine, king of Scots and Owain, king of Gwent and Ealdulfing from Bamburgh. They established a covenant of peace... at... Eamont Bridge: they forbade all adulterous practices and then separated in concord.

This manuscript illustration from ca. 930, depicts Athelstan (l) presenting a book to the patron saint of Northumbria, St Cuthbert, who died in 686. The image has less to do with the facts, and more with stressing Athelstan's piety and generosity to his new, Northumbrian subjects.

The sweetness and light of this Christian kingdom did not last. By 934 Athelstan was invading Scotland by land and sea.

Three years later, a combined force of Vikings from Dublin – led by Olaf Guthfrithsson, whose father had been ousted from York when Athelstan took over Northumbria – together with troops led by Constantine and the king of Strathclyde, marched south into England. Athelstan and his army met them at a place the *Chronicle* calls Brunanburh, around October 937.

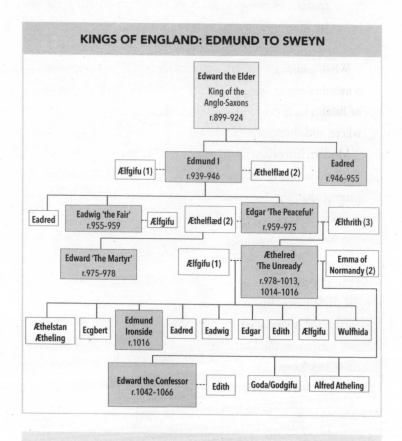

KINGS OF ENGLAND: EDMUND TO SWEYN

Edward the Elder
King of the Anglo-Saxons
r.899-924

Ælfgifu (1) — Edmund I r.939-946 — Æthelflæd (2)   Eadred r.946-955

Eadred   Eadwig 'the Fair' r.955-959 — Ælfgifu   Æthelflæd (2)   Edgar 'The Peaceful' r.959-975 — Ælthrith (3)

Edward 'The Martyr' r.975-978   Ælfgifu (1)   Æthelred 'The Unready' r.978-1013, 1014-1016 — Emma of Normandy (2)

Æthelstan Ætheling   Ecgbert   Edmund Ironside r.1016   Eadred   Eadwig   Edgar   Edith   Ælfgifu   Wulfhida

Edward the Confessor r.1042-1066 — Edith   Goda/Godgifu   Alfred Atheling

Brunanburh: The Battle That Made England
It was a day-long battle, culminating in a decisive victory: Athelstan's army crushed the alliance, killing five kings and eight Viking jarls. As the *Chronicle* jubilantly reports:

> Athelstan, lord of Warriors... won undying glory with the edges of swords... with their hammered blades, the sons of Edward clove the shield wall and hacked the linden bucklers... to defend their land, their treasures and their homes... The field grew dark with the blood of men. There lay many a warrior of the men of the north, torn by spears... likewise many a Scot, sated with battle, lay lifeless. Never before in this island... was an army put to greater slaughter by the sword.

Writing about 40 years later, the chronicler Aethelweard, a member of the Wessex Royal Family, wrote that 'the fields of Britain were consolidated into one, there was peace everywhere, and abundance of all things.'

Modern historians mostly agree that this battle confirmed England as a single state, and given its significance, it's surprising that the location of Brunanburh has remained a mystery. It could have been anywhere between Northumbria and Northamptonshire.

Athelstan's name became known throughout Europe. He forged diplomatic links with the courts of France and Saxony and arranged marriages for his sisters with the future Holy Roman Emperor, the Duke of the Franks and the Duke of Burgundy. King Louis IV of France took refuge at his court and Haakon of Norway was raised in England as Athelstan's foster son. A gospel presented by Otto, Duke of Burgundy, addresses him as 'Holy King Athelstan, renowned through the wide world, whose esteem flourishes and whose honour endures everywhere.' Otto clearly knew the way to Athelstan's heart, although, as the most powerful king in Europe, he probably needed no flattery.

Athelstan lacked the resources to administer such a large kingdom closely, but the meetings of his council took place right across Wessex and Mercia, indicating that King and court kept on the move, from Exeter to Abingdon and Faversham and – during times of peace – also York, Tamworth, Colchester and London. Rather than relying on a small, trusted coterie, he seems to have called in a range of advisers to witness his legislative acts and law codes.

Kings had always taken advice from their followers at court and powerful local magnates, but this now turned into a more formal arrangement. The *Witanagemot* seems to have begun as a means of witnessing royal grants of land, then evolved into a committee of nobles and senior clergy whom kings would consult on policies, and call upon to witness rulings and decrees.

Although the *Witanagemot's* meetings were ad hoc and its powers not clearly defined, it seems that by the mid-ninth century its approval was required for certain royal deeds and acts; kings could not exercise power alone. To rule over areas as disparate as Kent, Northumbria and Wessex, English monarchs relied upon the loyalty of men who were from such places, and wielded influence within them. Such local chiefs would become the regional baronage: the *ealdormen* who controlled the nascent shire counties, collected dues and taxes, supervised local justice and provided men for the army. The most powerful and influential became the monarch's counsellors, and they could also, at various points in history, become his critics and opponents.

After Athelstan died a bachelor in his mid-forties, five kings succeeded him in a space of 40 years – a sign of how swiftly a strong dynasty could give way to chaos. First was Athelstan's half-brother Edmund, assassinated by an outlaw in 946. He was succeeded by another of Edward the Elder's sons, the sickly Eadred, who was, according to the chronicler William of Malmesbury, writing 200 years later, 'unable to swallow more than the juices of the food he had masticated, to the great annoyance of his guests'. His teenaged nephew Eadwig succeeded him in 955, a lad allegedly scolded by his chief adviser Dunstan, Abbot of Glastonbury, for slinking off during his own coronation feast. Dunstan's biographer, Osbern of Canterbury, claims Eadwig had disappeared 'for caresses with loose women,' more specifically, a *menage à trois* with his future wife and mother-in-law. Dunstan was so appalled to discover Eadwig in bed between the two women that he physically hauled him out of it; at least, that's the story. The episode was more likely an invention, or at best, an exaggeration, inserted to dramatise Eadwig's conflicts with the Church, and the struggles between the future saint and a worldly king. These culminated in Dunstan's flight to Flanders, where he remained until Eadwig's four-year reign was over.

King Edgar (959–975)

Lest the spark of faith… should be extinguished by sloth and idleness [the king] began… to consider by what holy and deserving works it could be made to burn with the brilliance and ardour of perfection.

Aethelwold of Worcester, *Regularis Concordia,* ca. 973

Edgar brought welcome stability: inheriting the throne after his elder brother died in 959, he remained on it for 16 years, during which time he reached an amity with the Danes in the eastern counties, recognising their laws and customs. He also recalled Dunstan from exile, appointing the popular reformer as Archbishop of Canterbury, a shrewd move that won him the grateful support of the country's bishops.

Edgar further cemented his closeness to the Church by bringing the country's monasteries under his personal patronage, rather than leaving them to the mercies of local ealdormen. This came at a time of monastic reform, as the Benedictine rule replaced ephemeral religious groups with permanent, uniform communities. According to the *Chronicle*, Edgar threw his weight behind the revival. His gifts of land to monasteries probably meant that regional magnates lost out on revenues, but perhaps that was the plan. As their territory expanded, England's kings had to perform a complex balancing act in order to keep the support of various powerful individuals and institutions.

Edgar was certainly no paragon of Christian virtue: his mistress was a nun named Wulfthryth, and his law code went beyond even the draconian injunctions of the Old Testament, specifying that thieves should be blinded and scalped, have their ears, hands and feet cut off and their nostrils split – before being devoured by wild beasts.

Edgar was not crowned until 973, fourteen years into his reign. Generally, in this era and for many centuries after, kings were crowned swiftly to forestall challenges from rivals. Late as it was, Edgar's ceremony at Bath was elaborate and had Christianity at its heart. It may have been the first coronation to involve a formal church service, devised by Dunstan, and its high point was not the crowning of the king, but his anointing with holy oils, symbolising God's special favour and the monarch's difference from other men. An anointed king was untouchable, breaches of his authority bound to incur divine wrath.

By Royal Anointment

Anointing, a practice referred to frequently in the scriptures, remains the central and most sacred sequence of the coronation ceremony. In medieval times, the oil was believed to have

been bequeathed originally by the apostle St Thomas, but
nowadays it is a more humble blend of sesame oil and olive
oil (presumably obtainable from any good supermarket), per-
fumed with rose petals and jasmine and seasoned with musk,
civet and ambergris before being blessed by a bishop, or at least
a canon of Westminster Abbey.

Later that year, Edgar received the homage of six regional
kings at Chester: rulers from Wales, Scotland, Cumbria, Strathclyde and the Western Isles apparently rowed him across the
River Dee to a church service on an island, then back again, as
a symbol of their submission.

The absence of invasions or battles during Edgar's reign led
to him being called *Pacificus* – the Peaceful – and perhaps his
travels around the realm helped keep order. But all fell apart
in July 975 when he suddenly died in his early thirties, leaving
his son Edward with a contested inheritance. Archbishop
Dunstan, loyal to the last, declared Edward the legitimate
first-born heir, but others said the teenager had been born out
of wedlock, perhaps thanks to Edgar's liaisons with his mistress, the nun Wulfthryth. Edward's principal challenger was
Aelfryth, Edgar's second wife, who championed two sons of
her own.

Edward had a tendency towards violent rages, a trait that
probably alienated many retainers and potential allies, but his
downfall had more to do with rivalries between regional magnates. In March 978, as Edward arrived at the home of his stepmother Aelfthryth, Corfe Castle in Dorset, he was stabbed
to death by her servants. No one was held responsible and
Edward was buried unceremoniously, first at nearby Wareham,
then Shaftesbury, where miracles were soon reported by the
local clergy, probably to encourage lucrative pilgrimages. The

stroppy teenager was transformed into Edward the Martyr and then a saint. The *Chronicle* joined in: 'No worse deed was ever done... Men murdered him but God exalted him... In life he was an earthly king, but after death he is now a heavenly saint.'

Edward was murdered on behalf of Aelfthryth's second son, Aethelred, a child whose entire reign would be overshadowed by the way it had begun. The shocking murder of a rightful king, whilst a guest at his stepmother's house, amounted to two offences in one: overturning the rightful order of succession, and defying the conventions of hospitality. For these, and various later reasons, the next king would be called Aethelred the Unready, which had nothing to do with how ill-prepared he was for rule (although he was).

King Aethelred the Unready
(Reigned 978–1013 and 1014–1016)

Aethelred was not of the calibre of his forbears, but neither was he a complete disaster, and he reigned longer than any of his predecessors.

Oxford History of the British Monarchy

Aethelred's famous moniker probably dates from at least a century after his death, but he seems to have been regarded as ill-starred almost from birth: he allegedly crapped in the font whilst being baptised by Archbishop Dunstan (though this was a folk tale told of other unfortunate kings, too). Dunstan is said to have exclaimed that the grown-up Aethelred was *ignavus*, which can be translated as lazy, cowardly or ignoble. Writing more than a century later, William of Malmesbury described him as cruel, pitiable and disgraceful. Perhaps he did not improve with age.

The nickname derives from a modern mistranslation of the Old English *Unraed* meaning 'badly advised', which itself was a pun on his name: *Aethel* (noble) and *Raed* (counsel). He has had an almost unflaggingly critical press, from the first chroniclers down to the historians of the 20th century, and attempts at balance in recent years have had little impact. We know more about Aethelred's reign than almost any other Anglo-Saxon king thanks to the quantity of contemporary sources – but since they were all hostile to him, we have to accept that the picture is incomplete.

Written two centuries after Aethelred's reign, the *Chronicle of Abingdon* is unflattering both in its depiction and its descriptions of the hapless king. 'Aethelred, when he received the power of governing and commanding, committed himself to the advice of vicious men, and did many things for pleasure.'

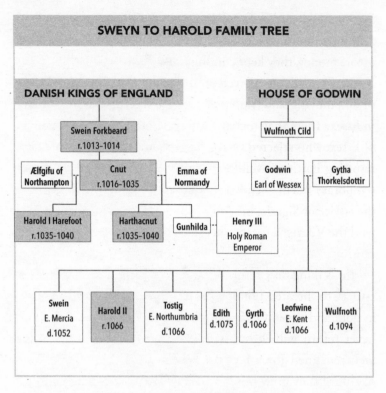

Nevertheless he held the throne for 38 years, and there is evidence from his charters that Anglo-Saxon government continued to operate: appointments were made, coins minted and taxes raised. But Aethelred broke the contract under which kings were given power in exchange for ruling justly and protecting their people. Estates were expropriated and handed to favourites, while regional chiefs did as they pleased without consequence. National morale sank, assisted by the return – after a century's absence – of Viking raids.

That was hardly Aethelred's fault, but his decision to pay the Vikings off several times over ensuing decades has defined him, perhaps unfairly so. He was not the first king to bribe the Vikings to go away – Alfred did the same – but it never worked. Once Olaf Tryggvason, future king of Norway and

Sweyn Forkbeard, king of Denmark (who may have sported a droopy moustache rather than a beard) realised they could extort money, they kept coming back.

Olaf's longboats arrived off the coast of Kent in the summer of 991, moving slowly up the coast into the Blackwater estuary in Essex. There they met an army led by Byrhtnoth, ealdorman of Essex, who rejected Olaf's suggestion of paying tribute. The resulting Battle of Maldon – commemorated in an epic contemporary poem – ended in a devastating English defeat. On the advice of Sigeric, his Archbishop of Canterbury, Aethelred paid the Vikings £10,000 'because of the great terror they were causing'.

The Viking fleet returned, and in 994 sailed up the Thames estuary to threaten London. This time they were paid £22,000 in gold and silver. Olaf – now baptised – promised he would never return with hostility. He went home, but some of his men remained for a few years as mercenaries in Aethelred's pay, until they grew bored and started attacking communities along the Devon coast and Severn estuary. In 1002, they were paid £24,000 to stop, but the raids continued. Archaeologists in Scandinavia regularly dig up coins bearing Aethelred's head: testimony to where all the money went.

At the time, these payments were called *gafol*, not Danegeld, which is a later, 11th- and 12th-century term for the money paid to those defending the country against Viking attacks (who were often Vikings themselves). Norman kings up to the reign of Henry II would raise Danegeld via a regular land-tax, in order to fund the island's defences, suggesting that they were already in a poor state by the time they invaded in 1066. This, in turn, might explain why Aethelred paid *gafol*: the defence-networks built up by Alfred in the ninth century had not been maintained, so repeated pay-offs were the only option.

It is less clear what motives lay behind the St Brice's Day Massacre on 13th November 1002, when Aethelred ordered the massacre 'of all Danish men who were in England'. The extent of the killing is disputed: it seems to have occurred in larger towns bordering the Danelaw, such as Oxford – where many families burned to death whilst sheltering inside St Frideswide's church – but also in Bristol and London. It was perhaps an act of vengeance after years of Viking attacks, and the chief targets may have been Danish mercenaries who'd reneged on their contract to defend the kingdom. Either way, it was an act of terror, and one for which Aethelred showed little remorse: a charter sanctioning the rebuilding of St Frideswide's a few years later spoke of a 'most just extermination.'

As a deterrent, it worked as poorly as the pay-offs: the raids continued and an astounding proportion of the national wealth was handed over in the hopes of stopping them: £36,000 in 1007, a further £48,000 in 1012, £21,000 two years later and £72,000 (plus £10,500 from London) in 1018. Amongst the raids and the bitter rivalries between the ealdormen surrounding the throne, Aethelred's rule broke down. A Ship Tax was raised, but before the new vessels could take on the invaders, they were destroyed in dock during a quarrel between nobles. Such divisions allowed the latest Danish raider, Thorkell the Tall, to rampage across the country with his army. The *Chronicle* for 1011 relates dolefully: 'They had by this time overrun East Anglia, Essex, Middlesex, Oxfordshire, Cambridgeshire, Hertfordshire, Buckinghamshire, Bedfordshire, half of Huntingdonshire... all Kent and Sussex, the district around Hastings, and Surrey and Berkshire and Hampshire and a great part of Wiltshire.'

These were not men who wanted to settle down and become farmers. When they reached Canterbury, they captured Archbishop Aelfheah and split his head with an axe. As the country was bled dry for money, Aethelred's response was to call for prayer and sue for peace. Written up by hostile monks after the reign ended, the *Chronicle's* verdict is damning:

All these misfortunes befell us by reason of bad policy in that tribute was not offered to them in time, but when they had done their worst then it was that peace was made with them. And notwithstanding all this they went about everywhere in bands and robbed and slew our unhappy people.

Thorkell eventually decided it was more profitable serving as a mercenary for Aethelred and settled with his army in Greenwich. But in late 1013, Sweyn Forkbeard, whose sister and her husband had been victims of St Brice's Day, marched into Wessex, forcing Aethelred to flee to Normandy, where his wife's brother was the duke. Sweyn briefly became King of England as well as Denmark, but died within six weeks.

The options now were Sweyn's son Cnut (or Canute), the return of Aethelred, or the succession of his son Edmund, known as Ironside, who had his own powerbase in Northumbria. The King returned from exile at the invitation of some – but not all – of the regional ealdormen, while others aligned themselves with Canute, against Ironside.

Crucially, those who invited Aethelred back did so on condition that he agreed to 'rule justly', and he consented to that. It was an implicit acknowledgement that, God-appointed or not, kings exerted their rule within the law – or not at all. Aethelred resumed the throne, but died just over two years later in April 1016, leaving Edmund and Canute's armies fighting it out across the country, before the Vikings won a decisive victory at Ashdon in Essex that October. Edmund died soon afterwards.

King Canute (1016–1035)

> Canute was a canny politician and a successful ruler, respected by his subjects… [He] brought peace and stability… much needed after the tumultuous reign of Aethelred.
>
> Marc Morris, *The Anglo Saxons*

Canute's victory was the first (and far less well-known) of two successful foreign invasions of England in the 11th century. It made him one of the most powerful rulers in Europe, already a military veteran in his early twenties: 'King of Englishmen, Danes, Norwegians and part of the Swedes', as he styled himself. There was a network of European connections: his mother was possibly Polish and one of his sisters, Estrith, was bequeathed to Robert, Duke of Normandy. Invader though he was, Canute's accession was welcomed by Anglo-Saxon nobles and churchmen, strong rule being preferable to the foregoing mayhem under Aethelred.

Canute was certainly strong, even ruthless, with rivals and hostages. In 1014, departing for Denmark after that year's campaign, he had dropped off his captives at Sandwich – minus their hands, ears and noses. Now, in 1017, it was the turn of Mercia's most powerful nobleman, Eadric, who had briefly supported Aethelred before switching loyalty to Canute. This mistake proved sufficient grounds for his capture and execution in London at Christmas. Even Thorkell, who had been the closes ally of Canute's father Sweyn, was banished from the kingdom and sent back to Denmark. Most of Aethelred's surviving relations fled into exile or were hunted down, except for his widow Emma, whom Canute married instead.

Yet as long as an Anglo-Saxon ealdorman proved loyalty, he would lose neither life nor land, and if he provided men for Canute's armies and naval ships, he was rewarded. The rise of men like Godwine, Earl of Wessex, Leofric, Earl of Mercia and Siward, Earl of Northumbria ensured that future kings would have to negotiate their rule with an increasingly self-confident powerbase of regional nobles.

This worked well for Canute, who knew he could count on the support of men he'd enriched. He could also rely on widespread, efficient collection of taxes in trusted coinage. The helmeted head of the King is depicted on the later coins of his reign, and it is thought that as many as 47 million silver pennies were minted in 1018, when Canute demanded £72,000 to pay for his army. This levy funded wars in Scandinavia, including a campaign to regain Norway from the Swedish-backed usurper Olaf Haraldsson. Later centuries would see the pattern regularly repeated: both foreign-born and native kings taxing the English people to pay for military action in distant lands. The resentment this caused would ultimately force monarchy to transform into something kings of Canute's era would not recognise.

Canute was generous to the Church and in return received the bishops' loyalty. Archbishop Wulfstan of York drafted his early law codes, just as he had for Aethelred, stressing that those who paid their taxes would have their property respected. Canute also made lavish gifts to churches and monasteries, appointed allies to bishoprics, and made pilgrimage to Rome. While he was there, just like any decent modern statesman, he negotiated a trade deal.

A Wave that Went Awry

The famous folk tale of Canute's vain attempt to turn back the waves, ordering the tide to recede as it lapped against the bank of the Thames at Westminster, is probably the only detail popularly remembered from his 19-year reign. It is almost certainly untrue, dating from a *History of the English* written in rhyming couplets by the Anglo-Norman chronicler Geoffrey Gaimar over a century after Canute's death. The episode was meant to demonstrate royal wisdom and humility: it depicts Canute making an ironic gesture in order to highlight his own limited power as compared with God's omnipotence. But gesture politics are prone to misinterpretation, and Canute's riverside enactment, real or not, has been interpreted by many later storytellers, artists and historians as an example of regal narcissism.

Capable as Canute was, his death in 1035 left a disputed succession between his sons. Harold Harefoot (a fast runner, apparently) and Harthacanute were half-brothers and sworn enemies. Harold was alleged to be the offspring of Canute's liaison with his mistress, Aelfgifu of Northampton, while the mother of Harthacanute, Emma (Aethelred's widow), had apparently secured Canute's word that her son would have precedence. Harefoot won the race temporarily in England, while Harthacanute was occupied with new threats to the Scandinavian territories. Alfred, another of Aethelred and Emma's sons, briefly joined the fray, only to be murdered whilst under the protection of Harefoot's ally, Earl Godwine of Wessex.

Harthacanute returned to England in 1040, when Harold's death left the path clear to the throne. Avenging Alfred's murder, the new King had his half-brother's corpse disinterred, beheaded and thrown into a swamp, but he did not live much longer himself, dying during a drinking bout at a wedding in June 1042. Since neither Harold nor Harthacanute had married or fathered children, the Danish dynasty ended after just over a quarter-century.

King Edward the Confessor (1042–1066)

Before Harthacanute was buried, all the people chose Edward as the king in London.

Anglo-Saxon Chronicle

In 1041, Harthacanute had invited his half-brother Edward to return from exile in Normandy, probably to name him as heir. According to one 12th-century account, Edward – the son of Aethelred and his second wife, Emma of Normandy – met with the English thegns and swore to uphold the laws of Canute, in return for being named successor to Harthacanute. Upon the latter's death, he succeeded to the throne in June 1042, apparently with the backing of his brother's murderer, Earl Godwine. He would become known as 'the Confessor' because of his supposed devoutness and peaceable nature, though he was not averse to earthly pursuits like hunting. The title was first used in the ultimately successful campaign for his canonisation, nearly a century after his death.

Though welcomed in London, the new King knew that Wessex, seat of England's most powerful magnate, Earl Godwine, could easily turn against him. To secure his position, Edward married Godwine's daughter Edith, who was some twenty years his junior. It was not an easy relationship: Edward had spent much of his life exiled in Normandy, he spoke more French than English, and he relied on a circle of Norman advisers. The couple had no children to bring them together, nor to secure the future succession.

The Godwines disliked Edward's favours to Normans, and when they objected to his appointment of Robert of Jumièges as Archbishop of Canterbury in 1051, the family was forced into exile in Flanders. A year later, they sailed back with a fleet too big for Edward to counter, and it was the turn of the Normans at court to flee. Archbishop Robert was replaced by Stigand, a Saxon, and the King was again at the Godwines' mercy.

By the 1060s, over 80 percent of England was effectively under the authority of Harold Godwine, Earl of Wessex, and his brother Tostig, Earl of Northumbria. The pair forged strategic alliances through marriage: Tostig was married to the half-sister of Baldwin, Count of Flanders, while Harold's wife was Ealdgyth, sister of Earl Edwin of Mercia – Tostig's chief regional rival.

The ageing Edward increasingly left them to it, spending his time hunting and overseeing the building of his great project, the abbey church at Westminster. It was finished just in time for him to be buried in it, in January 1066.

King Harold (January–September 1066)

> He met little quiet as long as he ruled the realm.
>
> *Anglo-Saxon Chronicle*

The last Anglo-Saxon reign began with four claimants to the throne, three of whom claimed it had been promised to them personally. Harold Godwine said he'd been named successor on Edward's deathbed. The *Witanagemot* believed him or, at least, believed he was the best contender, since they appointed him successor, and according to later sources, he was hastily crowned at Westminster the very next day. Meanwhile, William of Normandy, Edward's cousin, claimed the Confessor had promised him the throne when he visited England in 1051, while the powerful Godwines were all exiled. Harold Hardrada, king of Norway, argued that Harthacanute had offered it to him in 1036. And another, potentially stronger case came from Edmund Ironside's grandson, Edgar Atheling. Edgar's father, Edward the Exile, had been summoned from Hungary to the Confessor's court – perhaps to be named heir – but died en route in 1057. Yet if the King had intended Edward as his successor, he seems to have made no attempt to pass the succession to the teenaged Edgar, who had accompanied his father on the journey from Hungary.

The Norman Succession: A Promise Without Proof

Did Edward promise the succession to Duke William of Normandy? The Normans' claim to the throne rested not only on the Confessor's putative promise in 1051, but also on an alleged encounter in 1064, when Harold had been captured by William while on a mission to free two relatives being held in Normandy, and sworn his allegiance as a condition of his release. There seems to be no independent evidence for this. Indeed, as England's most powerful baron, it's likely that Harold would have had his own designs on the English throne. Still, he may have felt he had little to lose by swearing an oath to William while under duress in his custody; he could always break it once he was free. Whatever the truth, Harold seized his chance to become king, ensuring he was crowned at the Abbey on the same day Edward was buried there.

Harold's nine-month reign in 1066 would be one of the shortest but also one of the most consequential in the nation's history. The north had been in revolt before Edward's death, as local thegns complained about Tostig's heavy tax levies and demanded their own choice as Earl of Northumbria. Harold tried to conciliate them by marrying the sister of Edwin of Mercia, whom the Northumbrians preferred, and by forcing his brother Tostig into exile in Flanders. By May 1066, though, Tostig had returned with a fleet of mercenaries, harrying the south and east coasts before joining Harold Hardrada in Scotland to plan an invasion.

That summer, King Harold was on high alert, raising troops and gathering a fleet. William was openly recruiting an invasion force and building ships. But by early September, Harold was running short of money to pay his troops, and

1066: THE CONTENDERS

HAROLD GODWINE

Brother-in-law to Edward the Confessor (Harold's sister is the Queen).

Claims Edward named him successor on his deathbed.

The Witanagemot appoint him Edward's successor, and he is (according to later sources) crowned at Westminster.

WILLIAM OF NORMANDY

Cousin once removed of Edward the Confessor.

Claims that:

a) Harold swore allegiance to him in 1064

and

b) Edward promised him the throne in 1051, while the Godwines were out of favour.

HARALD HARDRADA

Is King of Norway, but also claims Danish throne (Harthacanute promised it to his father, Magnus). From 1064 claims England too, on the basis that it had been part of Anglo-Danish kingdom. Tostig backs him.

EDGAR ATHELING

Grandson of Edmund Ironside and great-nephew of Edward the Confessor

The Confessor summons Edgar's father, Edward the Exile to London, possibly to name him successor, but he dies en route, leaving Edgar to claim throne instead.

since no invasion had occurred, he disbanded the levies and moved his fleet to port in London, leaving the Channel open for the Normans.

That same month, Tostig and Hardrada sailed up the Humber and moved inland along the Ouse, making for York. In an extraordinary feat of organisation and speed, Harold's army engaged the invaders at Stamford Bridge, east of the city on 25th September, only four days after leaving London. He won a decisive victory, the greatest defeat the Vikings had suffered in England since Brunanburh 130 years previously, and both Tostig and Hardrada were killed. According to the *Chronicle*, sixty ships had carried the Vikings into Yorkshire, but only twenty-four were needed to take the survivors away.

Two nights later, though, William's Norman army set sail from the Somme estuary, and by 28th September it was disembarking on the Sussex coast. Harold was still in York when he heard the news, and he rushed south, reaching London by 11th October. Without time to summon troops from further afield, he moved to confront William. The two small armies – possibly only 5,000-7,000 men each – clashed just north of Hastings on 14th October.

The Embroidered Truth

The Battle of Hastings, the most decisive in England's history, is also one of the best-known thanks to the Bayeux Tapestry. Actually this unique cultural and historical artefact is no tapestry at all, but a 230-feet-long, 20-inches-wide embroidered cloth, sewn probably at Canterbury's embroidery workshop in the years immediately after the Conquest. It may have been commissioned by William's half-brother Odo, who was Bishop of Bayeux and Earl of Kent. Possibly he wanted it for his newly consecrated cathedral, though the earliest reference to it being there dates from 1476. The fine needlework would have been executed by women, possibly nuns, but the designer was probably a Norman male with court connections, and thus familiar with the physical appearance of William and Harold. In that sense, the tapestry serves as the earliest contemporary portrait of two kings of England; the relative size of William in the work tallies with written descriptions of a tall, imposing man, and on numerous further points, the story it tells is in accord with other contemporary accounts. We are fortunate that it has survived almost entirely intact. In 1792, only the heroic intervention of a local lawyer,

Lambert Leonard-Leforestier, prevented it from being cut up and used for blankets by Napoleonic soldiers; and in 1944, it narrowly escaped seizure by Himmler's SS.

The main body of the tapestry shows the English on the ridge of Senlac Hill, standing firm against the arrows raining down from William's archers. It goes on to depict their fatal blunder: they were tricked by the Norman cavalry into pursuing them, only to be slaughtered as William's knights wheeled round. One scene shows the moment when William lifted his helmet to silence rumours of his death (*Hic est Willelm Dux* – 'Here is Duke William') – a first depiction of that essential duty of kings: displaying themselves to their subjects.

Scene 55 of the tapestry, depicting Harold's death and William showing his face in victory

Somewhere in the mêlée Harold was killed, and the resistance crumbled. The Normans had archers and cavalry, and once the English lost their defensive position and their discipline, they were an easy prey. As the remaining English fled into the Sussex Weald, William's army cautiously followed them in a circular progress round the home counties before heading into London.

The *Witanagemot* appointed the 14-year-old Edgar Atheling as Harold's successor, but by then it was too late. At Berkhamsted in Hertfordshire, William received the formal submission of the English earls, the bishops and the leaders of London and from there he proceeded to the city, allowing his troops to ravage the countryside en route in a display of sheer military power.

William was crowned at Westminster Abbey on Christmas Day 1066, while his soldiers outside mistook the cheers coming from within the Abbey for a native uprising, and started setting fire to nearby houses. A monk writing 50 years later described the scene:

> The people in the church were thrown into confusion and crowds of them rushed outside, some to fight the flames, others to go looting. Only the monks, bishops and a few clergy remained. Though... terrified they managed to complete the consecration of the King, who was trembling violently.
>
> Orderic Vitalis, *Historia Ecclesiastica*, ca.1110–1142

Despite this fright, William was in near-complete control, and unlike Canute, who had allowed the English earls and local administration to remain in place, the new invaders were ready to remake the land in their image. It was the most divisive, consequential and long-lasting conquest in English history. Within a few years, the monarch and all sources of power in the country would be Norman, while the Saxons would become the dispossessed underclass.

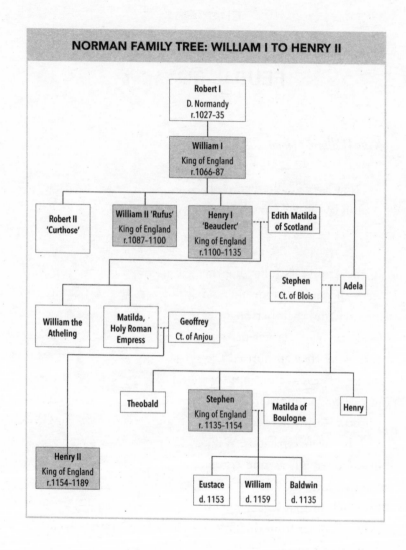

NORMAN FAMILY TREE: WILLIAM I TO HENRY II

Robert I
D. Normandy
r.1027–35

William I
King of England
r.1066–87

Robert II
'Curthose'

William II 'Rufus'
King of England
r.1087–1100

Henry I
'Beauclerc'
King of England
r.1100–1135

Edith Matilda
of Scotland

Stephen
Ct. of Blois

Adela

William the Atheling

Matilda,
Holy Roman
Empress

Geoffrey
Ct. of Anjou

Theobald

Stephen
King of England
r. 1135–1154

Matilda of
Boulogne

Henry

Henry II
King of England
r.1154–1189

Eustace
d. 1153

William
d. 1159

Baldwin
d. 1135

CHAPTER 2

FEUDAL ROYALTY

King William I (1066–1087)

> Now law rules the dignity of a king... if the king be without
> this law he will go astray.
>
> *The Song of Lewes*, 1264

In the 400 years following the Norman Conquest, monarchs
were the most important and influential individuals in the
country, and their personalities shaped its fortunes. All secular
land was held at their permission; their patronage ranged far
and wide; they authorised taxation, customs duties and other
means of revenue-raising; they established the laws by which
justice was administered. They were the wealthiest men in the
country – they needed to be, given all the wars they fought –
and they were rapacious. William the Conqueror 'loved greed-
iness above all', as one contemporary chronicler put it, and
Edward I was known as *Le Roi Coveytous*.

Much of that legacy remains. Queen Elizabeth II's private
income comes from the Duchy of Lancaster estates, originally
bequeathed in 1265 by Henry III to his son. It now encom-
passes 18,000 hectares of land, from Yorkshire grouse moors to
the Savoy estate in central London (site of a palace once gifted
to the Count of Savoy by Henry III) valued at £538m in 2020.

DL: Lancaster Castle: one of the best preserved castles in the country, dating back to Norman times. Used as a court and prison for many centuries; the Pendle Witches were tried and executed there in 1612.

DL: Mersey to Barrow foreshore: 98 lettings remain of this ancient parcel of land and coast, most recent being a licence to build a six-lane tollway across the Mersey. The Duchy's foreshore holdings include moorings, wildfowl licenses, grazing rights, sub-sea pipelines and fibre-optic cables.

DC: Dartmoor: some 368 square miles of South Devon moorland, home to stone circles, Army firing ranges and a prison, alongside populations of otters, adders and rare bats.

DC: St Enodoc's Church, Cornwall: on the dunes of the Camel Estuary, the building dates partly from the 12th century. It was almost entirely submerged in sand by the 1700s, when its vicar and parishioners had to enter it via a hole in the roof. Poet Laureate John Betjeman is buried in the grounds.

ROYAL ESTATES 2021

○ Duchy of Lancaster
18,000 hectares

● Duchy of Corwall
53,000 hectares

DL: Peveril Castle, Derbyshire: once the home of William the Conqueror's illegitimate son, the castle's keep was all that remained by the 17th century, when it was used as a courthouse. The imposing hilltop ruins were restored in the 19th century.

DC: The Oval: a couple of miles from the Queen's London home, the Oval cricket ground has been the site of international matches, and home to Surrey cricket club since 1845.

DL: The Savoy estate: various properties between the Strand and the Embankment, including the 12-storey Art Deco office block, Brettenham House, and the Savoy Chapel founded by Henry VII.

DC: Maiden Castle, Dorchester: the site of an Iron-Age hillfort, a mile and a half outside Dorchester; covering 47 acres, it is the largest of its kind in Britain and possibly Europe.

Prince Charles's private income has similarly ancient origins: the Duchy of Cornwall's 53,000 hectares, spread over 24 counties, were passed by Edward III to his son, the Black Prince, in 1337, and valued at around £1 billion in 2019.

Queen Elizabeth I on tour with her entourage

When kings toured England, visited their estates in Aquitaine or Gascony, or invaded Wales, Scotland and Ireland, crowds accompanied them: knights and men-at-arms, advisers, court favourites, clergy, cooks, grooms and horn-blowers. On a peacetime circuit of a king's own realm, the countryside through which he passed could be devastated.

> When it became known that the king was coming, everyone fled to the woods.
>
> Eadmer of Canterbury (c.1064-1124)

It was not a safe life: particularly from the 13th century onwards, kings faced armed challenges to their legitimacy, often from within their own families, and further stirred by barons and regional magnates wanting control over royal spending and a say in government. Six monarchs were deposed between 1327 and 1485 – such a heretical act became easier to contemplate the more times it was tried – yet monarchy, sanctioned by God, maintained by cunning and raw power, still persisted.

The country William inherited was wealthy, and its Anglo-Saxon kings had left a resilient central authority, with a local hierarchy of earls, sheriffs and bishops administering laws and raising taxes. It was not yet an embryonic modern state, but it was recognisably a nation. And it was about to be changed, utterly: although many of the local population must have cooperated with the invaders, England was rapidly and irreversibly altered to an extent not seen before or since. There would be a new official language – French – new architecture, new culture and a new ruling class taking over the land.

Above all, there was a new king with a different, more brutal way of doing business. He and his followers gazed south towards Normandy and France, not – as the Anglo-Saxon monarchs had – north towards Scandinavia, whose Viking inhabitants never seriously threatened England again. As a result of all these sudden changes, a bruising, niggling rivalry would endure between the English and the French for the next thousand years.

As Duke of Normandy, William the Conqueror paid homage to the King of France; he and his successors and followers devoted most of their time to defending their estates across the Channel. England was a useful source of revenue and manpower, whose fertile land could be used to reward followers or form part of a son's inheritance. Foreign-born monarchs would would continue to view the country that way for many centuries.

Not everything changed. The reason William was crowned so swiftly in Westminster Abbey was that Norman kings, like their Saxon predecessors, needed divine sanction. If they lost it during quarrels with prelates or popes, as William II, Henry II and John would all find out, they were in serious trouble. The Conqueror and his successors made full use of their patronage powers and, by keeping constantly on the move, they stayed visible to their subjects, in particular any potential rivals or challengers among them.

Some 90 percent of England's roughly two-million-strong population lived in the countryside, on subsistence farming. All land was the king's, held at his pleasure by regional magnates who were his tenants-in-chief: these were a dozen or so earls*, below them perhaps 200 barons, then some thousand knights of the shires and lords of the manor. Then came *villeins* (small farmers) and *bordars*, who ate at their lords' tables and had just enough land to feed their families while providing labour for their masters several days a week. Roughly 10 per cent of the population were slaves.

The Normans brought with them a feudal system long-established on the Continent: the earls swore allegiance to the king, and in doing so played a part in his accession and continuing reign. Those lower down the scale paid for the use of their lords' land with labour and, when necessary, military service. They could not travel without permission, especially at harvest-time, or own land. They were also taxed by the king, to fund his expenses and his wars. The king had responsibilities, too, to rule wisely and justly. If he did not, the loyalty of his nobles and therefore their followers could be strained and sometimes broken, as occurred in King John's reign. Feudal obligations strengthened an anointed

---

* The French title of *Duc*, or Duke, was not imported to England until the 14th century, and was reserved for members of the Royal Family.

king – they ensured obedience and provided men for warfare – but they also put limits on royal power.

England was thoroughly Christian, and had a network of churches and monasteries whose clergy were loyal to the monarchy and supported its rule. The belief in an all-powerful divinity, personified in a God who rewarded virtue and punished sin eternally, was universal, held by commoners and kings alike. A network of monasteries nurtured scribes and scholars, poets and artists, while the clergy administered God's blessings upon the throne. The king might treat bishops and clergy as personal servants, changing them if they displeased him, or seizing church assets if he needed money. But they represented a higher power – something that tended to concentrate his mind (or curb his excesses) if he fell ill and needed divine help, or fell out with them. The two archbishops would rank with dukes, while bishops and abbots of larger monasteries ranked with earls.

Firmly in place, William rewarded his Norman followers with land. By 1086, the *Domesday Book* tells us, the King held about 20 per cent of the land outright, the Church a further 25 per cent and Norman landowners 50 per cent. Only five per cent remained in the hands of the indigenous population. Forenames like William, Robert and Richard start dominating the historical record: by the end of the 12th century, people with Norman surnames owned 80% of the property in Winchester diocese. Wulfstan, Bishop of Worcester (a nephew of Canute's Wulfstan) was the only senior English cleric still in post after 1075.

But a more fundamental change occurred in the legal system. The shire courts, in which freemen served under *reeves* to administer justice, were replaced by manorial courts under the sole control of local lords, reinforcing the Norman caste's authority. The language of those courts was now Norman French; terms still in regular use today like *mortgage, chattel, tort* and *force majeure* remind us that England's legal matters were conducted, for centuries, in a foreign language.

William was the outcome of a liaison between Duke Robert of Normandy – Robert the Magnificent, or Robert the Devil, according to taste – and his mistress Herleva, reputedly a tanner's daughter, so he was not regally born. When he invaded England, he was nearly 40 years old and had been duke for around thirty. He owed his achievements to fighting – first against the French in Normandy; then against the English, Scots and Welsh; then against his eldest son; and finally against the French again.

He was reputedly a belligerent, harsh-voiced man, courageous, determined and occasionally displaying a chivalric sense of honour. He punished those who had hacked at Harold's corpse on the battlefield, and kept his rival contender Edgar Atheling safe at court, because he was of royal blood.

William was ostentatiously religious and ensured he had the blessing (and thus political sanction) of successive popes for his military campaigns, but he was ruthless otherwise, notably when tackling the last remaining pockets of English resistance. The so-called Harrowing of the North (1069-70)did not just defeat the rebels, it laid waste to the whole region, destroying villages, burning crops, killing livestock and wiping out the people. Those not put to the sword were left to starve; some resorted to cannibalism. The northern region, from the Humber to the Scottish border, remained desolate for years.

At first William tried to win over the English nobility, but heavy taxes, and the sequestration of their lands by the King's followers, prompted various uncoordinated rebellions. The last of these, led by the semi-legendary Hereward the Wake, occurred in the fens around Ely in about 1071.

> He caused castles to be built which were a sore burden to
> the poor.
>
> *Anglo-Saxon Chronicle*

The new King literally set his authority in stone, building a series of strategic castles from blocks of sandstone or limestone; an imposing and unfamiliar architectural style meant to intimidate the locals and defend his rule. Exeter, Warwick, York, Lincoln, Huntingdon, Cambridge, Chester and Stafford were all fortified, along with the Tower of London.

William's passion was hunting – useful training for warfare – and royal forests were set aside for the King's pleasure, such as the New Forest in Hampshire. A fifth of the land was wooded, but only the King and a few favourites were allowed to hunt the deer, a privilege guarded by new laws and a dedicated network of forest courts and officials. The Norman penalties for poaching, such as branding or mutilation, were savage, and a source of much resentment.

Taking Stock

The Conqueror needed to know how much money he could obtain if Denmark and/or Norway mounted another Viking invasion. In a bid to ascertain the sums he could raise in taxes from his new kingdom, he commissioned the *Domesday Book* in November 1085.

Initially, local magnates and officials recorded who owned what; this included William's Norman followers, who owed their estates to him, along with their tenants and under-tenants. Streams, buildings, livestock and even ploughs were listed, the current value of each property assessed against its notional value twenty years earlier. That first trawl took just nine months. Next, teams of commissioners were sent out to check the work of the first surveyors – care being taken that no official should assess an area where he himself owned land.

Before the final value was assigned, the shire courts hosted public inquests, which sometimes became fraught with old tensions and rivalries. Certain landowners were suspected of packing out the courts with loyal followers in order to get their tax bills lowered, while disgruntled tenants and political rivals saw the inquests as an opportunity for score-settling. The suspiciously light tax bill handed to Picot de Lascelles, sheriff of Cambridgeshire (see excerpt below), caused an onslaught of court challenges, possibly led by the monks of Ely, who called him 'a crafty fox' and 'a shameless dog'.

Domesday Book page referring to Babraham in Cambridgeshire, one the many possessions of 'crafty fox' Picot, and a classic example of formerly Saxon lands ending up in the hands of Normans. The text reads: 'In Babraham Picot holds 1/2 hide and 1/2 virgate from the King. This land lies in [the lands of] Chesterford and is valued there, at 30 shillings. Wulfwin held this land under Earl Algar; he could not withdraw or sell.'

Later readers can find many an interesting continuity in *Domesday*: a great number of the towns, villages and settlements that we know today already existed, and 80% of the area under cultivation in 1914 was under the plough at the time of *Domesday*. Not quite all of England was covered by the commissioners, though: the far north was still desolate and even in those parts of Yorkshire that were covered, it was clear that William's 'Harrying' had caused a steep decline. For example, the village of Cradwell was valued at 20 shillings in 1066, and two decades later, entered at only five shillings and four pence.

Domesday – as the name indicates – was intended as a final temporal judgement, just as God would eventually deliver a spiritual one on the last day. The survey was completed in less than two years – an astonishing feat of organisation then, as it would be now, and only possible due to the robust local administration inherited from the Anglo-Saxons. The two bound volumes of the survey, written in medieval Latin, were kept in a chest at Winchester. They are now in the National Archives at Kew, and are the most detailed record of any country in the 11th century.

When conflicts of interest arose, the King did not spare even his own family: his half-brother Bishop Odo was imprisoned in 1082, either for plotting to seize the throne after William's death, or perhaps because he had been planning an incursion into Italy to secure the papacy for himself. There were also disputes with William's eldest son Robert Curthose (thus called because he was short and stout), who rose against him in Normandy. William's death in September 1087 – he was possibly ruptured by the pommel of his saddle during the sacking of Mantes – meant a divided inheritance. Curthose became Duke of Normandy and the second surviving son, William Rufus, became King of England.

King William (Rufus) II (1087–1100)

Hateful to God and righteous men.

Anglo-Saxon Chronicle

The succession was far from settled. Rufus, so called for his red hair and perhaps his fiery temper, happened to be the man in place when William died. He raced from his late father's side at Rouen to Westminster, in order to be crowned William II less than three weeks later. Curthose challenged the new King, but was eventually mollified with 10,000 marks (raised by taxing the English) and departed to the Holy Land on the First Crusade.

Subjects rarely feel warm towards a king whose first act is a tax demand. Almost as swiftly as he alienated the general populace, William made powerful enemies within the Church, due to his tactic of leaving episcopal vacancies unfilled so that he could pocket the revenues. Fearing that a recent, serious illness was a sign of God's disapproval, he sought to make amends for his transgressions by appointing the zealous monk Anselm as Archbishop of Canterbury. Paradoxically, this turned the Church into an even more muscular adversary.

Anselm was a key figure in the Gregorian reforms occurring on the Continent. These stressed the power of popes over secular rulers, insisted that only the Church could make religious appointments, and made the clergy answerable solely to Church laws and courts. Over the centuries, these changes caused repeated clashes as monarchs sought to impose their authority over the Church.

In this instance, it was the clergy who had the last word – in writing, anyway. After Rufus was killed in a hunting accident in the New Forest in 1100, monkish writers delivered a critical verdict, emphasising Rufus's close friendship with his court administrator Ranulf Flambard, as well as his flamboyant fashion sense and his lack of a wife.

Rufus's demise, after getting in the way of an arrow aimed at a passing deer, was probably accidental, but his hunting companions feared they might not be given the benefit of the doubt, and they simply fled, leaving his body to be picked up by local peasants the following day. The beneficiary was Rufus's younger brother Henry, who had been in the hunting party himself and now raced to seize control of the Treasury at Winchester, and thence to London, being crowned within three days of the previous King's death. Robert Curthose, the oldest brother and presumed heir, was en route back to France from the Crusade, so speed was essential.

Robert did try invading England, but he was captured in Normandy in 1106 – a sign, according to the chronicler William of Malmesbury, that God had chosen Henry. In spite of this, Henry showed no Christian mercy to his brother, keeping Robert imprisoned in Cardiff Castle for the remaining 28 years of his life.

King Henry I (1100–1135)

> He treated the magnates with honour and generosity, adding to their wealth and estates and by placating them he won their loyalty.
>
> Orderic Vitalis, *Historia Ecclesiastica*, ca. 1110–1142

Divinely chosen or not, Henry I needed earthly backing, and swiftly issued his Charter of Liberties to secure it. The first royal, written proclamation of its sort, the Charter promised 'an end to all oppressive practices', removing the taxes Rufus had imposed on the barons. In return, they approved his coronation. This documentary acceptance of a king's obligations towards church and nobles set a template for the Magna Carta 115 years later. Although Henry's promises were ultimately unenforceable and he often ignored them, he did stick by some important elements: he renounced his right to consecrate clergy, and he accepted Pope Gregory's claim that secular rulers were not the deputies of God, but laymen, sub-

A VIEW of the COURT of EXCHEQUER

The Exchequer cloth in use in the 14th c.

ordinate to the clergy. Henry was more bookish than Rufus: he was known as *beauclerc*, meaning 'fine scholar', and according to William of Malmesbury, he was 'early instructed in the liberal arts and so throughout imbibed the sweets of learning'. Not that they made him any less ruthless than any other monarch of his era.

Centralisation continued through Henry I's reign. His chief adviser, Roger of Salisbury, was the first to use a chequered cloth to help count tax income in the royal treasury (hence 'the Exchequer'). While Henry was off campaigning in France, Roger was in charge, and he wielded his authority with zeal, having dozens of mint-operators castrated and blinded for debasing the currency.

Henry was not a popular king (taxes were too high for that) but the absence of a serious rival meant his position was secure. The future, however, was beyond his control. He'd sired more illegitimate children than any other monarch – probably 22, with six mistresses – but in November 1120, his only legitimate heir, William the Atheling, was very abruptly removed from the running.

> No ship ever brought so much misery to England; none was ever so notorious in the history of the world.
> William of Malmesbury, *Deeds of the English Kings*, 1125

Aged 17, the Prince had set sail in the White Ship from Barfleur harbour on the Normandy coast, heading for England in the wake of his father, who'd departed hours earlier. But the crew and all the passengers, who included many young nobles, had spent the day drinking (Orderic Vitalis notes that some wary travellers had even disembarked in port, the ship being 'overcrowded with riotous and headstrong youths') and the vessel hit a rock at the harbour entrance. William and all but one of those on board were drowned. Court advisers were so scared of the King's reaction that a pageboy was sent to break the news to him.

It was said that Henry never smiled again, although he did remarry a few months later, aged 52. He died in 1135 after a meal of lampreys – small eels which his doctor had warned him to avoid – leaving the throne to his daughter, Matilda. Having suspected that he might not produce another male heir, he had forced his barons to swear allegiance to her back in 1127. She had spent very little of her adult life in England, and probably had as much enthusiasm for the plan as the barons did.

Matilda had previously been married off, aged 12, to 28-year-old Henry V, the German Holy Roman Emperor; then, after his death, to Geoffrey, Count of Anjou (this time, she was 25, he was 13). Arranged marriages were a tool of strategic diplomacy. Indeed, it would be 300 years before a reigning king would marry an English bride.

Geoffrey's symbol was a sprig of the broom plant, known in dialect French as the *planta genista*. He is said to have worn it in his hat, or possibly planted it to provide shrubland cover for hunting. His descendants were the longest-reigning family in English history: a line of eight monarchs who ruled England for nearly 250 years, although their name – Plantagenet – only came into common use three centuries later.

King Stephen (1135–1154)

> Thus was the kingdom divided, some favouring and assisting the king, others the empress; and the divine saying was fulfilled: 'Every kingdom divided against itself is brought to desolation.'
>
> William of Newburgh, *History of English Affairs*, 1196–1198

As soon as Henry died, his nephew Stephen, Count of Blois, retracted his allegiance to Matilda, seizing the English throne and the Duchy of Normandy. As a grandson of the Conqueror, Stephen's claim was weaker than Matilda's, but he was a man, he was raised in England, and he was in the country when Henry died: reasons enough for the barons to switch their support to him. He was crowned king at Westminster Abbey on 22nd December 1135. As a monarch, Stephen possessed many personal advantages. He was said to be genial and charming, kindly and easy-going – and also a good soldier.

ANGEVIN/PLANTAGENETS FAMILY TREE: STEPHEN – EDWARD III

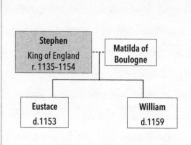

After the 20-year anarchy Stephen's surviving heir, William, was disinherited by his father (or perhaps persuaded to waive his rights to the Crown) in return for recognition of his rights to lands as Count of Boulogne and Earl of Surrey. This arrangement was essential for the peaceful accession of Henry II, grandson of Henry I and Stephen's first cousin once removed.

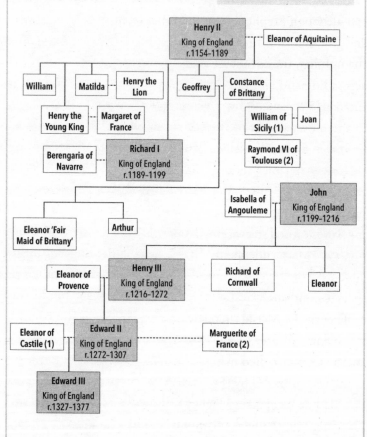

His anointing as king at his coronation made it difficult to challenge him. But Stephen had enriched some nobles at the expense of others, and by the time Matilda finally arrived in England in 1139, certain powerful individuals were disgruntled enough to support her. In support of her claim, her uncle, David I, King of Scotland, led an army into northern England while the Welsh princes began incursions along the border Marches. Unlike Stephen, Matilda did not win allies easily: it seems her personality was arrogant and lofty, and her second marriage was an unhappy affair, possibly because she resented being married to a mere count.

A 14-year civil war dragged on between the two contenders: although Stephen's side held the majority of the country and Matilda could never command more than a minority of the nobility, the advantage swung to and fro as the war spread across England and into Normandy. Stephen was captured at the battle of Lincoln in 1141 but released later that year, and in the snowy winter of 1142, Matilda escaped siege in Oxford by camouflaging herself in a white cloak and walking down the frozen Thames to reach supporters at Wallingford. With royal authority uncertain, local feuds broke out among the baronage, and the destruction of the countryside by marauding bands caused starvation. 'Never did a country suffer greater misery... Men said openly that Christ and his saints slept,' lamented the *Anglo-Saxon Chronicle*. 'We suffered nineteen years for our sins.'

Eventually, Matilda returned to France, leaving her young son Henry to carry on the campaign, and when Stephen's son and heir Eustace died in 1153, the ailing King gave up. A peace treaty was brokered by the Church, with Stephen keeping the throne, but recognising Henry as his heir instead of his own surviving son, William. Within a year, Stephen was dead, and the 20-year-old Henry, charismatic, energetic, thick-set and fiery, inherited an empire which would soon stretch from Scotland to the Spanish border.

King Henry II (1154–1189)

A human chariot, dragging all after him.
Herbert of Bosham, *Life of St Thomas of Canterbury*, 1196

King Henry II of England, also Duke of Normandy and Count of Anjou, had already negotiated marriage to Europe's most eligible bride, Eleanor of Aquitaine. Eleven years older than Henry, the formidable Eleanor had previously been wife to Louis VII of France for 14 years. That marriage was annulled: officially due to her consanguinity with Louis and failure to provide a male heir, but in fact mainly at her wish (she was bored with him). Eleanor would produce five sons with Henry II, three of whom would become kings.

With Aquitaine added to his empire, Henry controlled more of France than its own king did, and his was the first uncontested accession in a century. General war fatigue helped: the barons were looking to their own regional dynasties instead of challenging the throne, but Henry needed to spend long periods away, defending the substantial borders of his lands. He spent almost two-thirds of his 35-year reign in France.

The remainder of the time, 14 years, was spent in ceaseless circuiting of England and Wales, as well as a spell in Ireland, where Henry forced the submission of Strongbow, the King of Leinster, inaugurating 800 years of English interference. It was said that Henry's legs were bandy from spending so much time in the saddle. During his reign, he spent Christmas at 24 different places, crossed the Channel 28 times and the Irish Sea at least twice. Energetic as he was, he could not control the weather: in 1154 Henry had to wait a month to cross to England for his coronation, while in 1171 it took him several weeks to reach Ireland, and longer still to get back. This was what medieval kings had to do to maintain their authority, but Henry's efforts were unique. Peter of Blois, another chronicler dazzled by the King's stamina, wrote:

> He does not remain in his palace as other kings do, but going about the provinces, he investigates the deeds of all, judging those most strictly whom he had appointed judges of others... outsmarting his enemies: he mocks their plots with his sudden appearance.

Accompanying and advising the King was a fluctuating, informal council of individuals he trusted and respected. Alongside regional magnates like Robert, Earl of Leicester, were lesser gentry such as Ranulf de Glanvill, latterly Sheriff of Yorkshire, and men like Richard of Ilchester, a clerk in the royal household who rose to become the first King's Remembrancer, responsible for scrutinising the Exchequer.

What united this collection of nobles, squires, servants and friends was that Henry considered them incorruptible and trusted them to help keep the peace. Some fulfilled domestic, financial and administrative roles in England; others accompanied the King when he went abroad.

Increasingly the clergy scribes would be supplemented by men who had not taken holy orders, but were trained in the law. The first judges were senior churchmen and nobles, but by the end of the 11th century, trained lawyers had joined their ranks, too, and these were not necessarily men who had inherited titles and lands.

Monarchs might still proclaim laws, but these needed to be interpreted and implemented systematically. Trial by ordeal – seeing whether an accused person sank or not when thrown in the river, or whether they burned when grasping a hot coal – was no longer credible, and indeed the practice was banned for clergy by Pope Innocent III in 1215, effectively ending its judicial use.

Through the 11th and 12th centuries, the codifying of laws in documents such as Magna Carta became the hallmark of an increasingly orderly society, one governed by lasting rules instead of circumstances or individual royal whim. But the king's reach still extended into civil disputes and appeals, reinforcing the notion that all were subjects of the Crown.

Wherever the king might be, his permanent administration gradually relocated from Winchester to Westminster. The clerks of the royal bureaucracy were now full-time professionals, improving revenue collection, keeping records and transmitting royal charters across the country. The expansion of paperwork was exponential: thousands of documents remain, copies being made and kept on a routine basis from 1199 onwards. By the 13th century, a simple statistic shows the shift: the bill for sealing wax in the court of Henry III in the 1220s indicates that 3.6lbs were needed per week; by the 1260s, as Henry's long reign neared its end, the quantity was 32lbs.

One area remained beyond royal jurisdiction: the Church. Where did it sit in society? Was it part of it, and thus subject to its secular laws? Or was it beyond and exempt from earthly powers, including the king's? Such unsettled questions caused a series of clashes throughout the Middle Ages, the best-known involving Henry II and his Archbishop of Canterbury.

Following Rufus and Henry's acceptance of the Gregorian reforms, the clergy were subjects of the Pope, and governed by the Church courts. This was the source of the conflict between Henry II and his onetime favourite, Thomas Becket. Theobald of Bec, the 40th Archbishop of Canterbury, had recognised the talent of his young clerk, trusting him with increasingly important duties and eventually recommending him to Henry for the Lord Chancellor's role in 1155. The clerk from Cheapside was now 'second only to the king', so trusted that the heir to the throne, known as 'Henry the Young King', was raised in Becket's household. Things only soured after Theobald's death in 1162 prompted Henry II to give his friend the top church job, an appointment Becket himself had cautioned against, on grounds that a double role as Chancellor and Archbishop would prevent him from giving the King the undivided loyalty he deserved.

At this time, a sixth of the male population was in holy orders. Clerics accused of secular crimes could claim benefit of clergy and be tried in religious courts, avoiding the harsh punishments ordinary mortals faced: church courts could not shed blood, hence there were no executions, amputations or flayings. Henry wanted a single judicial system, applicable to everyone, issuing the Constitutions of Clarendon in 1064: a new law code to limit Church powers. He assumed his loyal ally Becket would back him.

Instead, the Archbishop renounced his role as Chancellor, and declared his opposition to the Constitutions. Accused of contempt and embezzlement, he then fled into exile in France. A compromise was reached, but when Becket returned in 1170, he promptly excommunicated those who had opposed him. It was this that prompted Henry's famously misunderstood – and probably misquoted – outburst. 'Who will rid me of this turbulent priest?' comes to us via a 19th-century translation. Henry's actual utterance was likely closer to: 'What miserable drones and traitors have I nourished and brought up in my household, who let their lord be treated with such shameful contempt by a low-born cleric?' This version, apparently transcribed a few years after Becket's death by Roger of Howden, who was a chronicler at the royal court, seems to have the best claim to authenticity, if not dramatic power.

A Becket pilgrim badge. Examples of these holy souvenirs have been found in France, Belgium, the Netherlands and Norway.

It is almost certain that Becket's murder, by four over-eager knights on sacred ground, was not what Henry had intended. His quick temper and loose tongue were legendary – earlier in his quarrel with Becket, he'd written to the Pope threatening to convert to Islam. But the consequences, this time, breached every protocol of decency, and they required swift reparations.

The King duly rescinded the more contentious clauses of Clarendon and paid penance, walking barefoot into Canterbury Cathedral and allowing himself to be whipped by the monks. He declined to punish Becket's assassins – signalling that he alone was responsible – but also offered them no help. They eventually sought forgiveness from the Pope, who sent them to serve as knights in the Holy Land.

The King survived unchallenged, his powers undiminished. But the Church and its privileges had not been much limited either. Meanwhile Becket was transformed from a fractious politician into a martyr, his tomb a focus of Christian pilgrimage for the next 350 years. At which point another king, still tussling with the Church, would have it destroyed.

The Becket affair undermined Henry's authority with the Church, but soon succession problems arose. When there were competing candidates, the naming of an heir remained a matter of calculation: who was eldest, whose the strongest claim, who the best candidate? Henry's own accession twenty years earlier had strengthened the hereditary principle: that the nearest legitimate heir should succeed (the barons readily adopted it for their own titles, estates and families) and it was not unknown for potential successors to be crowned as insurance against the current incumbent's sudden death. Back in 1170, Henry II's eldest son, known as Henry the Young King, had undergone coronation at Westminster Abbey (anointed by the Archbishop of York while Becket was in exile). Henry II had been ill, so he wanted the succession set and his various territories bequeathed in the way that best promised peace. The intention was that his second son Richard would become ruler of Aquitaine and Geoffrey, his third, should have Normandy. As the youngest, aged four, John was not given territory at that stage, and so became known as Lackland.

But Henry did not die, and within three years his three eldest sons, supported by their mother, rose against him, apparently because he refused to cede any power to them (a perennial complaint of royal heirs). That rebellion was quashed, but ten years later, Young Henry and Geoffrey revolted again, with Henry II this time supported by Richard. Then Young Henry died in 1183 and Richard, now the heir to England, was angered when the King tried to take Aquitaine from him and give it to John.

Richard forged an alliance with the French King, Philip II, and when John – the favourite son – joined them in 1189, this was the last straw for an ailing Henry. Forced to recognise Richard as his heir and to do homage to Philip, he was then carried to his childhood home at Chinon to die, murmuring, 'Shame on a conquered king.'

King Richard I 'The Lionheart' (1189–1199)

Our lion, our more than lion.

> Gerald of Wales, *De Principis Instructione*, ca. 1190–1199

Richard once said that he would sell London if he could find a buyer, a witticism containing truth, since his interest was military and financial. He saw it as a Christian king's duty to fight in a Crusade, and he needed to raise money for it by taxing his subjects. Although born and raised in England, he spoke and wrote little English, and spent only six months of his decade-long reign in his kingdom. Yet the tales of Robin Hood have given him folk hero status, and his mounted statue with raised sword presides heroically over the House of Lords' car park outside Parliament. History (and myth) has seen him as the chivalric Christian warrior-king, not the law-giver or ruler.

Contemporaries, like Gerald, the Archdeacon of Brecon, also saw him as a great Crusader knight, and he was seemingly an able general, whose behaviour – executing thousands of hostages – was unexceptional for the period. Whether his subjects in Aquitaine and England thought highly of him is less certain. They were obliged to pay a 'Saladin tithe', a 10-percent property tax to fund the King's crusade, and five years later, after Richard had been captured whilst returning home through Germany, a 25% levy which was, quite literally, a king's ransom. For his release, the Holy Roman Emperor was paid 150,000 marks, a sum equivalent to 100,000 pounds of silver, and two or three times the King's annual income.

Leonine decoration from Geoffrey of Anjou's tomb

Coats and Crests

Richard's reign bequeathed several symbols used by royalty ever since: the motto *'Dieu et mon Droit'* ('God and My Right') first flourished from a banner at the battle of Gisors in 1198; the three lions on the royal shield (he was, after all, *Coeur de Lion*) were also his, and the first use of 'we' as the royal pronoun. Probably ever since battles became large-scale affairs, warriors have used colours and symbols to identify themselves to their allies in the midst of the fray. By the 12th century, heraldic designs were becoming formalised, and continental nobles were adopting heraldic crests to be handed on to their descendants. Geoffrey of Anjou, Richard's grandfather, may have been one of the first, the shield on his tomb depicting golden lions on a blue background.

Richard I died aged 41 in 1199, wounded by a crossbow bolt at the siege of a minor castle in France. He bequeathed the throne to his untrustworthy brother John, who had schemed against him to get it (one truthful part of the Robin Hood legend), and supersede his 12-year-old nephew, Arthur of Brittany, whose disappearance and likely murder were probably down to John as well.

King John (1199–1216)

Hell itself is made fouler by the presence of King John.
Matthew Paris, *Historia Anglorum* ca. 1250–1259

King John's deeds blended cruelty, ineptitude and deceit, and from contemporary sources onwards there is strong consensus that his reign was disastrous. He failed at every duty of a medieval monarch: alienating nobility and Church, losing his overseas empire, succumbing to invasion by France, subverting the courts and depleting the Treasury whilst crippling the people with taxes. His personal hygiene left something to be desired as well: John's household accounts – the first to survive from a medieval monarchy – indicate that between 1209 and 1210, his ewerer (valet) provided only 23 baths over 16 months.

On the battlefield, John was outplayed by Philip II of France, who seized most of his lands in Anjou and Normandy. He was not assisted by a lifelong tendency to alienate those who might have supported him. The Barnwell Chronicler noted: 'He was generous and liberal to outsiders, but a despoiler of the inhabitants. Since he trusted more in foreigners... he had been abandoned before the end by his people.' In 1205, when John attempted to raise an army and fleet to regain Normandy, England's nobles refused to help and the expedition was cancelled.

Then in 1209, he was excommunicated, having quarrelled with the Pope over the appointment of a new Archbishop of Canterbury. Most English bishops fled into exile, and John seized Church property and revenues; as the subjects of a godless monarch, many ordinary English people now feared for their own immortal souls. The nobles, meanwhile, were increasingly resentful of John's taxes, and his habit of seizing lands and titles on a whim.

John's predecessors had accepted limits to their powers, presiding over a land increasingly governed and judged within a legal framework. John, however, saw his entire realm as an opportunity to be exploited. After losing his French territories, he spent all his time in England, becoming personally involved in legal suits, particularly those which offered some personal benefit to himself. The judicial system continued to develop during his reign, which meant the arbitrary nature of John's personal judgements, and his heavy tax demands, only caused wider consternation. So did the fate of the Earl of Leicester, deprived of his estates in 1207 because he could not meet a debt incurred to John. If a magnate so powerful could be brought low at the King's whim, then few were safe.

England's Jews, too, were targeted for heavy taxation, and as a result many of their debtors were pressured to pay off their entire loans at once. Nothing and no one escaped John's levies, from peasant farmers to burgeoning towns, and while nation-wide prosperity dipped, royal revenues soared. Between 1205 and 1211, they rose from £31,000 to £83,000, a 267% increase. John hoarded his gold at a network of royal castles, and by taking so much coinage out of circulation, he made further tax demands even harder to meet.

Had he been successful in battle, the discontent might have been contained. An opportunity arose in 1213, when he paid the Pope to reverse his excommunication, and to bestow bless-ings on a new invasion of France. But the outcome was a crush-ing defeat for John and the expensive German mercenaries he'd hired. With nothing to show for all the money he'd extracted, the King retreated back over the Channel, to find Wales in revolt.

By May 1215, the barons had had enough; renouncing their oath of loyalty, they issued a list of demands, formulated in what became the Magna Carta (the Great Charter). John accepted it by appending his seal to the document on 15th June, in a field at Runnymede, near Windsor Castle. The location expressed the level of mutual mistrust: an uneven, perpetually muddy water-meadow by the Thames, Runnymede would have made a poor choice for a surprise attack by either side.

The Magna Carta

The charter was probably written by Stephen Langton, the Archbishop of Canterbury whose appointment the King had opposed so disastrously. It contained 61 clauses: many dealt with immediate and local grievances, but others listed, for the first time, a series of more general principles. Three were of particular importance: that no taxation could be levied without agreement; that no free man should be arrested or imprisoned except by lawful judgement; that justice was not to be delayed or denied.

The barons knew exactly what John had been up to, as the wording of Clauses 39 and 40 suggests: 'No freeman shall be arrested or detained in prison, or deprived of his freehold, or outlawed or exiled, or in any way molested... except by the lawful judgement of his peers and by the law of the land. To no one will we sell, to no one will we deny or delay right or justice.'

For John, the hardest clause was the last: it imposed an advisory council of 25 leading nobles which, if necessary, could constrain a king to the extent of taking away his lands.

Magna Carta set precise limits on royal power for the first time, whilst enshrining the rights and freedoms of the nobles. Initially a temporary measure, the charter was amended and supplemented over the ensuing century, and later came to be seen as a fundamental statement of rights. It has been cited in laws and in courts, in England and across the world, including in the Fifth Amendment to the U.S. Constitution: 'no person shall be deprived of life, liberty, or property, without due process of law'. Although most of its clauses have been abolished or transferred into modern law, its status as a foundational document remains, as do four original copies: two in the British Library and one each at Salisbury and Lincoln cathedrals. Numerous later, revised copies from 1300 survive: one was discovered by chance in the town archives of Sandwich in 2015.

At John's request, Pope Innocent III swiftly annulled the charter, declaring it 'not only shameful and base, but also illegal and unjust'. In response, the barons rescinded all feudal obedience, inviting Philip's heir Louis VIII to invade England.

The following year, the French occupied London and Win-chester. The Welsh and Scots rose up again – the Scots got as far as Dover – and John had to resort to pillaging East Anglia and the Midlands. Most of the barons swore fealty to Louis and in October 1216, John went down with dysentery at King's Lynn. As he and his depleted army attempted to cross the Wash at low tide, they lost part of their baggage, includ-ing, it is said, a sizeable amount of money and treasure never since found. John reached Newark, then died. The chroniclers whose abbeys and churches had suffered under his rule spared no time in releasing their invective, few more colourfully than the Benedictine monk Matthew Paris, whose final verdict described John as 'a tyrant rather than a king, a destroyer rather than a governor.'

King Henry III (1216–1272)

> He acted imprudently and without the advice of his nobles, alike rejecting all deliberations and prudence. He ought really to have learned wisdom.
>
> Matthew Paris, *Chronica Majora*, 1258.

After the instability of John's chaotic reign, his son, who became Henry III, would remain on the throne for 56 years. Henry was a pious man, and so peaceable that he even disliked the mock battles of tournaments, although that didn't stop him campaigning vigorously – and expensively – to regain the French lands lost by his father. This, along with a similarly costly attempt to make his son Edmund king of Sicily, yielded nothing but empty coffers.

The funds that did not disappear into imperial follies were lavished on Henry's pet domestic project, the rebuilding of

Westminster Abbey as a shrine to Edward the Confessor. It was a statement both political and pious: the church where William the Conqueror, and every successive Norman monarch had been crowned, was dedicated to a holy Saxon king. In another unifying gesture, Henry named his eldest sons Edward and Edmund – Saxon names for Norman princes.

The Abbey: England's Symbolic Centre

The remains of 17 monarchs lie at Westminster, from Edward the Confessor to George II. When the vaults were opened in the mid-19th century, the coffins were found to have been haphazardly arranged: Elizabeth I was piled on top of her half-sister Mary, and James I's coffin, believed missing for 250 years, was found tucked into Henry VII's vault. From George III onwards, royals have been buried at Windsor.

The Abbey has also hosted 16 royal weddings – most recently that of Prince William and Catherine Middleton in 2011 – along with yearly remembrance services for the war dead. A number of prominent national figures are commemorated and interred there. Although Geoffrey Chaucer was renowned as a poet when he died in 1400, it was as a perk of his day-job as Clerk of the King's Works that he was buried in the cloisters. The custom of interring other notable citizens at the Abbey began in earnest under Oliver Cromwell, and continued when monarchy was restored. Scientists, poets, composers and politicians now share the sacred space with kings and queens, Westminster Abbey remaining, as Henry III intended, the unifying, symbolic heart of the nation.

Aged nine, Henry was crowned at Gloucester under the guardianship of William Marshal, England's leading knight, who had stayed loyal to John. Heredity clearly counted above all else now, and the accession was further assured by the support of the papal legate. The regency was kept stable, first by Marshal, then by Hubert de Burgh, both of whom broadly followed the provisions of Magna Carta. But when Henry came of age in 1232, he launched an era of personal rule – divinely sanctioned, in his view – bypassing the regional magnates and relying instead on the small circle of French nobles who had accompanied his young wife Eleanor of Provence across the Channel.

This, and heavy taxation – aimed particularly at the small Jewish community, whose money had helped the barons meet his tax demands – led to resentment and calls for the foreigners at court to be expelled. What followed was the first sustained attempt to seize control from a king.

In 1258, a group of nobles drew up the Provisions of Oxford. Building on Magna Carta, these reforms demanded the right to representation and consultation in government, a majority of nine seats on a newly-formed, fifteen-man Privy Council, and thrice-yearly parliaments to supervise royal appointments and expenditure, and look out for misrule. A *justiciar* would oversee the courts' administration of the law.

The provisions were published in French, Latin and, for the first time since the Norman Conquest, in English. The following year, they were further amplified by the Provisions of Westminster and Henry, who was by this stage desperate for money to fund his Sicilian venture, had to agree. But he also persuaded the new Pope, Urban IV, to absolve him of his oaths – whereupon civil war broke out.

The barons' leader was the Earl of Leicester, Simon de Montfort, who, as Henry's brother-in-law and closest adviser, had been part of the hated clique surrounding the King, until the two men quarrelled. In the first battle on English soil for nearly

50 years, de Montfort captured Henry and his eldest son Edward at Lewes in May 1264 and summoned a parliament in the King's name, to meet the following year. Each county and significant borough was told to send two representatives. This was not the first parliament – one had been summoned a decade earlier, but that had been at the King's instigation, and called solely to meet his demands for money. This time, the barons were in charge – temporarily – and for the first time, ordinary citizens were given a voice alongside the nobility.

Edward escaped his captors, and found an ally in the young Marcher magnate Gilbert de Clare, who had become aggravated by de Montfort's autocratic style. By August 1265, de Montfort was dead, killed in battle at Evesham, his body cut to pieces and scattered. He is now remembered as the progenitor of parliamentary democracy, but it all began with kidnap and murder.

Page decoration from a late 13th-c. MS., depicting de Montfort's grisly end

Henry was freed by his son, but by way of concession to barons, he agreed to the Statute of Marlborough in 1267, reaffirming Magna Carta and the Provisions of Oxford. Four of the statute's 29 chapters are still enshrined in British law – the oldest surviving legislation, governing the recovery of damages and the recompense of landlords. The format established by Marlborough – a king ruling jointly with a council and Parliament – initially lasted only 18 months, but a precedent had been set.

King Edward I (1272–1307)

> *Hic est Eduardus Primus Scottorum Malleus*
> Here lies Edward, First Hammer of the Scots
>   Tomb inscription of Edward I

The rulers of the Plantagenet dynasty followed a remarkably consistent pattern, from Richard 'the Lionheart' I to John, right through to Richard III's succession after Edward IV: warrior-kings were interspersed with ineffectual rulers and/or despots. Edward I was tall (he was nicknamed 'Longshanks'), athletic and ruthless, with a ferocious Plantagenet temper. Regarded as the ablest knight in Christendom, he was in Italy returning from the Crusades when he heard of his father's death in 1272. The realm was safe – his 35-year reign saw no challengers to the throne – and he felt so confident of this that he took two years to meander home.

On his return, Edward consolidated his overlordship by tackling the most powerful prince to emerge in Wales for generations, Llywelyn ap Gruffudd, who had declined to pay homage to him. The Welsh had been periodically waging guerrilla war against the English border lords for centuries. Now Edward envisaged a permanent solution; it would turn out to be one of the most expensive campaigns ever launched in the British isles. After an economic blockade, he sent a fleet to Anglesey, while troops invaded south from the Marches

Llywelyn was killed and his brother Dafydd executed for treason; it was the first such execution for 200 years and the first time a nobleman received the penalty of hanging, drawing and quartering. English supremacy was consolidated with a ring of crusader-style castles across the country, each one close enough to send troops to help its neighbour in emergencies.

Caernarfon, Harlech, Conwy and Beaumaris were constructed to inspire awe in the surrounding population, the foreign design a pointed reminder that the Welsh were now occupied. Edward made his own son Prince of Wales, and the eldest sons of English sovereigns have borne the title ever since.

Scotland was harder to subdue and would remain so for another three centuries. After the death of Alexander III, king of the Scots, in 1286, Edward pressed his claim to overlordship, betrothing Alexander's infant heiress to his own five-year-old son, but her early death thwarted the plan. Edward then asserted his right to choose Scotland's next king. But when he issued another round of tax demands to fund his war on France, the clan chiefs revolted, and his choice, John Balliol, joined them. In response, Edward destroyed Berwick and captured the Scots' leader William Wallace, who was brought to London and dismembered in the capital's livestock market, Smithfield.

When the century ended, the boundaries of England, Scotland and Wales were much as they are today. English kings would continue asserting their claim to French territory – it was only formally dropped in the reign of George III, and in the Channel Islands, Queen Elizabeth II still bears the title of Duke of Normandy. But whether they pursued imperial ambitions over the Channel, or focussed on peace at home, monarchs ruled less on the basis of what they wanted to do and more on what they *had* to do to get money. In 1290, the King needed funding for military campaigns in Wales. This led directly to him expelling England's small Jewish community, to whom the barons were deeply in debt. This indebtedness became a bargaining tool when a parliament was summoned and Edward demanded a 15% levy. Parliament agreed to Edward's tax, in return for him expelling the Jews and thus writing off the barons' debts.

Although the numbers were small – there were possibly only about 2,000 Jews in the whole country – the community had been convenient scapegoats, hated and persecuted for lending money, accused of being the killers of Christ, propagandised as the murderers of Christian babies and forced to wear badges of identity. They would not be allowed to return to England until Oliver Cromwell's protectorate in 1655, 360 years later.

Increasingly, kings would have to summon a parliament when they needed money. Edward's first was called in 1275, the year after he returned for his coronation. Knights and burgesses were summoned as well as barons, but this was not yet standard practice, and Edward would not summon a parliament so broadly representative again until 1295. On that occasion, there was a key difference in the way the institution operated. The year before, the French had seized Gascony, ushering in a costly war, which the church refused to fund, and the barons refused to provide men for. The King faced trouble to the north as well, as the rebellious Scots sought alliance with France. Accordingly, the Parliament of 1295 involved a significant *quid pro quo*. If the King received his money, then the members of his parliament would have an opportunity to discuss their various grievances with him. Granting taxes was no longer the institution's sole function.

Edward died in 1307 on his way north to tackle the remaining Scottish resistance, led by Robert the Bruce, who had declared himself king the previous year and was now leading an army in revolt. As Edward's tomb in the Abbey declared him: *Primus Scottorum Malleus:* First Hammer of the Scots – it might have added the Welsh, French and Jews – but however hard they were hammered by his successors, those nails would not stay down.

King Edward II (1307–1327)

> He was too familiar with his intimates, shy with strangers,
> and loved too exclusively a single individual.
>
> Sir Thomas Gray, *Scalacronica*, 1355– 1362

The old King had left his 23-year-old heir a hard legacy: an unfinished war in the North, and huge debts from previous campaigns. Edward II was the only male son of his father's first marriage to survive infancy; his reign would be characterised, like his great-grandfather John's, as a dismal failure, ending with his overthrow and probable murder.

Edward II's relations with the regional magnates foundered early because of his reliance on a favourite from outside their number – the young French knight, Piers Gaveston. The two men were clearly close, though not necessarily lovers as alleged. Edward's father certainly thought the relationship was too close, and as his reign ended, he had Gaveston exiled to his native Gascony. Edward II recalled him as soon as he became king.

The barons, led by the Earl of Lincoln, immediately tried to limit Edward's authority – as they would have done with his father, had he not been so powerful. Emphasising to the new monarch that their allegiance was to the office of king, not the person, they banished Gaveston again, this time to Ireland. Once again, Edward II defiantly recalled him, prompting the barons, led by Lincoln and Edward's cousin, the Earl of Lancaster, to issue Ordinances.

Some of these were sensible administrative and financial reforms: taxes and import duties were to be paid into the exchequer, not to foreign bankers. Others were undisguised constraints on Edward's activities: he could not wage war, or leave the kingdom without permission from Parliament. And

Gaveston was to be exiled once more. When he slipped back in again, he was imprisoned and executed in 1312.

The reign might have returned to an even keel, if Edward had not resumed his father's campaign against Scotland. At Bannockburn, in June 1314, Robert the Bruce's small, nimble army defeated a much larger English force sent to relieve the garrison at Stirling castle. More than 200 English knights were killed and many more held for ransom. The humiliation spread beyond the battlefield, with the Scots occupying much of northern England.

And the King soon had new favourites to aggravate the barons. Hugh Despenser and his father – also named Hugh – became Edward's chief advisers, receiving lavish gifts of lands and favours. They were a corrupt and manipulative pair, apt to use their powerful connections against rivals, challengers and anyone who fell foul of them. The King allowed it, as he was intent on punishing those who had caused Gaveston's downfall, such as the Earl of Lancaster.

The discontent was nationwide, as the years 1315 to 1322 saw a series of bad harvests and plagues, causing starvation, the death of livestock and rising prices. Having reached around four million by the end of the 13th century, the population would sink to 2.5 million in the mid-14th, barely recovering for decades afterwards.

Civil war broke out in 1321, the barons were defeated at Boroughbridge, and Lancaster and many leading rebels were executed or deprived of their lands. It was unprecedented for someone as high ranking as Lancaster, the King's own cousin, to be beheaded – few nobles felt safe, and hatred for the Despensers and Edward was widespread. The Marcher Lord and Lord-Lieutenant of Ireland, Roger Mortimer, escaped to France, where he began a relationship with Edward's estranged wife Isabella, who herself hated the Despensers. Gathering an army, they invaded England in 1326, killed the King's favourites and captured him.

The rebels argued that Edward had breached the Ordinances by leaving the kingdom without the permission of Parliament. This was a legalistic quibble, since Edward had merely headed for Wales, which his father had made part of the kingdom, but given this monarch's unpopularity, it proved sufficient. For extra validation, the Parliament of 1327 proclaimed that Edward had lost Gascony and Scotland through bad advice and 'caused to be slain a great part of the noble blood of the land to the dishonour and loss of himself, his realm and the whole people and... done many other astonishing things.' Declaring that he should no longer reign, they promptly crowned his 14-year-old son and heir, also Edward.

The King was held at Berkeley Castle and died there, though probably not by the insertion of 'a hot spit put through the secret place posterial' as a later chronicler claimed. He was more likely smothered – a method allowing for doubt over the true cause of death, and an important consideration, since the murder of an anointed king was so daunting an act.

The murder of Edward II was a historic decision: the first time a king was formally deposed, and a measure of how much power the barons and Parliament had assumed. Edward's mistake had been to ignore these power-brokers and place his faith in favourites like Gaveston and the Despensers, who only held power through him. But this was not an attempt to overthrow the monarchy, merely to replace the monarch with the rightful successor – his son.

King Edward III (1327–1377)

> Against his foes he was grim as a leopard, toward his subjects mild as a lamb.
>
>   Ranulf Higden (attrib.), ca. 1300

This 15th-c. depiction of the Battle of Crécy shows French crossbowmen falling prey to the superior English longbows. In retreat, the crossbowmen hampered a French cavalry charge, a further factor in Edward's victory.

Edward III did not make his father's mistakes: he was his own man, unchallenged by rivals or rebellions in England. But much of his half-century reign was taken up with pursuing his ambitions across the Channel. His title described him as *Rex Angliae et Franciae et Dominus Hiberniae* and he considered his realm to stretch down the entire western side of France, from Calais to the Pyrenees. Defending and expanding such a territory required loans from Italian bankers, as well as parliamentary approval for taxes and for a new source of revenue: customs duties on England's expanding international wool trade. Such commerce with the Continent should have made the nation flourish. Instead, throughout the 14th and 15th centuries, England was either waging war in Europe or preparing for it.

The Everlasting Fight

The Hundred Years' War lasted on and off from 1337 to 1453 and was essentially about English kings trying to win the French crown and territory.

There were three phases, with intervals, sometimes decades long, of peace (or at least no war). The period from 1337 to 1360 involved English offensives in western France alongside attempts to end French control over the Flemish cloth trade, and it delivered some huge but expensive victories. At Crécy in 1346, English archers scattered the undisciplined French knights, and at Poitiers, a decade later, Edward's son and heir – another Edward, later called 'the Black Prince' by Tudor historians – captured France's King Jean II.

Hostilities were brought to a close at the Treaty of Brétigny in 1360, when Edward renounced his claim to the French throne in return for untrammelled control over the Plantagenets' traditional lands in Aquitaine. A decade later, the fighting restarted when Edward revived his claim to the French crown, but they petered out again without any English gains, under the weight of the war's unpopularity and cost at home. War resumed in earnest in 1415, with Henry V taking advantage of the French King Charles VI's debilitating psychosis (he thought he was made of glass). Following England's unlikely triumph at Agincourt,

Henry was promised the French throne after Charles but both men died – Henry first – within weeks of each other in 1422.

England's triumphs were costly and brief. After a century of intermittent fighting, the outcome was the loss of most of England's French territory, and an end to its imperial pretensions in Europe.

The huge bills incurred by these campaigns could only be partly offset with the ransoms paid by captured rulers and nobles. Edward wisely called regular parliaments to agree funding, but the costs of these regular expeditions rose because of the Black Death epidemic sweeping England (and Europe and Asia) between 1348 and 1350.

In Sickness and in Wealth

The Black Death was an international disease, which killed perhaps 25 million across Europe. The plague arrived in England in June 1348, on a ship from Gascony. It swept the country in about 500 days, wiping out about a third of the population. Even at the pandemic's peak, the government continued to function, but the economic and social consequences were profound. Labour shortages caused rises in wages and prices, which the authorities tried to curb with the 1349 Statute of Labourers. This ordered workers to continue under the same contracts as before, causing resentment and unrest, and ultimately leading to the Peasants' Revolt of 1381. The plague ended the feudal system, as the link between lords and their workers became based on pay, not obligations of service. Afterwards, soldiers would have to be paid to enlist, and local barons had to use other means to control and coerce: the first Justices of the Peace were appointed in 1352.

By the 1370s, Edward was visibly declining, perhaps senile, and his eldest son, the Black Prince, was also dying from dysentery. The 'Good' Parliament of 1376 initially refused to levy more taxation for further French campaigns, and felt confident enough to elect the first Speaker, and impeach the King's younger son, John of Gaunt and his mistress Alice Perrers for profiteering. It gave way on the financial front, though, agreeing to a heavy poll tax of four pence from everyone over the age of 14 – another factor in the Peasants' Revolt five years later.

The profiteering charges were heard by the House of Lords – another innovation – but the Gaunt-controlled 'Bad' Parliament granted pardons the following year, as well as impeaching the Speaker and sacking the Lord Chancellor, William of Wykeham (leaving him free to found Winchester College and its sister institution New College, Oxford).

The Black Prince died in June 1376, followed nearly a year later by the King, probably after several strokes, if the twisted mouth on his wooden funeral effigy is accurate. This is the first

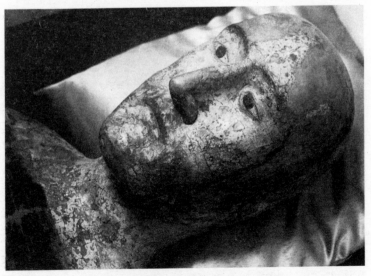

Edward III's effigy at Westminster Abbey

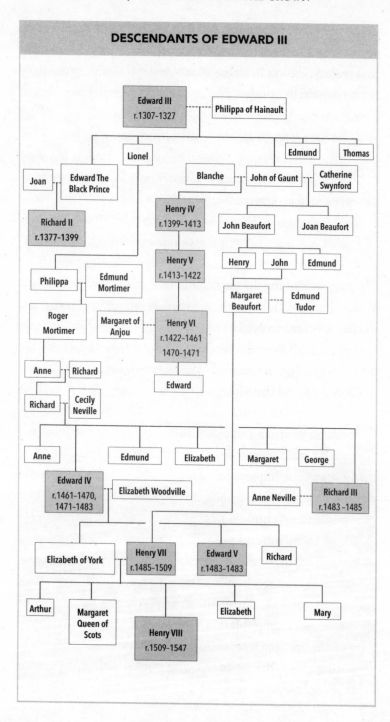

DESCENDANTS OF EDWARD III

contemporary and realistic statuary of an English king known to survive: from the 14th century onwards, more permanent and realistic figures in alabaster and bronze would increasingly adorn monarchs' tombs.

King Richard II (1377–1399)

> Capricious in his manners, prodigal in his gifts, extravagantly splendid in his entertainments and dress.
>
> *History of the Life and Reign of Richard II*
> by a 15th-century monk of Evesham

The successor to the throne was the 10-year-old son of the Black Prince, Richard II, leapfrogging the line of succession over his uncles, the Duke of Clarence, and John of Gaunt, Duke of Lancaster, who were the second and third sons of Edward III, respectively. The descendants of these two men would cause havoc in England throughout the next century.

We know what Richard looked like, from the Westminster Coronation portrait and the Wilton Diptych in the National Gallery. If his reputation derives largely from Shakespeare's play, that gives a false impression of passivity. Richard was active in pursuit of his prerogatives and privileges as king – insisting that subjects approach him on bended knee – and maladroit in his choice of favourites and political manoeuvres. He contributed much, personally, to the instability of the next hundred years.

Richard's courage, however, was in no doubt, as testified by his actions, aged 14, during the Peasants' Revolt of 1381. 'Peasants' is actually something of a misnomer, since the foot soldiers of the uprising were mostly farmers and small tradesmen, protesting about the poll tax being trebled to a shilling, and demanding an end to serfdom and wage restrictions. On 13th

June 1381, a mob from Essex and Kent arrived in the capital. Subsequently they broke into the Tower of London, slaughtered the Archbishop of Canterbury along with other leading government officials, and burned down John of Gaunt's Savoy Palace. On 15th June, at Smithfield, Richard calmly approached the ring leaders, and talked with their chief, Wat Tyler. As they spoke, Tyler may have placed an over-familiar hand on the

The Peasants' Revolt: Wat Tyler is struck down by the Mayor while the King looks on.x

young King, or looked as if he was about to strike him; the Mayor of London responded by fatally stabbing Tyler. Reassured by the King's promise that they would not be punished and that their grievances would be addressed, the mob dispersed peacefully. The royal pledge was immediately broken, and the surviving leaders hunted down. 'Rustics you were and rustics you remain... we will strive to suppress you,' the teenaged monarch told them.

Richard chose his own councillors, the 'chamber knights', a parvenu clique who were lavished with lands and titles. This alienated many powerful regional magnates at a time when taxes had risen to prepare for a potential invasion by the French. The 'Wonderful' Parliament of 1386 voted to impeach one of the favoured knights, the Chancellor Michael de la Pole (the son of a merchant, not an aristocrat). Two years later, the 'Merciless' Parliament purged the rest of the clique and executed many.

Richard had declared that he would not dismiss a scullion from his kitchen at the request of Parliament, but he was forced to backtrack when threatened with deposition. He grudgingly accepted a parliamentary commission to oversee his expenditure and limit the power he could grant to his favourites.

The insult was not forgotten, and Richard eventually turned on his enemies: in 1397 the Earl of Arundel was executed, the Duke of Gloucester murdered and the Earl of Warwick exiled. But when he sent Gaunt's hitherto loyal son, Henry Bolingbroke, into exile in 1398, Richard took a step too far. Gaunt himself died a few months later, and the King seized the family's estates: a fatal mistake born of greed.

The legitimate successor was seven-year-old Edmund Mortimer, offspring of Edward III's second son, the Duke of Clarence. Parliament had no wish for another child successor, though, so it gladly accepted Henry Bolingbroke, particularly when he promised that there would be no new taxes. He may not, originally, have sought to anything more than reclaim his family estates, but he wasn't shy of taking the throne when invited.

The lesson of Richard's reign was that kings could not alienate the power-brokers of the country or bend Parliament to the will of the Crown. But the ousting of an anointed monarch called into question the legitimacy of the House of Lancaster.

Kings had been deposed before: seventy years earlier, Edward II's deposition had been followed by the rightful succession of his son and heir. This time, however, the throne had been taken in a coup, and as a descendant of Edward III's third son, Bolingbroke's claim was weaker.

To bolster his legitimacy, he claimed his right 'by... line of the Blood coming from the good lord King Henry III' and the anointing oil used to crown him as King Henry IV was said to have come from the Virgin Mary, via Thomas Becket. The least secure medieval monarchs were keenest to emphasise their Christian kingship.

King Henry IV (1399–1413)

> This canker Bolingbroke
> *Henry IV, Part I* by William Shakespeare, ca. 1597

Henry IV's 14-year reign was beset by challengers: the Welsh landowner Owain Glyndwr rebelled, claiming the title of Prince of Wales. He was supported by the Earls of Northumberland, the Percy clan, who felt that they had not been sufficiently rewarded for helping Henry to take the throne. Both were eventually beaten off: Harry Hotspur, the Northumberland heir, was killed in battle at Shrewsbury, and Glendwr disappeared. But Henry's treasury was severely depleted by the cost of keeping regional magnates loyal and defending his rule – at one stage the King could not even afford to pay the royal messengers – and eventually he broke his promise on taxation.

Discontent followed, and Richard Scrope, Archbishop of York, tried to foment rebellion, only to be lured to a meeting with Henry and beheaded. It was a conspicuous sin against the Church, but, unlike the only other royal assassination of an

Archbishop (Becket in 1170) this did not have serious reper-
cussions for the King. It was, nevertheless, uncharacteristic for
Henry, who was a conciliator, able to pardon rivals and compromise with Parliament.

From 1406, his health was failing, apparently because of a skin
condition (possibly a symptom of syphilis). His relations with his
son were difficult, though not, as Shakespeare alleged, because of
Prince Hal's companions, but due to policy differences and the
age-old issue of the older man being reluctant to cede power to
the younger. A soothsayer is supposed to have predicted that the
King would die in Jerusalem, and so it happened, but not on a
crusade. On Thursday, 20th March 1413, Henry IV died in the
Jerusalem antechamber next to Westminster Abbey.

King Henry V (1413–1422)

> The myghty and puissaunt conquerour
>> *Vita Henrici Quinti Regis Angliae*, Tito Livio dei
>> Frulovisi, 1437

Tough and pious, Henry V had already established his cre-
dentials fighting the Welsh and the Northumberland Percys
on behalf of his father, as well as suppressing the proto-
Protestant Lollard sect. Aged 26 when he became king, he set
about reasserting the claim of his great-grandfather Edward III
to the western French territories once held by the Angevins.

Diplomacy failed. Envoys from the Dauphin, the heir to
the French throne, famously told the King he was too young
to make war with France and offered him tennis balls instead
('*he schulde have sumwhat to play with-alle, for hym & for his
lords*'). The French may also have tried to assassinate him by
bribing disaffected aristocrats. Henry enthusiastically prepared

for war, raising loans and getting Parliament to agree new taxes. In the summer of 1415, he invaded France.

A third of Henry's small army died of dysentery, and the campaign was a near-disaster, redeemed only as the King and his bedraggled army were staggering homewards towards Calais. The unexpected nature of the victory is exactly why the battle of Agincourt plays such a part in the national mythology: England's stroke of luck became England's character and destiny, the plucky underdog who triumphs against overwhelming odds.

Nevertheless, it was a considerable military achievement and a mark of Henry's own inspirational leadership. Contemporary chroniclers praised him to the hilt and Shakespeare's treatment would endorse the victory further, ensuring that later generations only remembered one medieval hero-king. Had the Bard adapted Crécy or Poitiers for the stage, perhaps Edward III might be recalled more widely.

After further campaigns, the 1420 Treaty of Troyes cemented peace with Henry's marriage to King Charles's teenaged daughter, Catherine. It was the triumph his predecessors had dreamed of, but it was short-lived. The King died two years later, still battling in France, leaving a nine-month-old heir whom he had never seen. Henry V was the first king since the Conquest to speak better English than French; yet he was regent and heir to the French throne, and he died in France.

King Henry VI
(Reigned 1422–1461 and 1470–1471)

A mild spoken, pious king, but half-witted in affairs of state
Chronicle of John Whethamstead,
Abbot of St Albans, 1465

Despite a long reign, Henry VI was largely unfitted for medieval kingship. A passive, indeed peaceable man – the Abbot (see above) went on to describe him as 'a son greatly degenerated from his father, who did not cultivate the art of war' – Henry was the only king of his era not to lead troops personally into battle. His perceived weakness allowed ambitious regional barons to vie for his throne, plunging England into the Wars of the Roses – the longest period of civil strife in its history.

Yet Henry's inheritance was enormous: the only dual monarchy in English history, requiring him to be crowned twice – first when he was aged eight, in 1429 at Westminster Abbey, and again in Paris two years later, on his first and last visit to the Continent. He never saw Ireland and went just once to Wales and Scotland, the latter while fleeing the war.

Other kings had inherited the throne as children, but Henry was the youngest, with the longest period under guardianship. His uncles Humphrey, Duke of Gloucester, and John, Duke of Bedford, took care of England and France respectively, assisted by his great uncle, Henry Beaufort, the Bishop of Winchester. Meanwhile his education was overseen by the Earl of Warwick from the powerful Neville clan. It was an uneasy coalition.

Wars with France dragged expensively on, punctuated by occasional truces, the campaigns subcontracted to a series of generals as territory was nibbled away. In 1445, a marriage was brokered between Henry and Margaret of Anjou, niece of the French king. She brought no great dowry. In fact, her uncle Charles VII demanded the western provinces of Maine and Anjou in return.

Henry's chief focus was on founding Eton and King's College, Cambridge, which he endowed lavishly, and on rewarding his friends at court. Charges of extravagance arose, leading in 1450 to a rebellion led by the Kentish yeoman Jack Cade, the first since the Peasants' Revolt seventy years earlier.

Even after coming of age in 1437, Henry remained under the influence of more ambitious and power-hungry men, although his loyalties vacillated frequently. In 1447, Duke Humphrey died in captivity, accused of treason by Henry's new favourite, William de la Pole, Duke of Suffolk. Three years later, Suffolk himself would be seized and executed as he fled into exile.

Henry was not simple-minded, as some contemporaries alleged, but he was inconsistent, naïve and unreliable: all major flaws in an era of personal kingship. In August 1453, he suffered a complete mental breakdown, possibly triggered by defeat at the battle of Castillon and the subsequent loss of Gascony. Not even the birth of his son and heir, Edward, in October, could improve his state of mind; Henry was in a catatonic state for over a year, unable to speak or recognise anyone. Diagnosis at a distance of almost six centuries is impossible, but the recorded symptoms suggest severe depression or schizophrenia.

With the King incapacitated and an infant as his putative heir, two powerful nobles were circling the throne: Richard, the Duke of York, and Edmund Beaufort, Duke of Somerset. Their rival claims dated back to key events in the previous century. First, in 1377, Richard II's accession had bypassed his uncles, the Duke of Clarence (whose descendants became Dukes of York) and John of Gaunt, Duke of Lancaster. Next, in 1399, Gaunt's son, Henry Bolingbroke had usurped the throne for the Lancasters – becoming King Henry IV – ahead of Richard II's rightful, Yorkist successor, Edmund Mortimer.

It was their descendants who were now eyeing up the crown in the mid-15th century: the Duke of York was Mortimer's nephew, while the Duke of Somerset, as grandson of John of Gaunt, was the new hope of the Lancaster dynasty. York had been regent while Henry was incapacitated – and had kept his rival Somerset imprisoned. However, Henry's recovery, at the end of 1454, altered the balance of power: the King freed Somerset, and the Duke of York was forced to flee the court.

The Wars of the Roses, between the Royal House of Lancaster (to which Henry VI belonged) and York, were the culmination of the rival dynasties' extended struggles, with the wan, bedraggled figure of the King stuck in between. Despite his brief rally, Henry was, according to the contemporary Pope Pius II, 'more timorous than a woman, utterly devoid of wit or spirit'.

The 'Roses' refer to the heraldic emblems of the clans – the Lancastrians' red rose and the Yorkists' white – though it wasn't until the 19th century and the writing of Sir Walter Scott that the conflict came to be known thus. Fighting would rage on and off for thirty years, encompassing some of the bloodiest battles on English soil.

Hostilities began in May 1455, as Somerset and his Lancastrian allies headed to Leicester to convene a Great Council and consolidate their control over the King. The banished Duke of York assembled an army and intercepted them at St Albans, where Somerset was killed and the King captured. He would be captured repeatedly as the rival clans jockeyed for primacy. York himself was killed at Wakefield in December 1460; three months later, in March 1461 – and thanks to the support of the powerful Earl of Warwick – York's son Edward declared himself king, and Henry was imprisoned in the Tower. For most of the next decade, England would have two, crowned and anointed kings.

Within weeks of assuming the kingship, Edward IV defeated the Lancastrians at Towton, reputedly the bloodiest battle ever fought on English soil. The new King could now claim the throne through right of battle, although that didn't bring peace. In 1464, the Earl of Warwick quarrelled with

Edward and switched allegiance, ostensibly because the young King had, without consultation, married Elizabeth Woodville, a commoner.

With Warwick's assistance, Henry VI was restored to the throne in October 1470, so feeble mentally that he had to be led by the hand as he paraded through London. Within eight months, both Warwick and Henry's teenage heir Edward had died in battle, the King had met his end during a final spell in the Tower, Edward was king once more, and the House of York triumphant. The official cause of Henry's demise was grief upon learning of his son's death, although murder on Edward IV's orders was widely suspected at the time, and corroborated by the exhumation of his remains in 1910.

Usurper though he was, Edward cut a more regal figure than his predecessor: he was 20 years younger than Henry, six feet four in height, athletic, handsome and a proven victor in battle. Many welcomed the change.

King Edward IV (1461–1470; 1471–1483)

> Edward was of a gentle manner and cheerful aspect, nevertheless should he assume an angry countenance, he could be very terrible to beholders.
>
> Dominic Mancini, *De Occupatione Regni Anglie per Riccardum Tercium* (after a visit to England in 1482–1483)*

Edward IV was the first king in three hundred years to marry a commoner, and the first ever to insist on being addressed as Your Majesty. He was ruthless, not just in his disposal of Henry VI, but also of his younger brother, the Duke of Clar-

---

* Mancini's report was probably written at the behest of one of the French king's closest advisers. It was lost for centuries, until being rediscovered by chance in the Municipal Library in Lille in 1934.

ence, whose execution Edward ordered on trumped-up treason charges (although tales of his being drowned in a butt of sweet Malmsey wine apparently stem from a dark joke Edward told about his late brother's favourite drink). Bad taste aside, Edward ruled more consistently than Henry, restoring the prior pattern of medieval monarchy: personal rule by the King, while his officials dispensed justice and gathered taxes. Edward's alternative streams of income meant the population wasn't too heavily taxed: the King did well from the wool trade and the customs revenue it garnered, as well as from investments in the City of London and his close relationship with the Medici banking family. Peace prevailed after he retook the throne in 1471, and the economy revived from a 20-year slump.

Edward was thus often able to avoid taxing the nation – and having to secure Parliament's permission to do so – but funds from all sources tended to be lavished on the royal household. Personally self-indulgent, he amassed a fine library, never stinted on clothes, jewels or ornaments, nor missed a dinner. Contemporaries described him as having grown fat and greedy, and he died suddenly, aged 41, in April 1483.

He left a much-depleted treasury and unpaid debts to the Medicis. Another unfortunate part of his legacy was putting his brother Richard, Duke of Gloucester, in charge of his twelve-year-old son and heir – also named Edward. On learning of his father's death, the Prince swiftly set out for London from Ludlow, where he had been raised by Lord Rivers, one of his numerous Woodville uncles, but before he could claim the throne, he was intercepted en route by Gloucester. He was taken to the Tower of London, allegedly for his own safety, and the date for his coronation was postponed. When Lord Rivers objected, he was accused of subverting the will of the late King, and executed. Gloucester's men then visited the boy's mother, who had taken refuge in

Westminster Abbey, and persuaded her to hand over her younger son Richard – claiming they wished to take him to Edward's coronation. He joined his elder brother in the Tower.

Within weeks, Gloucester was claiming that both of the 'Princes in the Tower' were illegitimate, the offspring of a secret marriage prior to Edward IV's union with Elizabeth Woodville. He also claimed that the late king, Edward IV, had been illegitimate, though he dropped this latter allegation once he was proclaimed King Richard III on 6th July 1483. A few weeks after that, the boys disappeared forever. Two skeletons found behind a wall 200 years later may be theirs.

The Princes in the Tower: an Edwardian depiction

King Richard III (1483–1485)

There is no creature loves me; and if I die, no soul will pity me
Richard III in William Shakespeare's *Richard III*

Richard III's action was not unprecedented – his brother Edward IV had done away with Henry VI and his own brother Clarence, after all. But it subverted the natural order of succession, while the disappearance and probable murder of the two defenceless princes in his care was a grave crime. Moreover, after executing Lord Rivers, Richard then murdered Lord Hastings, an enemy of the widowed queen's Woodville faction, who had not only advised Edward IV to make his brother guardian to the young Prince, but also tipped off Richard about the party leaving Ludlow for London. The new King looked very much like someone trying to cover his tracks.

Historians still debate whether Richard actually ordered his nephews' murder, but contemporaries thought so – he had means, motive and opportunity – and in the eyes of many of them, that undermined his legitimacy. The *Great Chronicle of London* lamented: 'Had he... suffered the little children to have prospered according to his allegiance and fealty, he would have been honourably lauded... whereas now his fame is darkened.'

Support seeped away and a Lancastrian challenger soon surfaced: the 28-year-old Henry Tudor, whose tenuous claim came through his mother Margaret Beaufort, a great-granddaughter of John of Gaunt's long-term mistress (and eventual wife), Katherine Swynford. Margaret had married into the landowning Welsh Tudor dynasty, just as Henry V's French widow Catherine de Valois had, a generation earlier. That happy coincidence meant that the King of France, Charles VIII gave his backing (and thus lent credibility) to the claim of young *Hari Tewdwr*.

In 1485, Henry sailed from France, landing in Wales with 3,000 French mercenaries to do battle with Richard at Bosworth in Leicestershire. The King had superior numbers, but his ruthlessness was ultimately his undoing. He'd taken Lord Stanley's son hostage in order to ensure his loyalty, but as commander of Richard's army, Stanley commanded more loyalty than the King. A swathe of Royal forces followed him in deserting to the Tudor side, Richard was killed – his crown apparently found hanging on a nearby hawthorn tree – and his naked body carted off to Greyfriars Abbey in nearby Leicester.

Shakespeare helped to spread the Tudor propagandists' message that Richard's misshapen body reflected the twisted nature of his soul. The bones recovered from underneath a car park on the former Abbey site in 2012 do suggest scoliosis, or curvature of the spine. Richard III's reign was the shortest of any crowned monarch since the Norman Conquest, and he was the first English king to be killed in battle since 1066. But he was not uniquely bad by the standards of his time, just ruthlessly ambitious, opportunistic – and, perhaps, unlucky.

An 18th-century engraving of Richard III

The Middle Ages did not end on a field in the Midlands one afternoon in August 1485, but Richard's death did mark the end of an interrelated family dynasty whose scions had ruled England for over 300 years. The Lancastrian and Yorkist factions were finally united dynastically through Lancastrian Henry VII's marriage to Elizabeth of York. Thus the Tudor dynasty was still descended from the bloodline of John of Gaunt, through Henry

VII's mother Margaret Beaufort, Gaunt's great-granddaughter*.

In the Plantagenet centuries, the feudal notion of service to one's lord in peace and war had eroded, and monarchs had realised that they could not rule alone. There was nothing approaching democracy, but to raise money, ensure allegiance and acquire consent, kings needed to call increasingly regular parliaments from amongst the nobility and knights of the shires.

In 1485, challenging an anointed king was no less of an undertaking, spiritually and legally, than it had been in 1185, but the mere fact of it being tried throughout the intervening centuries, sometimes successfully, had made it more conceivable. England's medieval kings were educated men, increasingly fluent in English, as well as French and Latin and fully aware of their Christian heritage and patronage (even if the numbers of their mistresses and illegitimate children showed faith more often in the breach than the observance).

In return for power, those kings had to govern justly, obey the laws they had agreed to with their nobles, and not exact more money than their nobles were prepared to give. If they breached such conditions, then they could forfeit their throne. That usually meant forfeiting life, too: of the 13 monarchs between Henry III and Henry VIII, only six were fortunate enough to die in their beds.

But even when kings were replaced, monarchy remained. English society became relatively stable under a network of locally administered laws, courts and administration, which kept running even during the Black Death and the Wars of the Roses. Kings still circuited their realm with entourages, but the machinery of government, from law-making to revenue-

---

* As were the Stuarts, through Henry VII's daughter Margaret, who married Scotland's James IV, and the Hanoverians and Windsors, linked through James I's daughter Elizabeth, grandmother of George I, and thus the great(x9)- grandmother of Elizabeth II.

counting, was based in London, and carried out by a salaried staff of laymen, speaking and writing in English.

The biggest strain on domestic stability was posed by the military ambitions of kings, which cost money and caused unrest. The loss of the French territories meant that kings eventually focussed their attention on England, but that often meant more time spent subduing the Celtic nations, with campaigns, soldiers, money and taxes. And wherever the money went, it was usually a waste. Victories like Agincourt, Crécy and Poitiers were exceptions, but they were eagerly ascribed to God's special favour, to the English nation, and to the monarchs He set over them.

They fed into an emerging myth of England as a nation uniquely blessed. As the leading 15th-century jurist, Sir John Fortescue put it: 'From of old, English kings have reigned independently and acknowledged no superior on earth in things temporal... there is no gainsaying nor legitimate doubt but that the customs of England are not only good but the best.' Since antiquity, Fortescue said, English law and royal government had made the country 'the mightiest and most wealthy realm of the world.' From believing their realm to be the best, it was, of course, just a short step to believing that they should conquer all the other ones. Monarchs would spend much of the next four centuries trying to do just that.

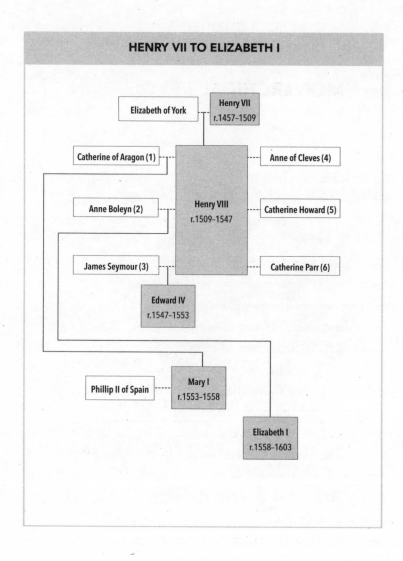

HENRY VII TO ELIZABETH I

Elizabeth of York

Henry VII
r.1457–1509

Catherine of Aragon (1)

Anne of Cleves (4)

Anne Boleyn (2)

Henry VIII
r.1509–1547

Catherine Howard (5)

James Seymour (3)

Catherine Parr (6)

Edward IV
r.1547–1553

Phillip II of Spain

Mary I
r.1553–1558

Elizabeth I
r.1558–1603

CHAPTER 3

MONARCHICAL REVOLUTION

> By the ancient laws of this realm this kingdom of England is an absolute empire and monarchy.
>
> Judgement in the Court of Queen's Bench, 1591

The Tudors seized power from the Plantagenets in a coup, and their dynasty survived for 118 years, petering out only because of a lack of heirs. Even so, in three generations they transformed monarchy by seizing control of the Church, its land and property, and moulding it into an instrument of the state.

They also stamped their image on the country with numerous licensed portraits and, in the case of Elizabeth I, by using masques and performances to create a cult around the monarch. They all employed ruthless means – and ruthless men – to maintain their rule and fortify it against challenges, real and perceived; this was an age of plots and spy-masters. And they often saw the law as a means to an end, rather than a way of establishing justice: seizing property and inflicting horrific punishments to attain their goals. Under Henry VIII especially, Tudor rule was despotic and terrifying.

Swift and severe: Bills of Attainder
Until the 18th century ended, monarchs would routinely

charge opponents with high treason, before serving them with a Bill of Attainder. The word 'Bill' suggests a process of deliberation and judgement, but their very attraction for kings was that, because of the treason charge, Parliaments could be coerced into passing them without the formalities, delays and uncertainties of a court trial. Attainders were draconian: aristocrats lost their lands, wealth and titles, meaning royal disfavour was visited on whole families and descendants. Reduced to the rank of commoner, the attainted could be subjected to torture, from which aristocrats were exempt. Monarchs found Bills of Attainder (and the mere threat of them) useful for ensuring loyalty and conformity, as well as for raising money: in return for 'fines' from penitent nobles, Richard III reversed 99 out of 100 attainders while Henry VI reversed every one of the 21 he'd issued.

The Tudors were less forgiving: attainders helped Henry VIII rid himself of two wives and his once-trusted adviser Thomas Cromwell. The U.S. Constitution forbids attainder and the 'corruption of blood': punishing heirs and successors for their antecedents' crimes.

Under the Tudors, parliaments met infrequently and briefly and were often ignored, but the previously hard-won principle of consent to taxation was upheld. If a monarch required extra money – to pursue wars, defeat uprisings or meet the costs of extravagant living in an inflationary age – they needed agreement. If they were wise, as Elizabeth I was, they cajoled and flattered the Commons. Those attending parliaments could now make their views known on other matters, if they had the nerve to do so, but it has been estimated that they were in session for only about eight years during the whole of the Tudor period.

The monarchs governed with the advice of their great councils, appointed by themselves and consisting of between twenty and forty favoured advisers and bureaucrats, consciously working at the monarch's pleasure and liable to dismissal or worse at a moment's notice, as some of Henry VIII's councillors found out. Those with the most power in Tudor government were not always from aristocratic backgrounds: Thomas Wolsey was an Ipswich butcher's son, Thomas Cromwell the son of a Putney publican and William Cecil, Lord Burghley, was descended from a line of social-climbing Welsh squires, the Seiysilles. Such men wielded considerable authority when monarchs allowed them to get on with government business – as Henry VIII and Elizabeth I did – but they knew they held office only on sufferance.

The royal court was another centre of power; its officers, the Comptroller and Lord Chamberlain, powerful figures organising the monarch's life and controlling access to him or her. It was now a highly public life for a ruler, of display and interaction from morning until bedtime, watched and entreated by a constant queue of nobles, prelates, ambassadors, lawyers and supplicants. Like their predecessors, the Tudors still interacted with ordinary people, especially those who came to be cured of scrofula – tubercular swelling of the lymph glands in the neck – by the 'King's Touch', thanks to the purported healing power of a monarch's hands.

Trialled from the 13th century onwards, the idea of ruling by consent was regarded as superior to the absolutist monarchy across the Channel. French monarchs might theoretically consult different strata of society, but rarely did so: the equivalent of Parliament, the *États Generaux*, was not summoned between 1484 and 1560, and ignored again between 1614 and 1789, by which time the bankrupted country was ripe for revolution. Whether English monarchs liked it or not, whether they called it 'consent' or something else, the last four centuries had proved that the land contained other, muscular sources of power, and that royal rule had continually to be negotiated.

King Henry VII (1485–1509)

> His appearance was remarkably attractive and his face was cheerful, especially when speaking. His eyes were small and blue, his teeth few, poor and blackish, his hair was thin and white, his complexion sallow.
>
> Polydor Vergil, *English History* ca. 1513

Henry Tudor was 28, he had vanquished Richard III and launched the most famous dynasty in English history, but his claim to the throne was weak. It was thanks to the Wars of the Roses that he faced so little competition: several leading aristocratic families had been wiped out. With the remaining nobles, Henry VII deployed a mixture of diplomacy, threats and financial exactions to ensure compliance and to secure the succession for his son. By the end of his 24-year term, the Tudors were not only rich, but dominant.

Following Henry's marriage to Elizabeth of York, the Tudor emblem of a combined red and white rose would adorn buildings across the country from then on. That did not stop some individuals from promoting alternative claimants, but they had to manufacture them. The first pretender, Lambert Simnel, was the son of an Oxford carpenter or cobbler, and said to look like the disappeared Edward V. Selected as the figurehead for a Yorkist rebellion by the Earl of Lincoln, Simnel was crowned Edward VI in Dublin in April 1487. But his ragged Irish army was beaten in battle near Newark and the 11-year-old was, mercifully, put to work in the royal kitchens.

A more serious threat came three years later from the Flemish Perkin Warbeck, who claimed to be the younger of the princes in the Tower in 1490. He found support at the French, Burgundian and Scottish courts, but gained little traction in England. He was eventually captured in 1497 and consigned to the Tower, where he admitted his imposture and might have redeemed himself, but an attempted escape led to his execution.

Henry VII was relatively conciliatory towards opponents. Participants in rebellions might be executed, but others paid fines and could even find their way into the royal service. That did not mean they were trusted, of course. Henry relied on a small coterie of close, loyal advisers such as John Morton, who became Archbishop of Canterbury. It was he who devised the so-called 'Morton's Fork' manoeuvre, to assist in extracting taxes from the nobility: nobles with frugal lifestyles could afford to pay higher taxes, the reasoning went, while those with lavish tastes evidently had more to give.

It's telling that, soon after Henry's death, revenge was exacted on Henry's two most loyal and zealous debt collectors, Edmund Dudley and Richard Empson. Pleading for clemency prior to execution, they said, tellingly, that they had only behaved 'as the King would have it so'. No monarch since has paid greater attention to the royal accounts, totting up the figures himself and scrutinising even routine documents, in the process gaining a reputation for miserliness. Judicial offices were sold, bonds and debts rigorously collected and crown lands efficiently exploited. But Henry's rapaciousness stemmed neither from a taste for high living, nor a desire to hoard riches. It was all about controlling the nobility.

However, there was something in it for the nobles, too. By paying bonds as guarantees of future good behaviour, they could buy access to inner circles and demonstrate loyalty. A web of obligation was thus created, with relatives drawn in as well, standing surety that the impositions would be paid. In this way, many regional magnates lost influence, their authority ceded to a class of 'new men': low-born, but educated urban officials. Burgesses were called to attend the King's Great Councils; since they were men with further to fall, they could be trusted more, and posed less of a threat.

Henry's regime filled the treasury without parliaments and it saved money too, by preferring diplomacy and trade to war. He was one of the first European rulers to sign a treaty with the new Spanish kingdom formed by the union of Ferdinand of Aragon and Isabella of Castile. As a condition, his eldest son Arthur was married, aged fifteen, to Ferdinand and Isabella's daughter, Catherine of Aragon, an accord that was barely disrupted by Arthur's death five months after the nuptials. Cathe-

Catherine of Aragon was a patron of scholars, which may explain her depiction in this early 16th-century painting as Christ's wealthy supporter, Mary Magdalene.

rine merely married the surviving son, Henry, who was now the heir – although not until some time after his coronation, and not without unforeseen consequences for the whole nation.

Shrewd deals, maximising England's dominance over the wool trade brought in fresh income, while two of Henry VII's daughters were also married off to secure alliances: Mary to Louis XII, King of France and Margaret to James IV, King of Scotland. By the end of Henry VII's reign, the country was, for the first time in generations, at peace with France, Scotland and Spain.

But Arthur's death in 1502, closely followed by Queen Elizabeth's – in childbirth, seeking to provide another spare for the remaining heir – shook Henry and made him paranoid about plots and conspiracies, which were exacerbated by his network of spies. The Italian diplomat and historian Polydor Vergil wrote of him:

> He began to treat his people with more harshness and severity than had been his custom... to ensure that they remained more thoroughly and entirely obedient... they considered they were suffering not on account of their own sins... but the greed of their monarch.

King Henry VIII (1509–1547)

> The most handsome potentate I ever saw, above the usual height, with an extremely fine calf to his leg, his complexion very fair... with auburn hair and a round face so very beautiful that it would become a pretty woman.
>
> Sebastian Giustinian, Venetian Ambassador to
> Henry VIII's court, 1515–1519

A copy of Holbein's classic depiction of Henry VIII, created 1536–7, when the King was in his mid-forties

When he died in April 1509, Henry VII was a king feared and obeyed, but not loved. So the accession of his 17-year-old second son, Henry VIII, handsome, accomplished and vigorous, was welcomed. Henry was undoubtedly a Renaissance figure who spoke – or at least read – Latin, French, some Spanish and Italian, could compose music, converse on theology and astronomy, write a book (with help), and exhibited prowess in all the riding and hunting skills expected of a courtly knight. He was also devout: one of his earliest acts was to petition Pope Julius II for permission to marry his dead brother's wife, Catherine of Aragon (on the grounds that her brief marriage to Arthur had not been consummated, despite the groom's bad joke on the morning after the nuptials*).

Henry remains one of the most familiar English monarchs, largely because of Hans Holbein's portrait, of which only copies remain since the original was destroyed in a fire at Whitehall Palace in 1698. It shows the King standing four-square, gazing imperiously at the viewer: the image of regal power and strength, despite lacking the traditional trappings of royalty such as crown and sceptre.

At first Henry and Catherine's marriage seems to have been happy, but the pressure to produce an heir steadily mounted. In 1516, the Queen gave birth to a daughter, Mary, but the all-essential son remained elusive. By the mid-1520s, having experienced numerous miscarriages and stillbirths. Catherine was entering her fifth decade and the relationship had cooled. It can't have helped when Henry fathered a boy by another woman; in 1519 his mistress Elizabeth Blount bore him Henry Fitzroy, later made Duke of Richmond. The child could have ended up as heir, even king, had he not died aged 17.

By 1526, Henry's eye was roving towards the 25-year-old Anne Boleyn (he had already an affair with her older sister), and he believed he had strong grounds for his present marriage to be annulled. These were based on a convenient prohibition in the Book of Leviticus against marrying the wife of one's brother. But Henry and his advisers misconstrued the scriptures: the prohibition only applied as long as one's brother was

---

* It was said that Prince Arthur had woken up and called for ale to drink, telling his servants that it wasn't surprising he had a thirst, having 'spent the night in Spain'.

still alive, not posthumously (indeed, in Genesis, a verse refer-ring to the fate of Onan suggests that marrying and conceiving a child with one's *late* brother's wife was divinely approved). Henry believed his argument was true, though, and he felt sure that Catherine's miscarriages were proof of God's displeasure.

In 1533, despite Rome's opposition, and after nearly seven years' fruitless petitioning, Henry married Anne and declared his marriage to Catherine void, leading the Pope to excommu-nicate him. English kings had argued with the Papacy before, but none had gone so far as to try to supplant the leader of the universal Christian church. In other circumstances, Henry might have obtained an annulment – it had happened before for other royals – but Catherine's nephew, Charles V, con-trolled Italy, and Pope Clement VII could not be as helpful as he might otherwise have been.

Catherine refused to return her crown jewels, and she died, a virtual prisoner in a Cambridgeshire castle, in 1536. Henry had always seen himself as a devout Catholic, but now he was chivvied towards religious reform by his advisers. Thomas Cranmer, the future Archbishop of Canterbury, and his evangelical colleagues were supporters of the Lutheran reform movement which was gaining ground across northern Europe (and which Henry had earlier condemned, receiving the title of *Defensor Fidei*, Defender of the Faith, from Pope Leo X). There was now a strong intel-lectual alternative to Catholicism, kicking against the Church's authoritarianism, its worldliness, wealth and corruption.

For Henry, though, the advantages were less spiritual, more personal and financial: lust was one factor, along with anxiety about the succession, sheer determination to have his own way, and the desire to replenish the treasury by appropriating the wealth of the Church. One of the dubious legal devices deployed for the latter was the Buggery Act, the first secular legislation against gay men, passed the same year Henry broke with Rome. It ordained death for perpetrators, and, crucially in its use against monasteries, empowered royal seizure of their property and wealth. By such means and others, 560 monastic institutions had been destroyed – or 'dissolved' – by 1539, with land worth £132,000 a year and valuables of £75,000 going to the King.

Henry's bid to marry Anne Boleyn inadvertently led to the creation of a new Christian denomination, which would eventually become the Church of England. This fundamentally changed the balance of Church and State, and the status of the clergy. It also released onto the market thousands of acres of Church land and property, which in turn had irreversible effects on the class structure and distribution of wealth in England.

Sale of the Century: the Dissolution of the Monasteries

The King needed money for his next planned war with France, and to finance his extravagance; rife inflation meant he was particularly hard up in the early 1530s. Abbots were required by Act of Parliament to surrender their monasteries 'of their own free and voluntary minds, good wills and assents,' if they knew what was good for them. If, like Abbot of Woburn, they didn't, then they were executed. Dissolution destroyed many fine medieval buildings – the 'bare ruin'd choirs' of Shakespeare's sonnet LXXIII – while others became private houses (e.g. Lacock Abbey, Wiltshire). It also precipitated the destruction and dispersal of many rare, ancient and priceless documents, books and collections: of Worcester Priory's 600 books, only six survived.

For properties not destroyed, Henry found a ready market amongst the local gentry and the rising class of merchants and lawyers. The family of Thomas Cromwell – Henry's chief minister between 1534 and 1540 – covered many of these shifting categories themselves. Cromwell's sister married the son of a Welsh brewer, who thanks to the court connection, acquired a portfolio of former religious houses in Huntingdonshire. By way of a tribute to his influential brother-in-law, he changed his surname from Williams to Cromwell. At the end of the century, this man's great-grandson would be born in one of these former monastic properties, and later bring about the downfall of a king.

The buyers of these monastic properties often found that there was a catch: before departing, the monks had cannily rented them out on extremely long leases. The purchasers now received this rent (minus 10% to Henry VIII) but since it was fixed long-term, it was subject to the ravages of inflation. The Hampden family of Buckinghamshire had to wait a century fully to access their property, in the interim ditching any loyalty towards the Crown and becoming key figures on (Oliver) Cromwell's side in the English Civil War.

Besides raising revenue, the sell-off had an additional benefit for Henry: it secured political loyalty, which may account for the relative peacefulness of the Reformation settlement, especially in the South. Many who joined in the land-grab were Members of Parliament, ensuring little opposition to Henry from that quarter. Many estates came with 'advowsons', which conferred the right to nominate clergy – further tightening secular control, as did the disappearance of all abbots from the House of Lords.

Opposition to Henry's religious reforms was strongest in the north, and it came to a head in the 1536 Pilgrimage of Grace. The loss of the old faith was at the heart of the northern protests, but inflation, poor harvests and heavy taxation also contributed. Sixty thousand people, rich and poor, joined the pilgrimage in Yorkshire and Lincolnshire, initially occupying York and demanding a Parliament there so they could air their grievances. Sent to quell the uprising, the heavily outnumbered Duke of York promised an amnesty to the ringleaders, knowing that the King would not endorse it. Henry promised to hear their grievances, then reneged and executed hundreds of them, including MPs, country gentry and even crown servants, in London and York.

Now, for the first time, individual religious and political beliefs were defined in statute. It was no longer enough to pledge loyalty to the ruler; ideological conformity was also demanded. To enforce the acceptance of this new order, in which Henry VIII replaced the Pope as the head of the Church in England, the treason law was widened. Twelve separate statutes were introduced between 1531 and 1544, making it a treasonable offence to criticise the King, his wife or his heirs, either in speech or in writing, or to suggest his actions were heretical. All males over 14 were forced to swear an oath of allegiance; bishops, clergy and all holders of public office had separate, additional oaths to swear. To ensure convictions, juries were rigged in treason trials. In 1537, one Margaret Tyrell was reported to have spoken critically of Jane Seymour, declaring that the son she'd borne – the future Edward VI – was not the rightful heir. She spent two years in the Tower, during which she was personally questioned by Thomas Cromwell, before finally being hanged, drawn and quartered.

Henry was not particularly interested in daily administration, by and large leaving it to officials, and trusting his closest advisers, low-born and ambitious men who depended upon his favour for their livelihoods, and even their lives. The first of these was Thomas Wolsey, who had entered court circles as a chaplain and won rapid promotion. Famously industrious,

Wolsey progressed through the Church hierarchy, becoming first a bishop, then Archbishop of York and a cardinal in 1515. He masterminded Henry's early diplomatic wranglings with

MOTHER SHIPTON AND CARDINAL WOLSEY.

Northern mystic Mother Shipton became famous after allegedly predicting the death of the Archbishop of York, Cardinal Wolsey.

France and instituted legal and administrative reforms, all the while becoming ever more ostentatiously affluent. But he floundered when it came to the King's divorce; having failed to secure it, he was on his way to prison when he died.

Wolsey was succeeded by his protégé, Thomas Cromwell, a lawyer not a cleric, whose political skills steered Henry's divorce and accretions of power through Parliament. He went unremembered for centuries until being rediscovered by modern historians and the novelist Hilary Mantel. His attraction is irresistible: a Machiavellian figure at the centre of a web of court intrigue, he was assiduous in devising ways for the King to get his divorce and remarry, first forging an alliance with Anne Boleyn, then abandoning her when she started to get her own ideas about religious reform (she wanted the proceeds of the monasteries to go to schools rather than to the King). By April 1540, when Henry made him Earl of Essex, the brewer's son from Putney might have felt he could climb no higher. And he would have been right; Henry was mightily displeased at the marriage Cromwell arranged for him to Ann of Cleves, and three months after receiving the earldom, he too, went to the execution block.

The careers of Wolsey and Cromwell indicate how capricious and dangerous the King could be. Some have suggested that his increasingly tyrannical behaviour was caused by a brain injury suffered when thrown from his horse during a joust in January 1536. His leg was also injured, limiting his movement and doubtless contributing to his growing obesity. The accident must have made Henry aware how vulnerable the succession was, should he die without a male heir: Anne Boleyn headed to the block not long afterwards, following a miscarriage.

Henry's legislative reforms were not part of a coherent policy or for the good of the nation. They were for the King's personal benefit, in accordance with his egotistical whims – especially those arising out of his 'Great Matter', the term for Henry's prolonged efforts to secure a divorce from Catherine and the subsequent fall-out.

Even if he had no agenda, and did not believe he was doing anything exceptional, Henry nonetheless brought about a step-change in royal power. In his view, the divine right of ordained kings could not be challenged within the kingdom: he was the Supreme Governor of Church and State, ruler and sole arbiter of clergy and lay subjects. It was rule by personal prerogative: an idea of monarchy that would reach its apotheosis under Charles I a century later, when it would lead to civil war.

The Wives of Henry VIII

1 **Catherine of Aragon (1485-1536)**

Daughter of King Ferdinand of Aragon and Queen Isabella of Castile

Married Henry, 11th Jun 1509

Gave birth to Mary, 18th Feb 1516

Marriage declared invalid, 23rd May 1533

Died (from cancer), 7th Jan 1536

Anne Boleyn (c.1501- 36) **2**

Married Henry, 28th May 1533

Gave birth to the future Elizabeth I, 7th Sep 1533

Beheaded on charges of adultery, incest and treason, 19th May 1536

Jane Seymour (c.1508–37) **3**

Married Henry, 30th May 1536

Gave birth to Edward VI, 15th Oct 1537; died nine days later

The only wife to be buried alongside Henry at St George's Chapel, Windsor Castle

Anne of Cleves (1515–57) **4**

A political match: Anne was the daughter of a German prince. Henry felt he had been deceived by her portrait , but couldn't risk his alliance with the Germans

Married 6th Jan 1540; annulled 9th Jul 1540

Anne became 'the King's Beloved sister'; died of natural causes in Queen Mary's reign, 16th July 1557

Catherine Howard (1523 – 1542) **5**

Anne Boleyn's cousin

Married 28th Jul 1540 (9 days after annulment with Anne of Cleves): she was 17, Henry was 49

Incriminated by a letter found in the bedroom of her lover, Thomas Culpeper

Marriage never annulled; sentenced without trial (by a Bill of Attainder)

Spent her last night with the chopping block, practising

Beheaded for adultery (and thus treason), 13th Feb 1542

Catherine Parr (c.1512 – 1548) **6**

England's most-married Queen: Henry was her third husband. She reconciled him to his daughters and, after he had her arrested for heresy, persuaded him to reverse the decision.

Married Henry, 12th Jul 1543

Married former lover Thomas Seymour four months after Henry's death in 1547

Died in childbirth, 5th Sep 1548

LENGTH OF MARRIAGE

23 years, 11 months and 12 days (longest)

2 years, 11 months and 21 days (3rd longest)

1 year, 11 months, 3 weeks, 3 days (4th longest)

7 months and 3 days (shortest)

1 year, 6 months and 16 days (5th longest)

3 years, 6 months, 16 days (2nd longest)

Divorced, Died, Beheaded: Henry's Wives

Henry's urgent search for a male heir defined him for posterity, yet it occupied less than half of his 38-year reign: from his initial disillusion with Catherine of Aragon in 1526 to his final marriage to Catherine Parr in 1543. The marriages themselves – Anne Boleyn in 1533, Jane Seymour in 1536 (10 days after Anne's execution), Anne of Cleves in 1540, (3 years after Jane's death in childbirth), then 6 months later the teenaged Catherine Howard and finally Catherine Parr (15 months after Howard's execution in 1542) – were the product of desperation. He could not have known that the little girl to whom Anne had given birth (and whom he was trying to declare illegitimate) would be one of the longest-reigning and most celebrated monarchs in English history. By contrast, the single, sickly son (by Jane Seymour) to emerge from this string of divorces, deaths and beheadings died in adolescence in 1553, six years becoming Edward VI.

Unlike his father, Henry was extravagant. On his accession in 1509, he had inherited 13 royal homes; upon his death in 1547, he bequeathed more than 60, stuffed with paintings and tapestries as well as more than 2,000 pieces of gold and silver plate. His candlesticks alone weighed a quarter-ton. Also unlike Henry VII, he was eager for military glory, to be seen as one of the great monarchs of Europe alongside the Hapsburg Holy Roman Emperor Charles V and France's François I, although ultimately, he lacked the means, manpower or territorial reach. The costs of his adventures fuelled inflation, caused the heaviest taxation for 200 years and, by deliberate debasement of the gold and silver content of the coinage, made the currency drop substantially in value.

On the international stage, Henry followed his Plantaganet forebears in trying to claim or reclaim territories in France. This mission led him into alliances with Burgundy and Aragon, which – like his bid to become Holy Roman Emperor in 1519 – would ultimately prove costly and fruitless. His military adventures were not confined to the Continent: he had designs on Ireland, Scotland and Wales, too. In the late 1530s, Wales was subdued, divided into English-style counties and brought under English law, its language and traditions suppressed by a king descended himself from a Welsh dynasty. The other territories proved more difficult and expensive to control: in Ireland, a revolt in the same decade was quelled at huge expense, yet without ushering in a lasting peace. In Scotland, King James V – the son of Henry's older sister – had displeased his uncle by marrying successive French brides to secure an alliance with England's old enemy. This led to an English victory over the Scots at the Battle of Solway Moss in 1542, along with the death of James, and a problematic legacy. At just six days old, James's daughter Mary became Queen of Scots, and her claim to the English throne would dog politics for the next 40 years. Henry's attempt to have Mary betrothed to his young son Edward (the so-called 'rough wooing', since it followed the invasion of Scotland) was thwarted by her French mother, Mary of Guise, who took her away to France. Mary would later marry the Dauphin Francis, heir to the French throne – a considerable diplomatic defeat for Henry VIII, whose realm was then encircled by threats, and not exactly peaceful within.

The Most Murderous Monarch

Henry was unable to brook criticism or questioning. He was also capricious, greedy, insecure and tyrannical, and executed more close advisers and associates than any other English monarch. The total is at least 56 (and of course this does not include all the lesser citizens sentenced to death for joining in uprisings or martyred during the religious upheavals over which he presided). In the circles fatally close to Henry, two wives, a cardinal, members of 20 noble families, four public servants, six attendants and friends and at least six abbots lost their lives – excluding a handful who died on their way to prison and probable death. Add the 216 or so participants executed following the Pilgrimage of Grace – the northern uprising of 1536 which posed the reign's most serious challenge – and Henry's rule has to be counted as one of the most blood-soaked in English history. Bluff King Hal may be the most recognisable king in English history, depicted in books, films – from Charles Laughton and Robert Shaw to Sid James – and television series. But he was a monster.

Incurable ulcers, gout and, eventually, a 54-inch waistline all contributed to Henry's death, aged 55 in January 1547. Like many kings in better health, Henry had drawn up elaborate plans for his resting place – incorporating items originally commissioned by Wolsey for his own tomb – but these were never completed.

King Edward VI (1547–1553)

I will see my laws strictly obeyed, and those who break them shall be watched and denounced.

Edward VI, aged 13

Throughout his reign Henry had been obsessed with securing the male succession, and he had at least achieved that by the time he died, although his son Edward was only nine years old. Edward VI faced no challengers, but even before his accession was proclaimed, there was an internal palace coup. Henry had intended a council of 13 advisers to act as regents, but instead the Prince was seized by his uncle Edward Seymour, his mother's brother, who appointed himself Duke of Somerset and Protector. Somerset and his rival and successor John Dudley, Duke of Northumberland were firm Protestants, who pushed the Reformation further than the old King had ever conceived. They were also both rapacious for wealth and land, and ruthless with rivals: Somerset would have his own brother executed for attempting a counter-coup.

Henry had entrusted Edward's education to the evangelical reformers, and at a young age the Prince displayed a certain fanaticism – when he was 11, he wrote a pamphlet entitled *A Small Treatise against the Primacy of the Pope*. His coronation oath was revised to reinforce the royal supremacy and religious reform, giving Cranmer and his colleagues free reign to dismantle the vestiges of Roman Catholicism. Churches were stripped of their images, relics and vestments, their murals painted over, altars replaced with tables. The Archbishop produced a new Book of Common Prayer, to be used exclusively, then the 42 Articles: a blueprint for the new faith.

This went down badly in many counties. In 1549 there were uprisings in the West Country and in Norfolk, where Kett's Rebellion was further provoked by land enclosures. Landowners were ruthlessly enlarging their estates to keep sheep and benefit from the wool trade. This was at the expense of the peasantry, and of the common land upon which they traditionally grazed a few animals that might, in a good year, mean a surplus, or in a bad one, the difference between life and death.

Somerset's rule proved chaotic, facing wars in Scotland and France along with domestic unrest, and a lack of funds. The currency was debased to raise money and inflation was rampant. The Norfolk rebellion was suppressed by Northumberland, who engineered Somerset's downfall and eventual execution, and then succeeded him as the boy-king's Protector.

By 1553 Edward was 15 and dying, probably from tuberculosis, with no chance of marrying or living long enough to secure English Protestantism with an heir. He was close to his sister Elizabeth, four years older than him and Protestant, but it was likelier that their older sister Mary would succeed, as Henry VIII had decreed in the 1544 Act of Succession.

Desperate to prevent the staunchly Catholic Mary from taking over, Northumberland found an alternative in the teen-aged Lady Jane Grey, who was Protestant and the same age as her cousin Edward (her grandmother had been Henry VIII's sister). To secure his own family's position, the Protector married Jane to his son, Lord Guildford Dudley, and bolstered by the *Devise for the Succession* document drawn up with and signed by Edward VI, bullied the regency council into accepting her 'and her heirs male' as the next in line.

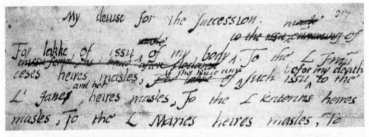

Not unlike a sample of Year 9 homework, Edward VI's 'Devise for the Succession' came complete with crossings-out

Queen Mary I (1553–1558)

Her Majesty, being now in possession of her imperial crown and estate pertaining to it, cannot forsake that faith that the whole world knows her to have followed and practiced since her birth.

Proclamation Concerning Religion, 18th August 1553

Northumberland failed to capture Mary, though, and she fled to Framlingham Castle in Suffolk, where, like much of England's east and north, loyalty to the old faith ran strong. Within a week of Edward's death in July 1553, Mary had the support of the East Anglian gentry and was heading to London with an army of 20,000. Northumberland could expect little mercy, although he bowed to the inevitable and accepted Mary's succession – as did Jane's father, the Earl of Suffolk. Both men were executed, though Jane herself survived, for a few more months.

Mary was the first Queen of England to reign in her own right, and her accession demonstrated that, even if the nation's religious landscape could be overturned, monarchy and the hereditary principle were untouched. It was also clear that large parts of England had not accepted the new religion introduced in the wake of Henry VIII's 'Great Matter'. Had Mary lived longer, and produced a male heir through her 1556 marriage to the Spanish Prince Philip, then Protestantism might have disappeared.

But the gentry would never willingly surrender the church lands and property they had purchased after Henry's dissolution of the monasteries – and Mary, wisely, did not try to make them. She had earlier resisted all pressure to renounce her Catholic faith, though in 1536, under duress, she did accept that Henry's marriage to her mother, Catherine of Aragon had been invalid, and that she was illegitimate. This had brought her back into her father's favour for the succession, but it had not led to her accepting Protestantism. When Nicholas Ridley, the Reformist Bishop of London, tried to change her mind, she told him: *'My Lord for your gentleness to come and see me, I thank you; but for your offering to preach before me, I thank you never a whit.'*

After a stressful early adulthood – barred from visiting her dying mother and attending her funeral, stripped of her title as princess – the iron entered Mary's soul and she became fixated on rooting out heresy. That might not, necessarily, have made her unpopular, but her choice of husband was another matter.

The population could welcome a legitimate Catholic queen, but not a Spanish Prince who spoke no English, and came with a large, expensive retinue. The Commons protested and Sir Thomas Wyatt raised a rebellion in Kent 'to prevent us over-running by strangers'. The rebels made it into London before being dispersed; the ringleaders were executed. So, too, was the blameless and unconnected Lady Jane Grey, solely because Mary feared she might become a figurehead for the rebels, or even a potential alternative queen.

Philip never viewed the marriage as a long-term arrange-ment. It was geopolitics – he wanted to gain an ally against France, which sat in between Spain and his possessions in the Netherlands. Mary was 38, a decade older than him, and no beauty. 'It will take a great God to drink this cup,' so one of the Spanish party (uncharitably) wrote home, and although Mary twice claimed to be pregnant, there was little chance that she was. Philip soon left for home, unimpressed by England.

Ridley had tried persuasion on Mary, but her own methods were limited to violence and the threat of it. Ridley, his colleague Hugh Latimer, bishop of Worcester and Thomas Cranmer were all burned at the stake, as were 300 other Protestants, mainly in southern England.

The persecution was not unusually harsh for the era – nor compared with the numbers executed by her father, or her sister. But it was barbaric enough, and combined with the unpopular marriage and effective Protestant propaganda, people swiftly came to see Catholicism, foreign invasion, tyranny and perse-cution as part of the same package.

Detail of a woodcut from *Foxe's Book of Martyrs*, depicting the burning of the Archbishop of Canterbury, Thomas Cranmer in 1556

The bloodshed was compounded by bad harvests, a further plague – the population dropped 6% in three years – and a lethal influenza epidemic. When Mary was pressured into sending troops to help her husband's invasion of France in 1557, the move was unaffordable and unpopular. National feeling soured further the following year, after Calais, the last remnant of England's claim to a continental empire, was captured by the French. It was a humiliating and symbolic blow, the end of almost half a millennium of English territory in France. Mary probably never said that 'Calais would be found engraved on [her] heart', but she might as well have done: it was a humiliation and an assault on her morale as well as the coffers, and she gradually weakened in 1558, perhaps from repeated bouts of flu.

Elizabeth was inevitably her heir, a prospect deeply unwelcome to Mary. The younger woman was not just Protestant, but the daughter of the woman who had supplanted Mary's mother as queen. She named Elizabeth as successor just ten days before her death in November 1558.

Queen Elizabeth I (1558–1603)

> I was never so much enticed with the potent name of a king, or royal authority of a queen, as delighted that God has made me his instrument to maintain his truth and glory and (save) this kingdom from dishonour, damage, tyranny, and oppression
>
> Elizabeth I, The Golden Speech, 30th November 1601

Sir Henry Lee commissioned this portrait in 1592 to mark Elizabeth's visit to Ditchley, his Oxfordshire home, after he'd temporarily fallen from favour due to his choice of mistress

Elizabeth was seventeen years younger than her half-sister, and considerably luckier. She would reign for nearly 45 years and by the time she died in 1603, Protestantism was firmly established. Her reign would be seen, not just by contemporary poets and

writers but by later historians as initiating a golden age of literature and exploration. Given lasting significance by Shakespeare's plays, Philip Sidney's poetry, Francis Drake's bucca-
neering explorations and the first English colonies in America,
Elizabethan England came to be celebrated as a beacon of
global success and domestic stability, an Arcadian age, the first
truly Global England, with the figure of the monarch herself –
Good Queen Bess – at its heart.

The Painted Lady

Elizabeth I was a propagandist of genius on her own account:
the first monarch whose image suffused the country, in regal
portraits, woodcuts, engravings and miniatures; no baronial
hall or privy chamber could be without one. According to
the historian Roy Strong, there are at least 80 surviving contemporary representations of the Queen, she figures in 20
group portrayals, 22 miniature portraits, 32 engravings and
23 woodcuts, many of them copied for wider distribution.
They are invariably flattering. She bestrides England framed
in sunlight and illuminated by lightening in Marcus Gheeraerts' Ditchley portrait, circa 1592. Carried aloft in glory
in Robert Peake's processional painting of 1601, she looks
about four decades younger than her age at the time, which
was 68. In the 'Coronation Portrait', painted about forty
years after the event, she is less woman, more Madonna,
with the orb and sceptre, symbols of earthly, English power,
replacing haloes and infants. These were, in the true sense
of the word, iconic representations, not realistic. Following
a proclamation in 1563, all royal images had to be licensed,
and painters were ordered to depict a youthful Queen.
Four centuries on, those images are the ones we know,
Elizabeth: forever young, and certainly not the wrinkled,

red-wigged, black-toothed figure whom later court visitors would describe.

Poets also larded their references to the Queen with allusions from the ancient world: she was a Biblical heroine like Judith or Deborah, a classical divinity like Diana or Cynthia. It seems Elizabeth really could inspire awe: 'When she smiled, it was pure sunshine that everyone did choose to bask in,' wrote her godson, Sir John Harington. 'But anon came a storm... and the thunder fell in wondrous manner on all alike.'

Like her predecessors, Elizabeth made tours of the realm, but in her case, only as far west as Bristol and north to War-wickshire. Civic leaders vied with each other to bestow lavish gifts: 'It was a good gift. I have but few such gifts,' she told the Mayor of Coventry, after he presented her with a silver cup filled with money. 'There is a great deal more in it: the hearts of all your loving subjects,' he replied, obsequiously.

These Canterbury premises are among the many inns, country estates and town houses where the perpetually touring Queen is said to have stopped off

The Queen's baggage train was three hundred carts long and her hosts faced enormous bills for feeding and entertaining everyone, usually more extravagantly than they could afford. If she was determined to visit, then attempts to deter or dissuade her – as the Archbishop of Canterbury Matthew Parker tried in 1573 by pleading a localised plague pandemic – were futile. The progresses served various purposes: they shored up regional loyalties, enabled the Queen to show herself to her people, they saved her personal expense and provided an opportunity for her palaces in London to be cleaned in her absence. Whilst she journeyed, people of all ranks could approach her for an audience. Foreigners were impressed. The Spanish ambassador told Philip II, Mary's former husband:

> She was received everywhere with great acclamations and signs of joy, as is customary in this country: whereat she was extremely pleased and told me so, giving me to understand how beloved she was by her subjects and how highly she esteemed this, together with the fact that they were peaceful and contented, whilst her neighbours on all sides are in such trouble. She attributed it all to God's miraculous goodness. She ordered her carriage sometimes to be taken where the crowd seemed thickest and stood up and thanked the people.

The image of her leaving Norwich in 1578 is irresistible: 'I have laid in my breast such good will as I shall never forget Norwich. Farewell Norwich!' she cried, shaking her riding crop, tears in her eyes. But that image was carefully cultivated: her speeches show a consciousness of being a woman in a man's world and using it to her advantage. Thus, her speech at Tilbury[*] in 1588, as the Armada threatened England's shores:

> Let tyrants fear: I have so behaved myself that under God I have placed my chiefest strength and safeguard in the loyal hearts and goodwill of my subjects... I know I have the body but of a weak and feeble woman, but I have the heart and stomach of a king and of a king of England too—and take foul scorn that Parma or any other prince of Europe should dare to invade the borders of my realm.

Her speeches mention her anointment by God, but also the consent of her subjects, and her grateful affection for them in return. Her 'Golden Speech' to the 141 Members of her final Parliament in November 1601 (see p.137) concluded thus:

> And though you have had, and may have, many mightier and wiser princes sitting in this seat, yet you never had nor shall have any that will love you better.

It is doubtful whether any previous monarchs (or most subsequent ones) ever spoke so winningly to their parliaments, or felt the need to do so.

But the succession was never fixed. Elizabeth spent the first two decades of her reign turning down various suitors, English and foreign, until she was past child-bearing age. Thereafter, she refused to name an heir, despite there being a good dozen potential contenders, insisting only that she was not to be followed 'by some vile person.'

---

[*] There are three versions of the Tilbury Speech. This one was apparently recorded as Elizabeth delivered it, by her chaplain and courtier Dr Leonel Sharp, so that he could read it out to more gatherings of troops later on.

Her reign came under repeated threats, including invasion and, as her Protestant advisers saw it, subversion from Catholic plotters. She also faced a long-standing potential rival claim to the throne from her cousin Mary, Queen of Scots, who had fled to England in May 1568 following a coup in Scotland. For the next 19 years, whilst being held under house arrest in various castles, Mary was the focus of numerous conspiracies, real and concocted.

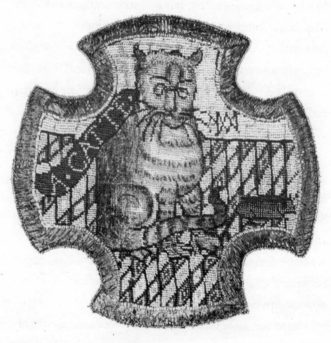

Mary took up tapestry to while away the hours of her imprisonment, encoding messages to her supporters within the embroidery. The symbolism of this image, a mouse cornered by a ginger cat, is hard to miss.

Unlike her father and half-sister, Elizabeth was reluctant to persecute opponents. Courtiers and advisers need not fear for their lives unless they openly rebelled, and many served her for decades. Sir William Cecil, later Lord Burghley, entered royal service in 1550 under Edward VI, subsequently working for Elizabeth until the end of the century, handing on to his son, Robert*. Such men might bear the brunt of her occasional rages, the Queen might ignore their opinions and advice (as they occasionally ignored hers), but she kept them on. As Burghley wrote to his son:

'I will not change my opinion... for that was to offend God to whom I am sworn first. But as a servant, I will obey Her Majesty's commandment and no wise contrary the same, presuming that she, being God's chief minister here, it shall be God's will to have her commandments obeyed.'

Parliaments and Privy Council

William Cecil was the dominant force on the Queen's Privy Council, which remains to this day a body of close, senior advisers to the Sovereign (privy meaning private/personal). Elizabeth trusted Cecil implicitly: he was largely responsible for the operation of her government, its cautious policies and its unity. It was no coincidence that after his death in 1598, the Council was riven with personal rivalries, largely between the Earl of Essex and Cecil's son Robert, which the now-elderly Elizabeth struggled to control.

Her father and grandfather used Privy Council to avoid summoning Parliament or the courts, whose decisions might not suit their wishes. Henry VII introduced a sub-committee of the Council, Star Chamber, which could issue any penalty, except execution, without a legal ruling. Henry VIII went further, assuming the power, via Privy Council,

---

* Asked how he'd survived high office under two Tudor monarchs, and even remained close to the court during Queen Mary's reign, he replied that he was 'sprung of the willow and not the oak.'

to scrap, change or make laws without any interference. The Council typically had around 40 members, appointed for life (or until another monarch took over) although in practice, far smaller circles or single individuals like Cecil were used to get things done.

Under the Tudors, Parliament met far less frequently than in many reigns of the 15th and 14th centuries. Henry VII called seven; his son, six (although the final 'Reformation Parliament' was really several, over six years). During Elizabeth's 45 years, it met 13 times, compared to 47 in the comparably long reign of Edward III, and 23 under Henry VI.

Excluding Henry VIII's attempts to legalise his religious upheaval, monarchs still only wanted one thing from Parliament: money. MPs could now air grievances, but sometimes they had little to say, as in the Queen's discussion with the Commons Speaker, Sir John Popham in 1581 (related by Sir Francis Bacon): 'Now Mr Speaker, what hath passed in the Lower House?' she asked, receiving the reply, 'If it please your Majesty, seven weeks...'

Elizabeth remained the Virgin Queen – wedded only to the state – pragmatic and cautious, as she was with many elements of her personal rule, and aware of the risks. A foreign prince could lead England into wars abroad (as Mary had found) and clashes at home, too. Philip II, the Hapsburg Archdukes Ferdinand and Charles and later the Duc d'Anjou and his unprepossessing brother the Duc d'Alençon (the origin of the rhyme 'the Frog who would a-wooing go'), all Catholics, were possible suitors at various times, as was the Protestant King of Sweden, Erik XIV. None passed muster.

Meanwhile, she knew that a domestic marriage could spark rivalries, like those that had caused the Wars of the Roses. The closest she came was her long dalliance with Robert Dudley, the Earl of Leicester, whose father, the Duke of Northumberland, was executed over the Lady Jane Grey plot. The Council forbade the match; in any case, Elizabeth was unwilling to take second place to any man – 'God's death my Lord, I will have here but one mistress and no master,' she told him – though he continued to woo her. When she visited him at Kenilworth in 1575, he laid on 19 days of celebratory revels, stopping the clock to show that time itself stood still when she was present. When he finally gave up and announced his intention to marry Lettice Knollys in 1578, Elizabeth was furious and banned him from court – but she didn't stop him.

'I grieve and dare not show my discontent,
  I love and yet am forced to seem to hate,
  I do, yet dare not say I ever meant,
  I seem stark mute but inwardly do prate.
  I am and not, I freeze and yet am burned,
  Since from myself another self I turned'

'On Monsieur's Departure', by Elizabeth I, is a poignant meditation on the conflicting forces of love and duty. It may refer to her affair with Dudley, or to her unsuccessful marriage negotiations with the Duc d'Alençon.

At the start of her reign, she was reluctant to persecute Catholics, provided they were discreet about their worship and did not threaten her rule. 'I would not make windows into men's souls,' she apparently declared, and there were even some

Catholics at court. She also disliked the more extreme Calvinist clergy: 'Mr Doctor, this loose gown becomes you mighty well; I wonder your notions be so narrow,' she told one, and in the first decade of her reign, the pace of reform was measured. The Book of Common Prayer was made compulsory, the Thirty Nine Articles defined the Church of England's doctrine, and Elizabeth became Supreme Governor of the Church of England (as opposed to 'Supreme Head', like her father: a position then and now reserved for God Himself).

But her tolerance faded in 1570, after Pope Pius V issued *Regnans in Excelsis,* an order of excommunication against Elizabeth, 'the pretended Queen and servant of crime', instructing Catholics in England and everywhere else of their Christian duty to overthrow her. It was a counterproductive move, causing the persecution of a sizeable group who had been loyal to Elizabeth, but could now not be treated as such. Effectively, it cemented Protestantism in England, too, ensuring that Elizabeth would provide safe haven for continental Protestants fleeing persecution, and committing Catholic rulers to wage war on her.

It also shaped the way Catholicism would be perceived in England for centuries: as a tyrannical, hostile, foreign and subversive threat, urgently in need of rooting out. If they failed to attend (Protestant) church services, English Catholics faced fines and the seizure of property and assets. If they met and worshipped in secret, they risked detection by Sir Francis Walsingham's efficient spy network.

But persecution in Protestant England never approached the levels seen in Catholic France and Spain. Approximately 200 Catholics were executed during Elizabeth's reign, compared with the 10,000-plus Protestants who were killed across France during the St Bartholomew's Day Massacre of August

1572. Despite the papal threats, moreover, Elizabeth declined to join a military alliance with Europe's Protestant rulers; just a few years later, she was considering deeply unpopular marriages to the French Catholic dukes.

The threat from Spain was hard to ignore, however. Thanks to its territories in the Americas, Spain had become a global power, and by the mid-1580s, was growing increasingly aggressive, not least because of attacks on its shipping by English privateers. Philip II was happy to back Catholic insurgents, who were

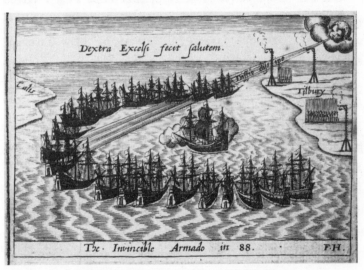

The failure of the Armada, and the belief that God had intervened on England's side via the weather, fostered a sense of exceptionalism for many centuries

plotting to replace Elizabeth with the imprisoned Mary, Queen of Scots. Coded letters, intercepted by Walsingham, eventually implicated Mary personally in a plan to assassinate the Queen. After long resisting the idea, Elizabeth was obliged to order her cousin's execution. Having obtained the Queen's signature on the death warrant, Burghley sent it off before she could have second thoughts and rescind it.

This led, in the summer of 1588, to the greatest external threat England had faced in centuries: Spain's attempt to invade and to end English Protestantism for good. Elizabeth had at last, reluctantly, forged an alliance with the Dutch Protestants, who were at war with their Spanish overlords. In retribution, Philip II sent an armada of 130 ships to Calais, the plan being to join the Prince of Parma's 30,000 troops and invade England. The Spanish fleet was harried up the Channel by blustery winds and the smaller, faster English ships, then trapped in the French port when Parma's army proved unready to sail. They were a sitting target for English fire-ships – vessels packed with gun-powder then set alight – which scattered the Spanish vessels into the North Sea; with no alternative, they had to sail north and west round Scotland and Ireland, many being shipwrecked on the rocky coasts en route.

Only sixty Spanish ships made it home, defeated. It was the largest attempted foreign invasion of England since 1066, and the greatest English naval triumph before the Napole-onic Wars. Celebrated around the land, commemorative coins depicted God Himself in the clouds over Philip's ships, rein-forcing the notion that the English were especially favoured by the Almighty. They belied an uncomfortable truth: but for the weather and Spain's incompetence, the outcome could have been very different.

The Armada was the highpoint of Elizabeth's reign. There-after her ships concentrated on plundering Spanish trade routes from the Caribbean and South America, producing private profits for investors, including herself. The increasing importance of the Royal Navy coincided with Elizabeth's army becoming costlier and less inefficient. The land invasion of the Netherlands, headed by the Earl of Leicester in 1585, was as dis-astrous and costly as the attempt to conquer Hugh O'Neill, the

Earl of Tyrone at the very end of the century, though both failures, in part, were caused by Elizabeth's favouritism.

She'd entrusted Leicester with the Netherlands and regretted it, yet proceeded to make the same mistake with his stepson. Robert Devereux, the Earl of Essex, was 32 years younger than Elizabeth; his energy must have been a tonic as the Queen's own health flagged, and trusted allies like Leicester and Burghley died (1588 and 1598, respectively). She made Essex Lord-Lieutenant of Ireland and, in March 1599, he departed to subdue the restive colony. Six months later, he returned, unauthorised and minus his army, having struck an equally unauthorised truce with the key rebel, the Earl of Tyrone. That was the end for Essex. Arriving at the palace, he burst in on the Queen, who was still in her bedchamber, without her wig or makeup on, to justify his actions. Instead he received censure and house arrest.

In its latter years, Elizabeth's court was riddled with corruption and conspiracies. The country was suffering from poor harvests, high taxation to fund the foreign wars and inflation as a consequence. In 1601 Essex stopped trying to win back Elizabeth's favour and led a coup in London, which fizzled out within hours, leading to his execution. The Tudor dynasty was also expiring. In March 1603, Elizabeth retired to her chamber where, propped up on cushions, she may – or may not – have finally indicated that James VI of Scotland should follow her. As she died, couriers were heading north to tell him so.

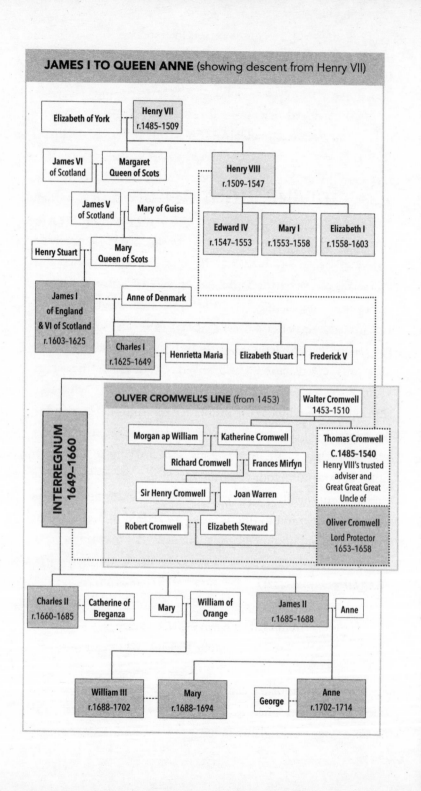

JAMES I TO QUEEN ANNE (showing descent from Henry VII)

- Elizabeth of York
- Henry VII r.1485–1509
- James VI of Scotland
- Margaret Queen of Scots
- Henry VIII r.1509–1547
- James V of Scotland
- Mary of Guise
- Edward IV r.1547–1553
- Mary I r.1553–1558
- Elizabeth I r.1558–1603
- Henry Stuart
- Mary Queen of Scots
- James I of England & VI of Scotland r.1603–1625
- Anne of Denmark
- Charles I r.1625–1649
- Henrietta Maria
- Elizabeth Stuart
- Frederick V

INTERREGNUM 1649–1660

OLIVER CROMWELL'S LINE (from 1453)

- Walter Cromwell 1453–1510
- Morgan ap William
- Katherine Cromwell
- Richard Cromwell
- Frances Mirfyn
- Sir Henry Cromwell
- Joan Warren
- Robert Cromwell
- Elizabeth Steward

Thomas Cromwell C.1485–1540 Henry VIII's trusted adviser and Great Great Great Uncle of

Oliver Cromwell Lord Protector 1653–1658

- Charles II r.1660–1685
- Catherine of Breganza
- Mary
- William of Orange
- James II r.1685–1688
- Anne
- William III r.1688–1702
- Mary r.1688–1694
- George
- Anne r.1702–1714

CHAPTER 4

DIVINE RIGHT REBUFFED

> A king is preferred by God above all other ranks and degrees
> of men, and the higher that his seate is above theirs: the
> greater is his obligation to his maker... The highest bench is
> the sliddriest to sit upon.
>
> *The True Law of Free Monarchies* by James I and VI, 1599

Personal monarchy of the Tudor sort demanded a strong and
stable personality, subtle in judgement, determined in nature,
able to flatter, cajole and overawe. Unfortunately the Stuart
heirs, James and his son Charles, lacked all these traits except,
perhaps, the determination. In their case, that meant a sin-
gle-minded mission to rule as God's anointed, unchallenged by
mortal men.

King James I (1603–1625)

> He tormented himself with fear of some sudden mischief
> Sir John Oglander, MP (1585–1655)

Succeeding his mother Mary, Queen of Scots, when he was
one year old, James had ruled Scotland for 36 years before he
became King of England in 1603. He was the first 'foreign'

monarch to be invited to take the vacant English throne, but he was nonetheless descended directly from Henry VIII's sister Margaret, and unlike his late mother, a Protestant.

James had been raised by Protestant regents (all four of whom had died violently) and educated by Protestant tutors. He never saw his mother after he was a year old, and his upbringing was frighteningly insecure, surrounded by threats, violence and even kidnapping. The English throne must have seemed a haven of stability and international prestige to the Scotsman – as well as a great reserve of wealth.

James had been the likely successor ever since Elizabeth passed the menopause without marrying, and he had been in secret correspondence with Burghley's son and successor Robert Cecil for years. The Privy Council were nonetheless anxious about last-ditch challengers, and invited him to become king on the day Elizabeth died. He set off southwards within a week, leaving his impoverished kingdom for a much larger, richer one. James could hardly wait, although he even had to borrow money to reach London. He only returned to Scotland once, fourteen years later.

The English certainly knew his views on monarchy in advance, for James had written them down, or authorised their writing a few years earlier, in two treatises concerning the divine right of kings, *Basilikon Doran* (*Royal Gift* in Greek) and *The True Law of Free Monarchies*. Anointed and chosen by God, he argued, kings could not be overruled by earthly powers and if they happened to govern unjustly while alive, they could only be punished by God Himself, once they'd died.

These were not new or novel arguments, having originated, as James himself maintained, in certain Biblical texts and then been asserted by monarchs ever since. But they ran counter to more recent doctrines (such as those of the Swiss cleric, John

Calvin) which argued that monarchs had a contractual relationship with their people, and that, if they broke the agreement, they could be legitimately overthrown. These, too, were
arguments that English nobles had deployed against their
kings over several hundred years. English parliaments were
increasingly used to asserting power over their rulers, chiefly by
denying them money. Kings could no longer easily buy these
influential figures off, as there were too many of them.

Many MPs were lawyers, non-aristocratic by birth, and a
large majority were now Protestant, in conformity with both
progressive thought and the law. Many, too, were related to each
other, through family ties, marriage or patronage. European
elites were (and still are) closed, but in England, birth was only
one way in. Particularly under the Tudors, men of talent and
ambition could become wealthy from commerce, or by service
to the monarch or other powerful individuals, then marry into
noble families or purchase titles.

No philosophical objections from a king were going to persuade Parliament to surrender its arduously-acquired authority,
and at the start of James's reign, the MPs asserted their liberties
robustly, telling him: 'The prerogatives of princes may easily
and do daily grow. The privileges of the subject... being once
lost are not recovered but with much disquiet.' James would
try to do without Parliament altogether, raising money by
selling honours (even inventing a new one: the baronetcy) to
the untitled wealthy, and offering the lower rungs of the nobility a chance to climb upwards, for a price. This was necessary,
mainly, because he spent so much. Elizabeth I's bill for gowns
had been £9,000 a year, James' robes cost four times that. In
1603, he inherited a royal debt of £100,000; within five years,
he'd made it £600,000.

The royal cistern [has] a leak which till it were stopped all
our consultation to bring money unto it [is] of little use.
John Hoskyns, MP for Hereford, Speech in Parliament's 5th
Session, October-December 1610

Were there limits to his powers: could he subvert or just ignore
the law? It was clear what James thought: even on his journey
south from Scotland, he had started doling out knighthoods
and making judgements. He freed Cecil's rival, the Earl of
Southampton, who had been held in the Tower since Essex's
rebellion, and as he passed through Newark, he ordered a
thief to be hanged without trial. All this he assumed was his
royal right, though it was unauthorised by custom, practice
or legal process. Later, in 1607, he clashed with Sir Edward
Coke, the Chief Justice of the Court of Common Pleas, after
intervening in a land dispute. As he overturned James's ruling,
Coke declared that the King had no power to judge, and that
although he wasn't subject to any other man, he was still subject
to the law. Coke lost his job as a result.

From the start it was apparent that Scotland and England
were going to find it hard to unite. Scotland did not wish to
become part of England and England did not see Scotland as
an equal partner. Even the naming of the joint kingdom was
contentious – should it be Britain, or Great Britain, and was
James King of Ireland, too?

He was initially welcomed in London, unlike his 'coarse and
beggarly' Scottish entourage – a phrase thought to have been
used by the English parliamentarian John Hare, though others
were just as rude.

A plant taken from barren earth and planted in fertile soil
will grow. And over grow... London can receive no more. No

more can the trade towns of England; all occupations are so over-burthened with artificiers.

Nicholas Fuller, MP for London,
Speeches to Parliament's 1st Session, 1604

Fuller, an outspoken Puritan, compared the Scots to cattle breaking into the 'rich pasture' of the kingdom; in sentiments frequently deployed against later immigrants, claimed they were taking jobs and causing overcrowding. In a 1606 conference with the House of Lords, he clearly went too far, claiming that in other nations, the Scots were rightly treated 'more like pedlars than merchants', an outburst for which he was 'shrewdly chidden'.

But it was King James's endless lectures, interspersed with insults, which most swiftly exhausted his MPs' patience. Unlike the English – he reminded Parliament in 1604 – the Scots had never been conquered, adding that opposing him would be like spitting in the face of God. It was no way to win support, and it is perhaps unsurprising that, in the same year, his proposal to be called 'King of Great Britain' was roundly rejected by Parliament.

Wherever he could, the King bypassed the MPs by relying on various handsome counsellors – first Robert Carr, then George Villiers, whom he made Duke of Buckingham. He also became close to the Spanish ambassador, Diego Gondomar.

James was not a Calvinist, but supported an episcopal church, governed (under him) by bishops. He had struggled with Scotland's Presbyterian kirk, which insisted on interfering in secular issues and resisted all attempts at control, by bishops or kings. But James's moderation did not extend to Catholics, whose pleas for toleration of worship were rebuffed.

That caused a group of gentlemen Catholics to take action.

The Gunpowder Plot of 1605 came close to its goal – blowing up Parliament and the King – the plotters managing to rent a cellar under the House and stuff it with explosives (though the powder was probably too wet to ignite). But their plans were known to the authorities in advance, at the eleventh hour, they were rounded up and later savagely executed. The planned act of terror cost moderate Catholics dearly in lost trust and led to several further centuries of persecution and discrimination.

Catholics shared pariah status with hard-line Puritans and non-conformists, who started looking abroad for tolerance. In 1620, one group would sail to America aboard the Mayflower in order to practice their own faith in their own colony, free from persecution (whilst persecuting those who disagreed with them).

Apotheosis literally means deification, and for depicting James I in such a state on Whitehall's ceiling, Rubens received a lesser elevation from the late god-king's son: a knighthood

King James was a poet as well as an author, and playwrights and artists flourished under him – in particular Shakespeare, whose theatrical company James began sponsoring shortly after his accession. In tribute, Shakespeare's *Macbeth* (1606) sent a dramatic message about the dangers of usurping rightful kings. At the King's behest, the architect Inigo Jones built the Banqueting House on Whitehall. Later, after James's death, it would be enhanced by Rubens's ceiling painting of the King's apotheosis, ascending to heaven in glory. James's son, Charles I would walk under it, on his way to his execution. At his suggestion and under his sponsorship, as well, the King James Bible was produced: a new translation and a rare example of a committee creating a masterwork – 54 scholars and bishops collaborating for seven years.

King Charles I (1625–1649)

> He has no vices or lusts, he is just but he is rather severe and serious than familiar... He is extreme in nothing except that he persists with his sentiments and anyone whom he has once detested may be sure he will never recover his favour... he will be very fortunate if he does not fall into some great upheaval.
>
> Anzolo Correr, Venetian ambassador in London, 1637

In 1625, James died in bed – unlike so many of his Scottish ancestors. He left a number of difficulties for his oldest surviving son, Charles I, including an unpopular arranged marriage with the daughter of the French king. In England, this had been greeted with only slightly less horror than an earlier planned match with the Spanish *infanta*, who had fortunately loathed Charles on sight when he went to woo her.* James also passed on heavy debts, an uneasy relationship with Parliament and an idea of kingship that would soon be tested to destruction.

---

* '*Infanta*' simply denotes the daughter of the Spanish monarch; the term has nothing to do with age.

James's eldest son Henry was, by all accounts, a bright and personable young man, who might have held things together. But he had died of typhoid aged 18 in 1612, and the second son Charles was sickly and awkward as well as self-righteous. The grand royal portraits by the court painter Sir Anthony Van Dyck exaggerate his stature and grandeur: seeing him bestride an enormous stallion, it is easy to forget that he was five feet, four inches tall.

Throughout his reign, Charles would clash with Parliament over a single issue. 'Parliament,' he said, 'is altogether in my power for their calling, sitting and dissolution. It is not a way to deal with a king.' Parliament disagreed.

Charles had delayed the opening of his first Parliament until he'd married the Bourbon Princess Henrietta Maria. Many felt this was an underhand tactic, deployed in order to forestall parliamentary objections to the marriage, and tensions were not eased when the Queen arrived in London with a large retinue of Catholic priests and hangers-on, openly pronouncing her desire for England's return to the true faith.

The furtive planning behind the royal marriage intensified peoples' fears of a Catholic revival, and made Charles seem a risky prospect as king, especially while the Thirty Years' War between Europe's Catholic and Protestant powers was laying the Continent to waste. The King's own religious tendencies also caused distrust, not least his growing reliance on William Laud, the conservative, authoritarian and staunchly anti-Puritan Archbishop of Canterbury, and his close colleague William Juxon, Bishop of London.

An early confrontation came when MPs refused to grant excise duties to the King for his whole reign, as per previous practice, but only for a year at a time. The King sensed they were trying to control him, and he was right – they wanted control over his expenditure. They went further in 1628, with a Petition of Right, expanding and updating Magna Carta. A king could not imprison opponents without trial, levy taxes without parliamentary consent, or maintain a standing army to bully Parliament. This progressive statement of legal rights became the template for similar declarations elsewhere in coming centuries, notably in France and North America.

In this period, parliaments were neither permanently in session nor elected to fixed terms (they were scarcely elected at all: seats were in the gift of regional nobles and knights of the shires or urban guilds and councils). The King called and prorogued them at his pleasure: three in his first three years, as he tried, unsuccessfully, to bend the MPs to his will.

In 1629 he dispensed with Parliament altogether – imitating the French example – and used other ways to raise money for the next eleven years, a period his opponents called 'The Tyranny'.

High inflation and parliamentary resistance had left Charles short of revenue, and like his father, he had expensive tastes. Peace treaties were concluded with France and Spain to avoid foreign military entanglements, and the King resorted to Ship Money, the medieval tax levied on coastal ports for defence purposes in times of war, which could be collected without parliamentary approval. Charles tried to make the whole country pay, on pretence of the threat from Barbary pirates. Like all taxes, it caused resentment; it also proved difficult to collect, especially inland, and only about 20% ever reached Charles.

In the late 1630s, Charles tried to enforce universal use of Bishop Laud's new High Anglican prayerbook, prompting a Presbyterian revolt in Scotland. It wasn't just the hint of Roman ritualism the Presbyterians objected to, but the whole notion of bishops imposing uniformity on congregations, let alone English bishops doing so to Scots.

When one portrait is not enough: 'Charles I in three positions' by Sir Anthony van Dyck, 1635-36 was one of many works of art commissioned by the King

In 1638, a royal army was sent to enforce obedience; it was woefully under-resourced and duly forced back. The same happened in 1640; this time the Scots invaded Newcastle and refused to leave unless Charles paid them. Ireland erupted too, as Catholics fearing a takeover by Protestant settlers plunged the country into a sectarian conflict, during which up to 20% of Ulster Protestants were killed.

Charles was obliged to call a new parliament in 1640 to raise funds: the so-called 'Short Parliament', annulled within three weeks after it refused him money for the Scottish and Irish campaigns. The Commons would not allow Charles to raise an army, in case he used it against them in England. A few months later he tried again, calling the 'Long Parliament', which would sit throughout the coming civil war until Cromwell dismissed the MPs thirteen years later.

The heavy-handed, autocratic behavior of Charles's two closest advisers, Bishop Laud and the Earl of Strafford, led to repeated clashes with the MPs. They eventually demanded Laud's impeachment and Strafford's arrest, and in a desperate attempt at peacemaking, the King sacrificed the latter to the axeman's block. 'Put not your trust in princes' was Strafford's rueful parting shot.

The House of Commons felt the same. Pushing its luck, the Long Parliament issued the Grand Remonstrance. This expanded the earlier Petition of Right, insisting that parliaments meet at least every three years, and that they could only be dissolved by MPs themselves. In addition, they should control political, military and church appointments, Ship Money should be ended and bishops banned from the House of Lords.

The Remonstrance would have stripped the King of most of his traditional powers. In January 1642, egged on by his wife, Charles marched into the Commons with troops and attempted to arrest the ringleaders. They had been forewarned, however, and slipped away by river. 'I see the birds have flown,' the King remarked. No monarch has tried to intervene directly in the House of Commons chamber again. To this day, the monarch's representative, known as Black Rod – due to his ebony staff of office – has to ask permission to enter the chamber on behalf of the sovereign.

Next the MPs' attention focused on the Queen, and armed mobs swarmed through London seeking her arrest. She fled to France with the royal children and the Crown Jewels (which she would pawn to raise money for the King) while Charles decamped to the Midlands, to recruit soldiers and retake control of his seething country.

The English Civil War

Mutual loss of trust, a lack of compromise, competing visions of monarchical government and widening religious divisions: all played a part in the English Civil War, although class did not. Both sides were led by aristocrats and gentry, and on both sides it was low-born foot soldiers and their families who suffered most. Nor was it ever a struggle to replace kings with something else, like a republic. It is better seen as part of a process begun six centuries earlier, when the exiled King Aethelred and his nobles struck a power-sharing bargain: if he promised to rule justly, he would be allowed to return to the throne.

In the days before political parties with distinct doctrines, there was a broad spread of opinion in Parliament. The majority of MPs were Royalists, or at least backed the King; some backed him despite being critical of his conduct; others believed that God had given him the right to rule unchallenged; others still were more concerned with the powers exercised by bishops. When war broke out, some left to join the King and his army; others stayed at Westminster. Even as the first clashes occurred in the summer of 1642 – when Charles demanded arms from the city of Kingston-upon-Hull, whose governor refused to comply – things were not black-and-white. The general of the Parliamentary forces, the Earl of Essex, claimed that his intention was to preserve the King's person, while rescuing him from his evil counsellors. There may be some truth in this claim: for many participants in the war, the goal was curtailing the powers of the King, not dispensing with him.

The war divided families and friends across the three parts of the kingdom: England, Scotland and Ireland. From a population of around five million, an estimated 200,000 were killed, either by wounds or disease. Casualties were proportionately higher in Scotland and highest of all in Ireland.

There were three phases in the war: the first, between 1642 and 1646, saw the King's forces defeated and Charles captured. The second (1648-49) followed a secret agreement between the King and the Scots, with Charles promising them bishop-free Presbyterianism, in return for a Scottish invasion to restore him to the throne – this ended in Charles' execution. In the third phase (1649-51), armed rebellions rose and fell in Scotland and Ireland, while the King's son and heir, the Prince of Wales, fled abroad after defeat at the Battle of Worcester.

Geographical divisions held fast from the outset: the south and east of England were Parliamentarian, and London was too. The King decamped to a new capital at Oxford, centre of a Royalist west and north. The Parliamentary side retained control of the navy and the main sea ports; their army would be the superior force as well, instilled with discipline by better, more determined leaders. Men like the commander-in-chief of the Parliamentarian forces, Thomas Fairfax, and Oliver Cromwell, a member of the Huntingdonshire gentry, risked losing everything, including their lives, for taking arms against the King, so winning was their only option.

The Royalist armies could never conquer London, although in November 1642, they reached the western outskirts at Turnham Green before being repelled. They were unable to score a decisive military victory either, and lost the major engagements: first Marston Moor outside York in July 1644, and then, catastrophically, at Naseby in Northamptonshire the following June, where the royal army was destroyed. In the battle's aftermath, Charles's papers were discovered, revealing his secret negotiations for help from the Catholic Irish and European powers.

In 1645, Charles surrendered to the Scots and they handed him to Parliament, in return for a ransom. En route to London, he was kidnapped by the army as a means of extracting their back pay from the Commons. They also insisted that Charles 'the man of blood' should be tried for treason against his people.

The trouble was that in law, treason was a crime *against* a king, not *by* him. Regardless of that detail, the army continued calling for the King to be put on trial, while the Long Parliament tried to negotiate his restoration. The balance changed in December 1648, when a former drayman named Thomas Pride – now a Parliamentarian colonel, backed by cavalry and a regiment of foot – entered the Commons and expelled those moderate MPs who wanted to restore the King.

'Pride's Purge' left a Commons of about 150 hard-liners who declared that treason went both ways for a King who 'trusting with a limited power to govern by and according to the laws of the land... hath traitorously and maliciously levied war against the present Parliament.' Their claim was rejected by the House of Lords, so the Commons abolished the Lords. In January 1649, the Rump of the Long Parliament announced that 'the People are under God, the origin of all just power' and their acts alone had the force of law.

A commission was set up to try the King. Of the 135 judges appointed, 53 dared to show up, and they agreed on the charge that Charles had 'a wicked design totally to subvert the ancient and fundamental laws and liberties of this nation and in their place to introduce an arbitrary and tyrannical government'. He therefore deserved 'exemplary and condign punishment'.

It was a contentious strategy, risking a popular uprising out of loyalty to the King, or even a foreign invasion to rescue him. If the King pleaded to the charge, guilty or not guilty, he would be implicitly accepting the Commons' authority over him, in which case, there would be no need to execute him, and a strong likelihood of some deal being struck. If he refused to plead, thereby denying the Commons' supremacy, then, in Cromwell's words, they would have to 'cut off his head with the crown on it.'

That represented an awesome undertaking, going not only against a monarch but the God who had anointed him. And they'd be committing treason *against* the King as the penalty for what they claimed was treason *by* him. In consequence, Cromwell and his judges ought properly to order their own executions, not the King's.

Charles would not bend to his accusers, and he would die defending divine right. Perhaps he welcomed the chance to do so, or he thought no one would ever dare to execute him. Kings had been killed before, in battle, or in secret, but never by judicial process, and especially not by newly-invented law.

Fairfax, for one, thought it inconceivable and refused to attend the trial, which was eventually conducted by the radical lawyer John Bradshaw. When brought to Westminster Hall for the proceedings, Charles refused to accept the court's jurisdiction or enter a plea. Bradshaw told him he was being tried in the name of the people of England 'of which you are elected king,' and Charles replied: 'England was never an elected kingdom but a hereditary kingdom for near these thousand years...' before adding, 'The King can do no wrong' and asking how Parliament could represent the people when the Lords were excluded. Charles was right to say that kings were not elected, but wrong about the thousand years of hereditary kingship, and, as several of his predecessors had already discovered, mistaken on the matter of the king being unable to do wrong. Nevertheless, Charles would not accept the sovereignty of the Commons, and they would not accept his supremacy.

This judicial stand-off was not ended by law or argument,

but sheer political power. The King was condemned and three days later, he was beheaded outside his father's Banqueting House in Whitehall, arguing to the end that only a sovereign had a divine right to rule. At the same time, he expressed a desire that his subjects should have their liberty and freedom: *'I am a martyr of the people.'* Published a few days later, the *Eikon Basilike* (Royal Portrait), consisting of a collection of Charles's writings and prayers, became an influential work and established his martyred status in the minds of monarchists.

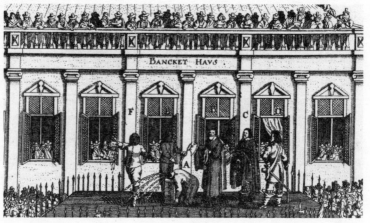

This contemporary German woodcut provides a graphic depiction of the regicide

The Interregnum (January 1649–May 1660)

> I would be willing to live to be further serviceable to God and His people, but my work is done.
>
> Oliver Cromwell, 1658

If the beheading answered one question, it raised another. Who was in charge now? The war had not been fought in the name of republicanism and few had considered a non-monarchical government. Its options limited, the radical Rump Parliament declared a Republic of the People under God, with the supreme power shared amongst MPs. Monarchy was abolished, along with the House of Lords and the established Church of England. Otherwise things stayed the same: the legal system still functioned, property rights were protected against radical fringe groups and, while the religious sects fell out amongst themselves, Anglican worship was widely, if quietly, practised. It was a very bourgeois revolution.

Politically, the Rump could not agree on much. It sold off the lands of the Crown, of the Church and of the defeated Royalists in order to pay the army and fund its response to the ongoing Irish rebellion. In the autumn of 1649, Cromwell's troops crushed the revolt with the mass slaughter of Catholic soldiers and civilians in Drogheda and Wexford.

By 1653, the faction fighting in the Commons was out of control. Cromwell, commander of the army since 1649, dismissed the Rump in terms no king had dared to use: *'Ye are grown intolerably odious to the whole nation. The Lord hath done with you. Go, get out, make haste ye venal slaves, be gone...'* A period of personal, military rule ensued, with Cromwell in charge, and Parliament replaced by an 'assembly of saints'. These were hardline Puritans, drawn mostly from the tradesmen classes, but also including gentry and Scots representatives. This 'Barebones Parliament' was named after the Member for the City of London, a leather seller called Praise God Barebone (apparently christened under the longer name of Unless-Jesus-Christ-Had-Died-For-Thee-Thou-Hadst-Been-Damned Barebone, though what his intimates called him is unclear) but it lasted only five months before dissolving itself. A small group of radicals remained, telling a Colonel sent to clear the chamber that they were seeking the Lord, to which he replied: 'Then you may go elsewhere, for to my certain knowledge he has not been here these twelve years.'

Cromwell was now Lord Protector. He refused to become King Oliver, leaving that to the future jazz cornetist, clearly aware that becoming monarch would have constrained his powers. He was endowed, said the Earl of Clarendon, adviser to Charles I and Lord-Chancellor to Charles II: 'with a greater power and authority than had been ever exercised or claimed by any king.'

Backed by an army council of state, his priority was to return the nation to belief in his sort of God: a 'reformation of manners', as it was called. He was tolerant, to a point, of differing religious practices, provided they were not Catholic – hence Christmas and carols were banned as popish, whilst he invited the Jews to return. But there was little tolerance in the way Cromwell imposed his deeply conservative religious values on the nation, and his rule – which ignored duties and rights enshrined in law since Magna Carta, such as no imprisonment without trial – was more repressive than most monarchs'.

Uniformity was imposed on Scotland and Ireland, while England was divided into ten militia-controlled regions or 'associations', each headed by a major-general and trusted ally of Cromwell. Theatres were closed, the playing of games was banned, and adulterers faced execution. Such fanatical commandments, imposed by a theocratic regime, were not wildly popular. Nor did the regime manage to create an alternative constitution: four were drawn up in the 1650s, each rejected. And when Cromwell died in September 1658, he upheld the monarchs' hereditary principle by making his ineffectual son Richard – 'Tumbledown Dick' – his successor.

At this point, coherent government broke down as the army and Parliament wrestled for dominance. Within 18 months, one of the Parliamentary generals, George Monck, governor of Scotland, was marching south with an army to restore public order. The surviving MPs of the Long Parliament were recalled and took up a petition previously presented to Cromwell before his death, calling for the restoration of the monarchy. A new ruler was required to reunite the country, and there was only one non-divisive candidate. He was the Prince who had already been crowned in Scotland, the dead King's oldest son: Charles II. But if he was to return from the Netherlands as king, conditions would be attached.

Charles II (1660–1685)

> Here lies a great and mighty king
> Whose promise none relies on.
> He never said a foolish thing
> Nor ever did a wise one.
> The Earl of Rochester's impromptu 'Epitaph' for Charles II

> This is very true: for my words are my own and my actions those of my ministers.
>   Charles II, in reply to Rochester's 'Epitaph'

Charles responded to Parliament's invitation by pledging pardon for those who had fought against his father, except the signatories of the death warrant. He also promised that all property purchased during the Interregnum would be protected, and that the army would be paid. Crucially, he accepted the supremacy of Parliament and agreed to meet one every three years. This was a considerable advance. Parliament responded that 'Government ought to be by King, Lords and Commons' and invited him to return as 'King of Great Britain and Ireland'. On 29th May 1660, his 30th birthday, Charles entered London to near-universal rejoicing. The eleven-year experiment was over, more than over: Parliament declared that Charles II had been England's rightful monarch ever since the day his father was executed. It was if the civil war had never happened.

Since his narrow escape after the Battle of Worcester, Charles had been living precariously on the Continent, dependent on loans and handouts from other monarchs, such as his cousin Louis XIV. If he shared his father's idea of monarchy, he was also more cautious and pragmatic; there would be no attempt to create an absolute monarchy like France's.

Nonetheless, when the mostly Royalist Parliament passed the Militia Act of 1661, Charles II was given command of a permanent standing army, seemingly a significant extension of royal power. Up to then monarchs had relied on ad-hoc, local levies, plus personal protection from two small armed units, the Yeomen Warders of the Tower of London and the Yeomen of the Guard, both formed in Tudor times. Now, based on the Parliamentarians' New Model Army, and even containing some of its veterans, there would be a full-time, regular national army with a regimental structure. But Charles's command was symbolic (like the Queen's today). Parliament held the true authority, renewed annually by the passing of an Army Act, which stands to this day as a safeguard against dictatorial control of the military.

In exile, Charles had resisted all pressure to convert to Catholicism – privately, he would convert on his deathbed – and he remained acceptably Protestant. The Royalists back in control of Parliament proved far more hard-line than him: the 1662 Act of Uniformity insisted that clergy subscribe to Anglican doctrine, and as a result, a thousand Puritan clergy lost their livings. Dissent was being pushed to the fringes.

Charles's policy was to leave politics to his ministers, whilst indulging his interests in hunting, horse racing and mistresses, such as Nell Gwyn: he was not called the Merry Monarch for nothing. He sired at least 14 illegitimate offspring, but none by his Portuguese wife Catherine of Braganza; those who reached adulthood were inducted or married into the peerage.

The reign's initial crises – the Great Plague of 1665 and the Great Fire of London in 1666 – could not be laid on the monarchy, although Protestant politicians still tried to blame Catholics and foreign plotters for the fire, which was certainly accidental. The Second Dutch War of 1665-7 was more problematic for the monarchy (the First Dutch War had occurred during the Interregnum, provoked by attempts to curtail Dutch overseas trade). It resulted in the Dutch sailing up the Thames estuary, attacking and partly destroying the fleet in the Medway, after British sailors refused to fight without first being paid. Peace was restored, but the episode was a national humiliation, and in the fallout Charles's Lord-Chancellor Clarendon was exiled.

In 1670, Charles had come to a secret arrangement with Louis XIV, accepting private French subsidies in return for supporting France's war against the Dutch, and promising to convert to Catholicism. Eight years later, Parliament found out, beginning the long-running Exclusion Crisis. The revelations about a covert French deal confirmed MPs' suspicions about the Royal Family's true allegiances, and they retaliated by rejecting all the religious toleration measures proposed by the King in the 1672 Declaration of Indulgence. In place of them, the Test Act of 1678 barred Catholics from public office, excluding all those who did not accept Church of England rites. Catholicism was equated with absolutist government, as exemplified by France and its Sun King, who in 1685 had revoked the Edict of Nantes protecting Protestants from persecution. In such a context, with hostilities between France and the Netherlands, Charles accepting money from the French king was akin to backing the enemy. It fuelled the prevailing atmosphere of suspicion about Catholicism and the Royal Family's susceptibility to it – an atmosphere in which plots, conspiracies and sheer fable flourished.

Titus Oates and the Popish Plot

The Popish Plot emerged in 1678, thanks to the revelations of a renegade Anglican priest called Titus Oates. This barely credible figure, who had previously fled the country to avoid perjury charges, now claimed to have infiltrated the Jesuits, and uncovered a plot to seize the throne, assassinate the King and install his brother James, the Duke of York in his place. James was known to have converted to Catholicism and had been married to a Catholic, but that was the extent of the truth. Nevertheless, all the old fears were stirred and a witch hunt began, with Oates himself given a squad of soldiers to hunt down and eradicate supposed Jesuit plotters.

The 'eminent pen' reviving knowledge of the 'almost forgotten plot' in this 1683 pamphlet was, of course, none other than Titus Oates.

By the time the claims finally blew over, or were shown to be false, 35 people had been hanged, drawn and quartered for treason, including James's former private secretary. Oates, who had managed to secure a state pension and a royal apartment, was discredited and eventually, after James succeeded his brother, jailed for sedition and perjury. Charles gave the plot no credence: 'No man in England will take away my life to make you king,' he told his brother, and he personally interviewed Oates and proved him to be lying. Out of pragmatism, he did little else, aware that directly ending Oates and his fantastical allegations might sit badly with Parliament, at a time when the issue of the succession was threatening an even deeper crisis.

Charles was more successful against Parliament when it came to the succession of his brother – who under the terms of the 1678 Test Act was barred by his religion from becoming king – but he sent James into temporary exile while the heat was on. The Exclusion Crisis rumbled on through three parliaments and only blew over when the King declined to summon a fourth in 1681. For the remaining few years of his reign, he did without the Commons, relying on more money from Louis.

James was not just openly Catholic. He was autocratic; a military man rather than a politician like his brother, drawing different lessons from the Civil War: 'Compliance was the fatal rock on which (my) father miserably split,' he erroneously confided. James seems to have converted in 1669, convinced that Catholicism was the only key to personal eternal salvation. After the passage of the Test Acts, he resigned as admiral of the fleet rather than abjure his religion, and following the death of his first wife Anne Hyde, Clarendon's daughter, he married Princess Mary of Modena, Italian and, naturally, Catholic. At that point, James's sole heir was Mary, the daughter of his first marriage, who had been raised Protestant and was married to the equally Protestant Prince William of Orange. But what would happen if his second wife produced a son, who would clearly be a Catholic, and leapfrog over his half-sister Mary to the throne? It did not seem likely: James was approaching his fifties and Mary had not conceived in seven years of marriage.

By the time Charles died following a stroke in February 1685, the crisis seemed to have run its course, but the religious divisions remained. They produced the first glimmerings of rival political parties, known by their nicknames and mobilised on the different sides of the Exclusion Bill debate. The Whigs were named, derisively, after Scottish fundamentalists – the Whiggamor Presbyterian cattle drovers who had fought the imposition of bishops in Scotland. They supported the Bill and a Protestant succession, with the monarchy governed by the constitution and excluding Catholics. The Tories, named after Irish Catholic bandits, supported the King and the natural order of succession.

King James II (1685–1688)

> He had no true judgement and... was obstinate against all other advice.
>
> Bishop Gilbert Burnet, *A History of My Own Time*, 1723

James's succession was received in a relatively positive mood: there were reports of public rejoicing and his first parliament was generous to him. For his part, James promised forgiveness to anyone who'd opposed him. Soon afterwards, Charles's illegitimate Protestant son, the Duke of Monmouth, made an attempt on the throne with a small, ill-equipped peasant army, but it was swiftly suppressed by the King's professional army. Following the Battle of Sedgemoor in the marshy Somerset levels in July 1685 – the last battle on English soil – Monmouth was captured and ignominiously executed, along with many of his followers. The Bloody Assizes in Dorchester and Taunton, presided over by the famously draconian Judge George Jeffreys (a Protestant himself) and others, sentenced to death 250 of the 1,300 brought to court, and a further 850 were transported to forced labour in Barbados. The condemned were hanged, drawn and quartered in their own towns and villages and some women – including the elderly Lady Alice Lisle, who had merely offered a night's shelter to some rebels – were burned at the stake. For the time, these were not excessive penalties for treason, but they horrified the West Country and convinced others of the alien brutality of Catholicism.

James took this early victory as a sign that God wanted him to return the realm to Catholicism. Lacking his brother's pragmatism, he attempted to appoint fellow Catholics to the army and bishoprics whilst enforcing toleration, not just for Catholics but certain dissenter groups (Quakers were released from prison) in his *Declaration of Indulgence*, which he publicised in a speaking tour. Too far, too fast: the Commons refused and James prorogued its sittings. He then tried to enforce toleration without Parliament and swiftly became embroiled in quarrels with the judiciary, the Church of England, the army and universities. The Vice-Chancellor of Cambridge was dismissed and the King's choice of a Catholic President for Magdalen College, Oxford caused a revolt by the fellows, who were all expelled. Seven bishops, including the Archbishop of Canterbury disobeyed his instruction that the *Declaration of Indulgence* be read from the pulpits. Prosecuted by the King for seditious libel, they were acquitted. In the counties, the Lord Lieutenants were asked if they would support the lifting of penal laws against Catholics; those who refused were dismissed. The King effortlessly and wilfully alienated one group after another.

Even so, James might have survived. People feared another civil war more than they feared absolutism, and the mutterings among the political classes never stretched to violent insurrection. But in June 1688, his wife gave birth to a son, and the still-unresolved Exclusion Crisis blew up again. A key reason for James's acceptability as king had been the perceived unlikelihood of him and his wife having children. So the arrival of a male heir, supplanting his older, Protestant sisters Mary and Anne in the line of succession, provoked fears of an imminent, absolutist, Catholic dynasty. Meanwhile, on the other side of the North Sea, someone had an answer.

Present and Correct

Whig propaganda quickly claimed that the child, James Francis Edward Stuart, could not be legitimate because of his parents' age, and must be some substitute smuggled into the royal bed in a warming pan. His father produced some 70 witnesses to prove this accusation false, but it created a State custom that lasted well into the 20th century. A government minister, latterly successive Home Secretaries and Archbishops of Canterbury were required to be present at every royal birth to witness legitimacy (though usually they stayed outside the room). Queen Elizabeth II's birth on 21st April 1926 was formally witnessed by Sir William Joynson-Hicks, the Tory Home Secretary, who broke off from dealing with the prospective General Strike to confirm the birth of the then-third in line to the throne at 2.40am. The practice was only formally abandoned in 1948, when Labour Home Secretary James Chuter Ede informed the Palace that no politician was going to waste time on 'the custom of past ages'. Prince Charles was the first royal whose birth went un-witnessed.

William III and Mary II (1689–1702)

His Majesty left a quiet, retired, completely happy condition, full of honour... to come over hither at your own request to deliver you from the encroachments and tyranny... of your prince. Ever since he has been your mere journeyman, your servant, your soldier of fortune.

Daniel Defoe, 1705

The Dutch husband of James's oldest daughter Mary, Prince William of Orange, had been secretly negotiating with potential British supporters for some time. In the late autumn of 1688, with the winds in the Channel veering from the east – a Protestant wind, it was said – he landed in Devon with a large and experienced army. Thus began the Glorious Revolution. Rather than confront the formidable Dutch force, James's troops simply deserted, and the King was permitted to flee to France, leaving a governmental void. A Convention Parliament was formed – following the precedent set in 1660, when Cromwell had died and there was no monarch to summon MPs to Westminster. The Convention declared that by breaking the original contract between king and people – a contract Charles I had refused to recognise forty years earlier – James II had abdicated. It then offered the throne of Great Britain and Ireland to William and Mary.

So James's daughters, first Mary and then Anne, would inherit the throne in succession, while his baby son, James, 'the Old Pretender', never would. Both Mary and Anne had been

This broadside ballad from 1688, welcoming William of Orange to London, is
part of a vast collection amassed by the diarist Samuel Pepys

raised Protestants at the insistence of their uncle Charles II, and
both, to their father's chagrin, supported William's succession.
Anne told him: 'The Church of Rome is wicked and dangerous,
their ceremonies... plain downright idolatry.'

Under pressure from Louis XIV in 1689, James II reluctantly
landed in Ireland as part of a campaign to provoke a Catholic
uprising and ultimately regain his throne, but William defeated
him at the Battle of the Boyne – a victory still celebrated by
Ulster's Presbyterians – and he returned to French exile until
his death in 1701. Louis' Catholic rivals, Spain, Austria and the
Papacy, cheered William's victory. A Scots Highland rising by
John Graham, Viscount Dundee – 'Bonnie Dundee' – also
foundered in 1689, after which the clan chiefs were forced to
swear allegiance to the new monarchs. When the Macdonalds

of Glencoe were slow to respond, they were massacred by loyalist Campbell troops, to whom they had given hospitality.

To Parliamentarians, the choice was simple: William or anarchy. William's claim wasn't the most tenuous; he was James II's nephew, and he was married to James II's eldest daughter Mary – although she made it clear that she would never reign alone, telling the Convention she was 'never meant to be other than in subjection to [William].' So William was given executive power, and Mary acted as regent during his absences in Holland, until her death from smallpox in 1694. Their joint reign has thus far been the only one in Britain's history.

William, a diminutive and dour Dutch soldier, understood Britain's tangled intrigues well thanks to his mother – daughter of Charles I, sister to Charles II and James II – but he had no particular loyalty to the place. It was strategic: with him on Britain's throne, France was encircled by enemies. He might have refused to accept restrictions on his power, he said, 'but for the condition of his affairs.'

He also agreed, under the Bill of Rights (called the Claim of Right in Scotland) passed later that year, to free elections and freedom of speech in Parliament, no peacetime standing army, no taxation without Parliamentary approval, the right to petition and just treatment in the courts; a reassertion of the rights originally outlined in Magna Carta. This acknowledgement of a shared sovereignty was an acceptable price for what the Whigs were soon calling 'the Glorious Revolution'. The term 'contract' was not in the Bill, but it implicitly accepted that divine right was dead and that monarchs ruled by consent: an idea articulated by the philosopher John Locke in his 1690 work *Two Treatises of Government*.

The conditions were not particularly onerous for a king whose attentions were elsewhere, and he agreed to meet Parliament every year, instead of calling it just when he needed revenue. Parliaments were now regularised and MPs kept control of the royal finances.

> When princes have not needed money, they have not needed us.
>
> Sir Joseph Williamson, MP for Thetford, 1689

William was no different from any other monarch in terms of needing money, but he needed a lot of it. Fortunately, Parliament had backtracked on abolishing the army, and also permitted William, via taxation, to expand his military might considerably for his ongoing war with France: before long 100,000 men, 2% of Britain's population, would be under arms.

The agreement also helped to regularise the royal finances and in parallel, the Bank of England was founded in 1694, initially to manage war expenditure, but also providing the means to manage the national debt. This gave the prosperous classes further reason to support a stable regime and the constitutional settlement.

The war ended in 1697, but resumed after the Spanish Hapsburg King Charles II died heirless in 1700, leaving the European powers to fight over the succession. Louis XIV claimed the throne for his grandson, while a Dutch, Austrian and British alliance championed the son of the Holy Roman Emperor, to keep France in check. James II died in exile ten months after the Spanish King, and to stir the pot, Louis recognised his teenage son, the 'Old Pretender', as Britain's rightful heir. Within six months, William was dead, too – he broke his collarbone when his horse stumbled on a molehill* – and his sister-in-law Anne became queen.

---

* *'The little gentleman in black velvet'* was supposedly toasted by Jacobites following the mole's inadvertent intervention in the monarchy.

Queen Anne (1702–1707)

> I know my own heart to be entirely English
>   Queen Anne, 1st Speech to Parliament, 11th March 1702

Married to the stolid Danish Prince George, Queen Anne had no heir. Just one of her children, William, Duke of Gloucester, had survived infancy, only to die aged eleven, and after 17 miscarriages, still births and infant deaths, it was clear that she would bear no more children. This gruelling pursuit of an heir had ruined Anne's health, so the succession was a matter of urgency. It could not be the Catholic Old Pretender – the Bill of Rights had declared it 'inconsistent with the safety and welfare of this Protestant kingdom to be governed by a popish prince', so Parliament had to find another suitable, foreign and Protestant heir to follow her.

Suitable Heirs: The Act of Settlement

The nearest candidate was the 70-year-old Electress Sophia of Hanover, granddaughter of James I. Her right of succession was enshrined in the Act of Settlement of 1701, which also barred any Catholic, or any prince or princess who married a Catholic, from the throne. In addition, it insisted that monarchs swore allegiance to the Church of England, that they resided in England and did not travel abroad without Parliamentary approval. (The latter clause was later abolished, so that George I could retreat regularly to his German estates.) The Act further tightened Parliament's hold over the monarchy.

The main act is still in force, recent reform attempts complicated due to its also being law in the 14 other countries where Britain's monarch is Head of State. Catholics are still barred from the throne, because the monarch is supreme head of the Church of England, but the Crown Act of 2013 permitted monarchs to marry Catholics. It has been pointed out – something not considered in 1701 – that the Act does not bar the monarch from marrying a Muslim, Hindu, Jew or atheist.

Anne has often been described as a dull figure, but her 12-year reign as the last Stuart monarch was in itself momentous. It was a bridge between the fractious power struggles of the previous 250 years and the more settled times to come, just as it was a bridge between the rule of two foreign monarchs. Despite frequent illness, she regularly presided over ministerial meetings, and played an active part in political debate. She was not averse to taking sides between the Whigs and Tories, leaning towards each in turn, and she was the last monarch to veto a Parliamentary Bill. The Scottish Militia Bill of 1708 proposed setting up an armed force in Scotland, to repel a predicted invasion by James Stuart. Anne feared that the militia volunteers might turn out to be James' supporters – Jacobites – themselves, and blocked the Bill. In the event, the invasion was thwarted, but no monarch has vetoed legislation since then.

A year earlier, the Act of Union united England and Scotland, after much arm-twisting from London, anxious to prevent the Stuarts' return. The Scots gave up their Parliament and the right to choose their own kings, sending representatives to Westminster instead, and gaining the certainty of frictionless, border-free trade (across the largest such area in the world at that time). After centuries, England had secured her northern border, and the nation formally became Great Britain.

The War of the Spanish Succession broke out two months after Anne's accession and lasted until a year before her death.

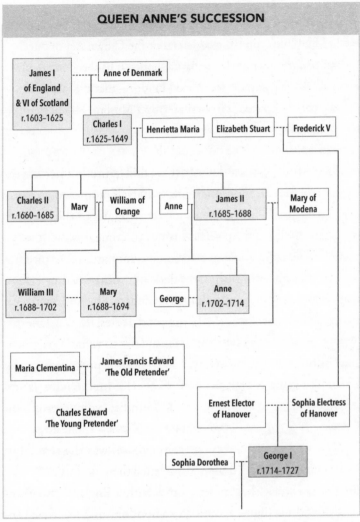

QUEEN ANNE'S SUCCESSION

James I of England & VI of Scotland r.1603–1625

Anne of Denmark

Charles I r.1625–1649

Henrietta Maria

Elizabeth Stuart

Frederick V

Charles II r.1660–1685

Mary

William of Orange

Anne

James II r.1685–1688

Mary of Modena

William III r.1688–1702

Mary r.1688–1694

George

Anne r.1702–1714

Maria Clementina

James Francis Edward 'The Old Pretender'

Charles Edward 'The Young Pretender'

Ernest Elector of Hanover

Sophia Electress of Hanover

Sophia Dorothea

George I r.1714–1727

During this conflict, John Churchill, now the Duke of Marlborough, won various military victories across Europe as head of the Grand Alliance – composed of Britain, the Dutch Republic and the Holy Roman Empire – against the French. He was rewarded with the Woodstock estate in Oxfordshire, where construction began on Blenheim Palace, named after his greatest victory in Bavaria in 1704. The bill was met partly by the state and partly by the Queen, though both baulked at the spiralling cost of the Baroque palace, and the final bill was settled by Churchill himself.

He and his wife Sarah – initially a close friend of the Queen – were associated with the Whig faction, ardent supporters of the war with France. However, the Queen came increasingly to favour the Tories, who were critical of the never-ending foreign conflict and its mountainous costs, and suspicious of the Churchills' influence at court. In 1710, the war ended in the Treaty of Utrecht, more trade-off than treaty: the ageing Louis XIV recognised the Hanoverian succession in Britain, in return his grandson got the Spanish throne, Britain got Gibraltar and access to the Spanish slave trade.

Her health waning, Anne evaded demands from Electress Sophia's son Georg about settling in England before he succeeded to the throne. This prompted rumours among the Whigs that she was backing out, and contemplating a Stuart succession. Her Tory ministers, Harley and Bolingbroke, were indeed holding secret talks with the Old Pretender James, urging him to convert to Protestantism if he wanted the Crown. 'It is for others to change their sentiments,' he replied loftily – a true obstinate Stuart. By 1714, it was clear that Anne would not live long, but her putative heir Sophia, 35 years older, died seven weeks before her. On her deathbed, Anne sacked Harley and Bolingbroke and appointed a moderate Whig, the Duke of Shrewsbury to replace them. A Protestant succession was assured.

The Scottish Stuart dynasty invited to England in 1603 had a clear idea of monarchy: the divine right of kings to rule unchallenged and uncompromised. A clash was inevitable: a would-be authoritarian king who needed money faced a parliament determined to uphold its right to decide on taxes and spending. The result was a bloody civil war across the British

Isles and ultimately, parliaments stronger than any future monarchs. Monarchy itself was only temporarily replaced, though. When a Catholic king succeeded, a family coup by his Protestant daughter and her foreign husband replaced him, but even then, Parliament dictated the conditions for it.

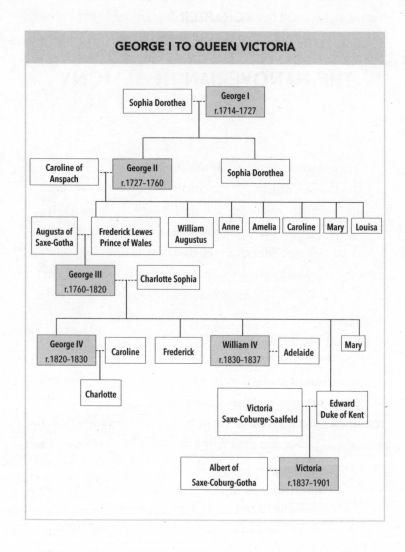

GEORGE I TO QUEEN VICTORIA

Sophia Dorothea - - - George I
r.1714–1727

Caroline of Anspach - - - George II
r.1727–1760

Sophia Dorothea

Augusta of Saxe-Gotha - - - Frederick Lewes Prince of Wales

William Augustus

Anne

Amelia

Caroline

Mary

Louisa

George III
r.1760–1820 - - - Charlotte Sophia

George IV
r.1820–1830 - - - Caroline

Frederick

William IV
r.1830–1837 - - - Adelaide

Mary

Charlotte

Victoria Saxe-Coburge-Saalfeld - - - Edward Duke of Kent

Albert of Saxe-Coburg-Gotha - - - Victoria
r.1837–1901

CHAPTER 5

THE HANOVERIAN HEGEMONY

The first two [Georges] are usually dismissed as stupid...
The third... tried to ape the Stuarts and in so doing, lost
the American colonies... The public life of George IV is
usually ignored and attention focused on the elegance of
his furnishings. Poor creatures, they have all been judged by
standards which were not their own nor their contemporaries'.

J.H. Plumb, *The First Four Georges*, 1956

The Glorious Revolution of 1688 was no revolution in the
modern sense and scarcely glorious either, but it was at least
peaceful. Almost inadvertently, due to William's need for money,
it shifted the power from Crown to Parliament. Monarchy
remained the central executive institution, but its autocratic and
managerial power was gradually handed over to politicians and
ministers. The process was accelerated in the 18th century by
a series of expensive foreign wars and foreign kings, who were
unable or unwilling to engage in daily government.

The accession of Georg Ludwig, the Elector of Hanover
and Duke of Brunswick-Lüneburg in 1714, was accomplished
remarkably peacefully considering that the Old Pretender still
presented a threat, and that should the public mood and legislation shift in favour of allowing Catholics on the throne, he was

a stronger claimant than Georg. But as he'd done often before at crucial points, James drew back from the challenge. He took almost four months to join a Jacobite rebellion in Scotland in 1715, by which time the rising was all but over. After a few weeks, he caught a chill and retired wanly to France.

King George I (1714–1727)

> In private life he would have been called an honest blockhead... he was more properly dull than lazy and would have been well contented to have remained in his little town of Hanover.
> Lady Mary Wortley Montagu, *Account of the Court of George I On His Accession*, ca. 1715

George I, as the new king became, was hardly inspirational. A dumpy, ageing figure (five years older than Anne) he spoke French, but very little English and had only once visited before, 34 years earlier, in order, unsuccessfully, to woo Anne. He barely tried to endear himself to his new kingdom, and the indifference was mutual. He was the second European prince to be invited to take the throne in 25 years, and the third foreign-born monarch in just over a century. George professed the right religion, but he had little else to recommend him. He preferred the company of his German retinue and he returned to Hanover as often as possible. His chief interest in England (apart from wishing to see root vegetables cultivated in St James's Park) was to enlist help and resources for expanding his German territories towards Bremen on the Baltic, at that time controlled by Sweden and Denmark*.

---

* The Germans had little time for English customs. George soon put an end to the centuries' old tradition of the King's Evil, touching sufferers of scrofula. Unsurprisingly, George thought it superstitious nonsense and probably unhygienic.

The King's absenteeism suited the Whigs, who consolidated their influence over the government, assisted by the creation of a new political appointment: the Prime Minister. It was a post for a new era, one of disengaged kings and powerful Parliaments, one where ministers, not monarchs, conducted government business: 'Ministers are the kings in this country. I am nothing there,' moaned George II – but he did not try to change it. The arrangement suited the first two Georges, who did not trust the Tories. For their part, the Tories viewed the Hanoverians with suspicion, seeing them as interlopers, who had usurped the hereditary monarchy, though few were prepared to do anything about it. Tories would accordingly be kept out of government for 40 years, resentful of the Whigs' monopolisation of place and patronage, but unable to change things.

The Hanoverians were bolstered by the established Church, sharing its wariness of dissenters and its intolerance of Catholics. There was a slight loosening of the grip, though: despite being viewed as a fanatical sect by some, Methodism was permitted to develop outside the episcopal structure of the Church of England. On the walls of some of the oldest Methodist chapels, boards can still be seen which affirm support for the Hanoverian monarchy.

Public office was still limited to Anglicans, though, and no changes were considered to the Test and Corporation Acts (1661 and 1673). All MPs, military officers and local magistrates had to be at least nominally observant. Medieval kings had struggled against nobles and clergy alike. Now their descendants joined forces in a way that shored up the monarchy as well. All the power and influence lay in the hands of practising Anglicans, who were naturally supportive of the Church of England and its hierarchy, and of the monarchy, too. This became a powerful, stabilising social force in 18th-century England. In such conditions, the fires of real persecution could no longer burn, as they still did in France. If religion became a more mundane and less fanatical sphere, however, people soon found other, dangerous obsessions. Like the stock market.

The Burst Bubble

The long war with France had produced a burgeoning national debt, borrowed from various sources, including the then-private Bank of England and other financiers. The interest alone swallowed a third of all annual revenue and to manage this – not unlike the 'consolidated loan' deals advertised today to people in dire financial straits – the government packaged its debts into monies owed to a single company, which it had established in 1711.

The South Sea Company was granted the monopoly on trade with South America, a lucrative prospect, in particular the slavery element, provided everyone overlooked the fact that Britain had no monopoly to grant in the first place. Spain was the dominant power in that region, and it was at war with Britain.

Trading in the company's shares by individuals and companies – including the Royal Family and half the government – grew frenzied, under the mistaken premise that the South Sea Company was guaranteed to return profits. To keep the stock price rising, board members bribed ministers and MPs with free shares. Other companies sprang up to take advantage of this burgeoning market, some naïve, some impractical and some transparently corrupt – like the business inviting investments in 'a company for carrying out an undertaking of great advantage, but nobody to know what it is'. The market was unregulated and thousands of small investors were left unprotected. Stock worth

£100 in 1719 was selling for £130 in April 1720 and £1,000 by July. By that point, it had become a Ponzi Scheme: creditors and early investors reassured by 'profits' which were actually just the funds more recent investors had sunk into the company.

When the shares crashed that autumn, they took with them, not only the fortunes and savings of thousands of investors, but also the credibility and trustworthiness of the government.

'The South Sea Scheme': a satirical engraving published by Hogarth ca. 1721. Prospectors scramble onto a perilous merry-go-round while in the foreground, 'Honesty' is broken upon the wheel by 'Self-Interest', 'Honor' is flogged by 'Villainy' and a monument records London's destruction.

Robert Walpole, a Norfolk squire and junior member of the Whig administration, stabilised the government and managed the political fall-out. Some ministers were disgraced, the Chancellor of the Exchequer went to jail. Aided by the downfall of his colleagues, Walpole assumed power, becoming Britain's first Prime Minister in 1721. He would prove a true master of the Commons, cajoling and occasionally bribing his colleagues over the next 20 years in office.

For Walpole, managing the independent-minded though loyal country gentlemen of the Commons was easier than his other role: he served as go-between for the King and his eldest son and heir, Georg Augustus. For the next century, a common feature of court life would be Hanoverian fathers not getting on with their sons. In 1717 the baptism ceremony of George's first grandson was interrupted by a father-son quarrel that led to Georg, the Prince of Wales, being evicted from St James's Palace. Worn down by such battles and increasingly unpopular after the South Sea crash, George I suffered a fatal stroke on a trip back home to Hanover in 1727, making him the last monarch to die abroad.

King George II (1727 – 1760)

> In truth he hated the English, looked upon them all as king killers and republicans, grudged them their riches as well as their liberty, thought them all overpaid and said... that at Hanover he rewarded people for doing their duty and serving him well, but here he was obliged to enrich people for being rascals and buy them not to cut his throat.
>
> John, 2nd Baron Hervey in *Lord Hervey's Memoirs*, written
>
> 1727–1737

Swiftly settling into middle age, tetchy and dull, George II proceeded to reign 33 years. His lasting claim to fame was being the last monarch to lead his troops into battle, at Dettingen against the French, in 1743. No monarch since has needed to.

As his dying wife, Caroline begged him to remarry in 1737, he delivered one of only two memorable quotes, replying, '*Non, j'aurai des maitresses.*' ('No, I'll have mistresses.') The second supposedly occurred when asked for his opinion on Hogarth's painting *The Road to Finchley*, which depicted troops on the way to counter the Jacobite invasion of 1745: 'I hate all boets and bainters'.

The failure of that invasion, led by the Old Pretender's son, Charles Edward Stuart (also known as Bonnie Prince Charlie, or the Young Pretender), showed how established the Hanoverians had become. The impoverished Catholic Highland clans who supported the last Stuart claimant found scant support beyond their own ranks. Most of Scotland, including Edinburgh, the Lowlands and major clans such as the Campbells remained loyal to the Hanoverian monarchy, and when the Jacobites crossed into England, few joined them. Even so, by 4th December they had reached Derby, 130 miles from London, before a retreat became inevitable. Their defeat at Culloden in April 1746, the last battle on British soil, was inflicted by a professional army, led by George II's son, the Duke of Cumberland, and it marked the end of challenges to the royal dynasty. Around 7,000 Highlanders fought in the battle, but ten times that many would have been needed to conquer Britain. By the 1740s, even romantic Jacobites were too comfortable and prosperous in a stable, peaceful country to risk it all for an old cause. The Bonnie Prince retired to Rome, fractiousness and eventual alcoholism, never to return to Britain during the remaining 42 years of his life.

When George II died of a stroke, sitting on the toilet one morning in October 1760, five days before his 77th birthday, the best encomium the writer Horace Walpole (Robert's son), could find was: 'What an enviable death! In the greatest period of the glory of this country, and of his reign, in perfect tranquillity at home... to die without a pang.'

Painted here in 1785, three years before his death at the age of 67, the Bonnie Prince became estranged from his father and brother, his European allies and two wives. His remains are in St Peter's Basilica in the Vatican, where a monument was erected to the Royal Stuarts in 1807, funded by, among others, the future King George IV.

King George III (1760–1820)

> I glory in the name of Briton.
>
> George III, to the House of Lords, on his accession

The crown passed to 22-year-old George III, grandson of the previous incumbent, since his father, the Prince of Wales, had died suddenly in 1751. The country he inherited was a prosperous one. Agriculture prices were buoyant and productivity was up, thanks to innovations like 'Turnip' Townsend's crop rotation scheme and Jethro Tull's seed drill. The middle and upper classes had money spare to purchase the luxury goods coming onto the market: Wedgwood's china, Chippendale's furniture – chosen by catalogue, delivered by the developing network of canal and turnpike roads. Consumers could buy tea from China, sugar from the slave plantations in the West Indies. Factories were springing up too, with newly developed machinery using abundant water power. New markets for British goods were opening globally: the country was importing raw materials and exporting finished goods such as textiles and tools. 'Our trade is the most considerable of the whole world. And indeed Great Britain is of all other countries the most proper for trade,' stated 1758's edition of the annual directory *The Present State of Great Britain*.

The population expanded too: from an estimated 5.3 million to around 8 million between 1730 and 1790. By mid-century, it is calculated that one family in five derived its income from trade and distribution. London had become the largest and most developed city in the western world: a mercantile centre, home to one in 12 of the population. Other cities were growing rapidly, too: Liverpool, Bristol and Glasgow, port cities on the western coast, becoming rich partly on the profits of slavery. These were vibrant places, but with volatile populations, prone to riot. If violence was the outlet of the disenfranchised, more influential sectors of the population would increasingly lobby Parliament to get things done: most notably the abolition of slavery, a moral-political crusade fuelled by evangelical and non-conformist religious groups – though that campaign would take a long time.

The Gordon Riots of June 1780

The largely working class Gordon Riots were stirred by the unbalanced rabble-rouser Lord George Gordon. He took advantage of enduring anti-Catholic sentiment following the Catholic Relief Act of 1778, which allowed a moderate relaxation of the restrictions, such as giving Catholics the right to buy and inherit property. He had not objected when the Act was first proposed, but subsequently became frenzied about it, prophesying the imminent return of foreign, Papist absolutism, and stoking the fears of the London mob. He grew strangely disconcerted when the anger he'd stirred resulted in Catholic properties and Embassy chapels being attacked, while crowds began massing outside Parliament. The army was called in and at least 200 people were killed before order was restored. After the worst disturbance in the capital since the Middle Ages, Gordon was acquitted of incitement and treason. A year later, however, after converting to Judaism and defaming Marie-Antoinette, he received a five-year prison sentence and died in Newgate.

Expansion and prosperity were enabled by stable government in the first half of the new century, facilitated by non-interventionist monarchs, a free indigenous population and a free press, which included satirical cartoons of politicians and the royal family. Society was open in a limited way, both to innovation and social advancement. Money could be borrowed for new ventures, and debt funded by the City of London. A few members of the landed aristocracy took advantage and became businessmen, like the Duke of Bridgewater, who not only extracted coal from his Lancashire estate, but built a 40-mile-long canal to send it to Manchester. More commonly, successful members of the mercantile class became aristocrats, marrying into titles or buying them. Neither kind of social mobility was tolerated in France and Germany.

This all contributed to a country looking outwards, to new markets and new sources of raw materials, and to find money for the campaigns and wars that followed, especially, in mid-century, the Seven Years War (1756–63) between Britain, France and Spain. By now, English settlements had been spreading down the eastern seaboard of North America for more than a century. Many were composed of religious dissenters, who were tired of the persecutions and restrictions imposed on them by the State-Monarchy-C. of E. triumvirate. The expatriate British population increased fivefold between 1675 and 1740, bumping up against French settlers to the west and north, and the Spanish in Florida. The Scots had also conducted a colonial experiment: building a settlement at Darien in central America in the 1690s, but its financially (and mortally) disastrous outcome contributed to Scotland accepting the Act of Union a few years later.

Now those early colonies would be added to, usually at the expense of France: much of India was conquered for the East India Company, and with the capture of Quebec in 1759, the eastern seaboard of Canada came under British control as well. That year, said Horace Walpole, the bells of Britain were 'worn threadbare with ringing for victory.'

George III is remembered chiefly for the loss of the American colonies and of his mind. But the American War of Independence ended 20 years into his reign, and madness only incapacitated him after 28 years on the throne.

He was the first British-born king since James II, and the first for 50 years whose native language was English. Dogged and diligent, he reigned for nearly 60 years, the third-longest of any British monarch. He was interested in the arts, endowed a large national library, followed developments in science and technology, and was happy talking to his subjects when he encountered them on his holidays in Weymouth or when pottering around Windsor Great Park. He did not travel abroad, and never visited large parts of his own country, including the Midlands and the North as the Industrial Revolution took off, and Scotland, Wales and Ireland. Unlike his predecessors, he was devoted to his wife, Charlotte, by whom he had nine sons and six daughters.

One of a series of prints by James Gillray poking fun at the moderate habits of King George III and Queen Charlotte

Monarchs Undercover

There are many tales of monarchs not being recognised by their subjects. George III was chatting to a farmer near Cheltenham for a quarter of an hour before the man asked if he'd ever seen the King. 'Our neighbours say he's a good sort of man,' continued the farmer, 'but dresses very plain,' to which the King replied, 'Aye, as plain as you see me now.' On another occasion, he chatted to a pig-herding boy in

Windsor Great Park who said that the land belonged to 'Georgy – he be king and lives in the castle, but he does no good for me,' which turned out to be untrue, since the King gave him a job on one of his farms. More recently it is alleged that, whilst walking on her Balmoral estate in tweeds and a headscarf, Elizabeth II was asked by a passing group of foreign tourists whether she had ever met the Queen. 'No,' she answered, pointing to her accompanying detective. 'But he has.' Such stories are endearing to the British, demonstrating an admired lack of royal pretentiousness. Queen Elizabeth II's popularity was only enhanced by the disclosure that she keeps her breakfast cereal in a Tupperware box – just as James Gillray's cartoon of George III and his wife abstemiously eating boiled eggs scarcely diminished popular respect.

Two of the longest-lasting features of George III's reign appeared at the start. In 1761, he purchased Buckingham House – soon to become, after much rebuilding, Buckingham Palace.

It was a London home, close to, but removed from the formal official ceremonies of St James' Palace just across the park, modest by continental standards, like the King's court and retinue.

Versailles housed 10,000 courtiers, ministers and officials, all with ample space to plot and scheme together and kept at lavish royal expense – a situation which contributed eventually to the overthrow of the French monarchy. By contrast, George III kept a court of fewer than 2,000, who were not permanent residents. In spite of his (relatively speaking) modest requirements, some still felt that the royal living arrangements needed reining in. When a developer wanted to buy land next door to the palace, George III pleaded to Parliament for an extra £20,000 to buy the land and avoid being overlooked when he walked in the grounds. It was refused.

Buckingham Palace: Fit for A King

Originally built by the first Duke of Buckingham in 1703, Buckingham Palace has had several rebuilds since George III bought it. George IV employed his favourite architect John Nash to redesign the state rooms and added a marble arch at the front. In the 1840s, that arch was moved (just across Green Park, where it became Marble Arch) in order to add more accommodation for Victoria's growing family, an extension designed by Edward Blore, built by Thomas Cubitt and paid for partly by the sale of the Royal Pavilion in Brighton. In 1913, Sir Aston Webb resurfaced the main façade to take on its now familiar appearance, with the balcony where the Royal Family appear on ceremonial occasions. The exterior is monumental and grandiose, the interior somewhat formal, cold, draughty and unloved by many members of the family. Although a London residence, it is also the headquarters of the monarchy, with no fewer than 92 offices on top of the 19 state rooms, the 188 staff bedrooms, 52 guest bedrooms and just 78 bathrooms.

More important than the royal home, however, was the royal salary, revolutionised by the creation of the Civil List. Previously, since the onset of regular parliaments, monarchs had received an annual grant, decided at the time of accession, and remaining unchanged for the duration of their reigns (though for Charles I, the agreement had been only for five years – an initial source of friction between the new King and Parliament). These grants were usually inadequate, and deliberately kept that way, to curtail royal extravagance and maintain parliamentary oversight. From this stipend, monarchs were expected to pay for all royal expenditure, the administration of the royal household, including the servants' wages, along with salaries and pensions for officials such as judges and ambassadors. The bill also included the nation's military costs – appropriate for eras when monarchs had principally passed their time waging war, or raising funds for it, but increasingly anachronistic by the mid-18th century.

George II's stipend, from 1727, had been £800,000 a year. The same sum was offered to George III 33 years later, but it was clearly inadequate and would only become more so with inflation as his long reign continued. From the start, he needed to beg Parliament for more, in order to pay for his coronation, a bill which included buying back the Crown Jewels for £54,000, since they'd been bequeathed by his grandfather George II to his uncle, the Duke of Cumberland.

An arrangement was reached with Parliament: the King would hand over all the hereditary revenues from the Crown's estates in return for an agreed fixed sum to cover official expenditure each year. He could keep his private income from the Duchy of Lancaster estates, and the Government would take responsibility for the costs of other national institutions, such as the army and navy and the civil service. Ministers would become more accountable to MPs than they were to the monarch.

The Civil List formula remained essentially the same until 2012, when it was replaced by the Sovereign Grant: a consolidation of funds from various government departments into a single sum, based on 15% of revenues from the Crown Estates, reviewed by the government every five years. In 2021–22, the grant was £86.3 million.

Unlike his predecessors, the young King did not let Whig politicians conduct all the business; he was determined to assert royal authority over ministers against the party system. Painfully, and slowly, he learned that he needed allies for this: men with sufficient power to manage the Commons and thus secure measures with which he might agree. Men with that sort of power, of course, could also do things he disagreed with.

George initially tried to impose as Prime Minister his former tutor Lord Bute, a Tory with little political experience. This was a snub to the elder William Pitt, a Whig, whom George once described as a 'madman' with the 'blackest of hearts', but who was still the dominant, if divisive, political personality of the period.

During his 317 days as Prime Minister, Bute became so unpopular that he was frequently subjected to physical attack. He was widely seen as a manipulator, who exercised undue influence over the King and had connived to force Pitt out of office. Eventually, he was compelled to step down. In desperation, with all other options exhausted, the King was now forced to offer the job to Pitt; a humiliating U-turn. Pitt's own powers were waning, however, not helped by ill health and mental instability, but if he had been brought in to help earlier, he might have prevented the humiliation of the revolt by the American colonies.

The loss of America followed a long drawn-out crisis, over attempts by successive British governments to make the colonists pay for their own defence through taxation. The Seven Years' War – a fight for global dominance between Britain and France – had been won at a heavy cost. It doubled Britain's national debt to nearly £4 million, nearly half the normal peacetime revenue, and the need to defend the American frontier was estimated to cost an additional £225,000 (and 10,000 troops) a year*. The impasse dragged over several years, as successive governments tried to exact revenue and some – by no

---

* Some American politicians objected on principle to being taxed without Parliamentary representation, although the rates of tax proposed were generally lower than they were in Britain.

means all – colonists grew more militant in their demands for independence. Inevitably, it ended in war.

Inevitable and Unaffordable: the Fight for America

The American War of Independence was one of the greatest blows to the monarchy's self-esteem, but not ultimately to Britain's economic expansion. It was a costly, unwinnable conflict, against determined and resilient expatriate opponents thousands of miles away, as foreseen by many politicians including Pitt and even the Tory Prime Minister at the time, the affable Lord North. But faced with the loss of the colony, the defeat of his army and the decline of his prestige, George refused to listen. The final spark came when France and Spain intervened to help the colonists, mounting a naval blockade against ships bringing supplies and reinforcements to British troops.

After the British surrendered at Yorktown in 1781, there was one consolation: intervention had been ruinously expensive for France (and when Louis XVI was forced to call a parliament in order to raise taxes, it led to revolution). The only other plus was that, as one British negotiator allegedly told his American counterparts, they might have lost the war, but the Americans would speak English. Pro-British colonists were forced out, mostly north to Canada, which retains its independence of the USA, and Britain's monarch as its Head of State. Remarkably, given the significance of the War of Independence in the USA's national psyche, no nation has a greater fascination for the minutiae of the British Royal Family.

George had stubbornly supported the war, and even drafted an abdication document after it was lost: 'His Majesty with much sorrow finds he can be of no further utility to his native country which drives him to the painful step of quitting it for ever.' It was never issued, however, and when John Adams, the first American ambassador, arrived in London in June 1785, the King managed a gracious speech: 'I was the last to consent to the separation but (it) having been made and having become inevitable, I have always said, and say now, that I would be the first to meet the friendship of the United States as an independent power.'

Regrettably, George III's reign would see another conflict with the USA: during the messy 1812–15 war, the British burned Washington and the Americans smashed the British at New Orleans, unaware that a peace treaty had already been signed in far-off Ghent, in what is now Belgium. But by then George III had no idea what was happening.

Despite the national humiliation of the war and the loss of Britain's most valuable colony, the industrial revolution kept her economy strong: by 1800 exports were 80% higher than in 1775. Politics proved far less stable, as the King tried to hold on to his unhappy Tory Prime Minister, North, who spelled out the facts to his master: 'In this country the prince on the throne cannot with prudence oppose the deliberate resolution of the House of Commons.' But North's plain-speaking was still more tolerable to George than working with the radical Whig, Charles James Fox, who happily described the King as a blockhead. Naturally, in keeping with Hanoverian tradition, the King's eldest son, George, Prince of Wales, sided with Fox and the Whig radicals against his father.

The King struggled to find a Commons coalition to form a government. His chance came with the India Bill of 1783, which proposed that the private British India Company should hand control of the sub-continent to the government, with commissioners appointed by Parliament – and thus, at that time, likely to be Whigs. George III let it be known that anyone who voted for the legislation would be his enemy, and the bill fell – narrowly. It was an extraordinarily blatant, partisan royal intervention in Parliamentary business – 'little less than a declaration of open war between the King and his subjects,' said Lord Camden – but by then George had found a new Tory minister, 24-year-old William Pitt the Younger.

To bolster his support, the King agreed to pack the Lords by awarding peerages to Tory supporters – a tactic of Queen Anne's era that would recur as a threat in 1832 and 1910. But it wasn't needed this time: Pitt won a Parliamentary majority and he would master the Commons, serving as Prime Minister for 19 of the next 23 years until his death. In 1799 he introduced the first levy of income tax to fund the war against Napoleon: a sliding scale, from tuppence in the pound to two shillings (10%) for incomes over £200.

In 1788, after over a quarter-century on the throne, the King suffered a disabling mental breakdown that would compromise his remaining 32 years as ruler.

The Madness of King George

The nature of the so-called 'Royal Malady' remains debated. The first bout may have occurred as early as 1765, but a complete collapse occurred in 1788: the King became agitated, occasionally violent, talking incessantly and suffering stomach cramps. Under the instructions of the 'Mad Doctor' Francis Willis, he was confined in a straitjacket and a restraining chair, while preparations were made for his son, George, Prince of Wales – later George IV – to stand in as Regent. Pitt and the Tories were aghast, as the Prince supported the radical Whig leader of the Opposition, Charles James Fox. On that occasion the King recovered, but three more bouts followed, the last in 1810 after the death of his favourite daughter. George spent his final decade permanently confined at Windsor Castle, often chattering for days on end, but by now blind, deaf and in a world of his own.

In the 1960s, it was suggested that the King's dementia stemmed from porphyria, an inherited metabolic disease of the nervous system causing psychosis (as well as deep blue discolouration of the urine). The latest favoured explanation, however, is that George suffered from a form of bipolar disorder triggered by stress. Contemporary doctors had no idea how to manage, let alone cure the condition except with close confinement, which the King rightly feared. In an age long before the advent of psychiatry, the royal doctors resorted to physical restraints such as straitjackets or chaining to a chair, as well as purging and bleeding.

1993: Clive Merrison plays Dr Willis and Nigel Hawthorne the troubled king in Alan Bennett's original stage-play 'The Madness of George III'.

Shortly after the King's first recovery, the French Revolution broke out. At first it was greeted in Britain with glee: an old rival had been brought low. The beheading of the French King in 1793 changed attitudes; even more so the prolonged ensuing period of massacres and executions, which terrified not just the Tories and the aristocracy, but the whole political class. They would remain terrified well into the 19th century: some future holders of high office witnessed the uprising in Paris as students or young gentlemen on the Grand Tour, among them Lords Liverpool and Castlereagh. As Tory ministers a quarter century later, they would do all they could to block change, and suppress those calling for it with the harshest measures.

The Royal Family shared their view, with some justification. In 1812, the Prime Minister Spencer Perceval would be shot (by a disgruntled businessman rather than a revolutionary) in the lobby of the Commons, and there were periodic labour protests, some edging close to mass unrest. Amidst fears of chaos if things were allowed to go unchecked, the French Revolution drew Britain into war with France for the next two decades.

Inspired by the American and French examples, some of Ireland's Catholics and Protestants joined in armed revolt against British rule in 1798. Pitt's response was threefold: a union of the island of Ireland and the rest of Britain, including the abolition of the separate Irish parliament, and granting voting and election rights to the majority Catholic population. The Union went through, but emancipation foundered for thirty years, largely because George III and then George IV opposed it. The Coronation oaths, they argued, included a promise to uphold the Protestant faith, so the King would have to abdicate. Having not consulted the monarch in advance on the issue, Pitt resigned, returning to office three years later as the Napoleonic wars rumbled on, but dying within 18 months, worn out at 46.

Within a few years, the King was oblivious to outside events, including the momentous conclusion of the Napoleonic Wars at Waterloo. Yet the institution of monarchy stayed strong enough to withstand an absent and incapacitated king. In fact, the longer George III's reign endured, and the less he intervened in affairs of state, the more his subjects revered him. Patriotic ceremonials, like the Garter ceremony inaugurated in 1809, and George III's golden jubilee in the same year, were celebrated in what was described as 'a spirit of loyal enthusiasm'. Public performances of the National Anthem also became more frequent.

As the historian John Cannon writes of the King's life in the *Oxford Dictionary of National Biography*: 'George was an unlucky man whom life treated badly and whose talents did not quite fit the situation in which he found himself. But he cannot be faulted for want of effort. "I do not pretend to any superior abilities," he wrote, "but will give place to no one in meaning to preserve the freedom, happiness and glory of my dominions and all their inhabitants, and to fulfil the duty to my God and my neighbour in the most extended sense".'

The historian Linda Colley has calculated that 'God Save the King', first published as a patriotic song in the 1740s, was only sung publicly four times in the first two decades of George's reign, but 90 times in the next twenty years. Other countries had occasionally adopted unofficial national songs, but Britain's was the first to enjoy quasi-official status, although the tune quite possibly came from abroad. Later, the French, German and American anthems would extoll, respectively, a revolution, a unified nation and victory over a foreign foe. By contrast, Britain's anthem centres firmly on the monarch and the preservation of the institution.

The King's eldest son, the dissolute and spendthrift Prince

of Wales, had spent more than 20 years waiting. His moment finally came in 1811, when he was made Regent. Some visibly monarchical figure was needed, both in the final years of the Napoleonic Wars and in the aftermath. The country seethed with dislocation as soldiers returned home. Agriculture was suffering from repeatedly bad harvests, inflating food prices and creating hunger. The largest volcanic eruption ever recorded, at Mount Tambora in the Indonesian archipelago in 1815 had spread a dust cloud across the northern hemisphere, affecting weather patterns for several seasons. It is no coincidence that mass unrest, and demands for change, occurred in so many of the nations affected. In Britain, many people fled the land to the growing cities, where regular work for only marginally higher wages barely compensated for the conditions of the most poor.

The era saw protests by Britain's disenfranchised, combined with harsh legal measures to suppress them. In 1815, Lord Liverpool's government introduced the Corn Laws, protecting and boosting landowners' profits at the expense of those struggling to feed their families. The authorities, government ministers and local magistrates may have had their fears of a French-style revolution stoked by an increasingly vocal press, but few voices were calling for a Reign of Terror. Demands focussed on affordable food, better working conditions and, increasingly, for parliamentary reform, to make legislators accountable for the laws they passed. Even the most potentially dangerous of the era's insurgents, the Cato Street conspirators – caught plotting to assassinate the existing Cabinet in 1820 – had not been directly seeking to overturn the new King George, who succeeded his father in January that year.

King George IV (1820–1830)

> What eye has wept for him? What heart has heaved one throb of unmercenary sorrow? If George IV ever had… a devoted friend in any rank of life, we protest that the name of him or her has not yet reached us.
>
> *The Times*, 15th July 1830, Obituary for King George IV

Rather than seeking to behead George IV, his subjects mainly ridiculed him, and he gave ample cause for it. Unlike his monogamous parents, George IV conducted serial affairs, the most serious at the age of 23 when he secretly married a widow named Maria Fitzherbert, who was Catholic, breaching not only the Act of Settlement but also the Royal Marriages Act (which required him to obtain his father's permission to marry).

Nine years later he abandoned Maria for an official, arranged marriage to his coarse, malodorous and promiscuous cousin Caroline of Brunswick – 'I feel faint, a glass of brandy if you please,' he apparently exclaimed on first meeting her. Both partners led separate lives with other lovers, but not before they had produced a Princess, Charlotte, whose death in childbirth aged 21 in 1817 ended any chance of a direct line of succession. So public and acrimonious was George's split from his wife that when Napoleon died in 1821, and a courtier told the King that his greatest enemy was dead, George replied: 'Is she, by God?'

He attempted to have his marriage annulled after becoming king in 1820, but lengthy public hearings in the House of Lords only increased Caroline's popularity at his expense. By the time of George's coronation in 1821, relations were so bad that she was barred from the ceremony by bouncers, and died a few weeks later. Inspired by the press, dislike of the King was expressed as public outrage at the late Queen's treatment.

His reputation was not helped by regular cartoons expounding on his gluttony and lechery, which he failed to censor, even by bribing the cartoonists. No monarch has ever been so widely and publicly ridiculed. He was a man of taste and wit, kind to children, attached to animals and could rarely bear to approve the execution of criminals, but he also behaved like an entitled buffoon: 'a spoiled, selfish, odious beast,' as the diarist Charles Greville wrote.

George IV rages at his younger brothers Frederick (far left) and William for refusing to back his divorce from Princess Caroline, while George's mistress, possibly Lady Conyngham, eggs him on.

Ironically most of those cartoons only exist today because George's private secretary was sent out to buy them up from the print shops of London, and they remained sequestered in the Royal Collection for a century until George V sold them to America to raise funds for his stamp collection.

George's lasting legacy remains in the architecture he commissioned and encouraged, from the Brighton Pavilion to the elegant curved façades of Regent Street spreading south from Regent's Park. George's jaunts to the South Coast popularised the idea of the seaside as a holiday destination and health-giving experience. Brighthelmstone had been a rather grubby fishing village, which the King helped to turn into fashionable Brighton, not least by building himself an ersatz Far Eastern pavilion near the shoreline. (Queen Victoria sold it in the 1840s, partly because she hated errand boys in the Brighton streets sticking their faces under her bonnet to see what she looked like, opting instead for the seclusion of Osborne House on the Isle of Wight, and the Balmoral Estate in the Highlands).

Far less appreciated were George's mountainous debts, paid off, reluctantly, by a succession of Parliaments: £60,000 in 1783, £161,000 in 1787, £65,000 per annum granted to go towards a debt of £630,000, £60,000 in 1803. By 1793, ten years after moving into Carlton House on Pall Mall, he had run up more debts of £500,000 in decorating it with paintings, including a Rembrandt, Gainsboroughs and Reynoldses, Sèvres porcelain and other treasures. The extravagance continued throughout his life, including his coronation – for which he designed his own robes, and which cost £240,000. The bill for William IV's coronation ten years later came to just £42,000 and it was not until the 1930s that another British coronation matched the figures spent on George's.

The King did become modestly popular with his Celtic subjects, simply by going to see them. His 1821 visit to Dublin was the first time a British king had set foot in Ireland since William III, 130 years earlier. Scotland, the following year, had not been graced since Charles I's visit in the 1630s. In Edinburgh, despite his ludicrous, be-corseted appearance in a kilt, worn over flesh-coloured tights, George's tour was pronounced a success. Sir Walter Scott organised what was called 'the King's Jaunt' north of the border, one correspondent, the lawyer and author James Simpson, describing it thus:

> Their first glimpse of that being called a king – Britain's king – Scotland's king – their own king! The moment came, the first in their lives, when they could compare the actual thing called Majesty, with all they had from childhood dreamed and fancied of it!

The thing called Majesty was himself thrilled – the reception was so different from London, where people regularly threw stones at his carriage. Scott's careful choreography set a template for later royal tours: the orchestration of pageantry, uniforms, reviews and military parades, balls and receptions, informal public appearances and waving to the crowds. Even George's short, Royal Stuart tartan kilt drew praise: 'The more we see of him the better,' said Lady Hamilton-Dalrymple. It was as important for monarchs of the early 19th century to be seen as it had been for those of the early 12th.

George IV emulated his father by opposing emancipation for Catholics, despite it becoming ever more clear that the policy was doomed. Voters in Ireland were repeatedly attempting to elect a Catholic candidate, Daniel O'Connell, to represent them and violence was threatened if they were thwarted again.

By 1827 George was forced to accept George Canning as his Prime Minister, a man whom he deplored, not only because he supported Catholic emancipation, but because he had supported Caroline in her legal wrangles against the King. Canning died within four months of taking office, but two years later, even the reactionary Duke of Wellington, who had succeeded him as Prime Minister, was urging George to change the laws regarding Catholics (and other non-Anglican groups).

George was forced to give way, broadening voting rights in Ireland and allowing Catholic participation in politics. It was becoming futile for a monarch to oppose the will of the government. When George died in 1830 – 20 stone in weight, still a glutton, warding off his various ailments with alcohol and laudanum – there was little weeping. George IV had stretched the bonds of the monarchical contract to their limit, and exasperated his ministers.

William IV (1830–1837)

> Whatever his faults may have been... he was not only zealous but most conscientious in the discharge of his duties as a king. He had a truly kind heart and was most anxious to do what was right.
>
> Queen Victoria on her uncle, William IV

George's successor was his younger brother William, the Duke of Clarence, who inherited as next in line by virtue of the death of Charlotte in 1817 and then of his older brother Frederick, Duke of York (the nursery rhyme's Grand Old Duke of York) who had died in 1827. Previously William had led a life of quiet obscurity as a retired naval officer, cohabiting for many years with the Irish actress Dorothea Jordan, with whom he had fathered ten illegitimate children. He had only married a German princess, Adelaide, in 1818 when the remote possibility of him becoming king turned into a distinct probability, and George III's ageing and unmarried sons competed to find their own, suitable brides. Although William and Adelaide had two daughters themselves, neither survived infancy, while the Duke of Kent and his wife produced the princess who would become Queen Victoria.

A William IV sovereign depicting the King's trademark hairstyle

William IV, the oldest monarch so far to succeed to the throne at the age of 64, was known as The Pineapple due to the shape of his head, surmounted by a crest of white hair. He was a slightly more endearing, bluff and garrulous figure than his brother, though he took time to get used to the constraints of monarchy. He found, for instance, that he could no longer wander out for a stroll along Pall Mall unmolested. The first time he tried to do so, he was embraced by a prostitute, and had to be rescued from the gathering crowd by members of nearby White's Club.

> When he might very well have sat himself quietly down and rested, he must needs put on his plain cloathes [sic] and start on a ramble about the streets, all alone too... he got back to the palace amid shouting, bawling and applause.
>
> Charles Greville, *Journals*, Vol. III, published 1874

This early attempt at a royal walkabout was not a success.

William was obliged to be more flexible than his brother about parliamentary reform. By the early 1830s, the Whigs had accepted the expansion of voting rights and were attempting to address certain flaws of the election system. These included the Rotten Boroughs, whose MPs, especially in southern England, were elected by a tiny handful of voters, while the new industrialised towns of the north and Midlands had no representation at all. It had suited the Tories to keep this unreformed Commons in place, with many MPs chosen for Pocket Boroughs, thanks to the patronage of aristocratic landowners. The Whigs, out of power for seventy years by this point, were determined to change that.

It was a struggle. The Tories followed the Duke of Wellington in arguing that reform would lead to revolution, and that reducing patronage would undermine landowners' property rights. But they were unable to form a government, and having initially rejected the Whig PM Lord Grey's request for 50 new peers to force the reform through the Lords, William was obliged to give way, just as his brother had over Catholic emancipation. In the end the extra votes were not needed: the Tory-controlled Lords capitulated and passed the bill, on Wellington's advice. William surrendered gracefully, writing to Grey that as an individual he would have taken a different view, but 'as a sovereign it was [his] duty to set those feelings and prejudices aside.' The King was acknowledging that Parliament could overrule him: a further important step in the shift of power.

He seemed to grasp as much himself. 'We all of us mean well,' he told the Whig politician Lord John Russell. 'I have my view of things and I tell them to my Ministers. If they do not adopt them, I cannot help it. I have done my duty.' Elizabeth II would have occasion to say the same: an acknowledgement that sovereigns could warn and advise, but not impose their will.

The Great Reform Act abolished 60 rotten boroughs, and 47 seats which had previously returned two MPs were reduced to one-member constituencies. The hitherto unrepresented major cities of industry were given MPs and the franchise was widened from 400,000 to about 650,000 property owners – still a minority of the population, and still excluding women. The Whig reformers went on to outlaw slavery in the Caribbean, to limit factory working hours for children under the age of 13 and to introduce the workhouse system under the hated 1834 Poor Law.

Given his advanced age at the time of his accession, William's reign was bound to be short. His successor would be Alexandrina Victoria, the teenaged daughter of his deceased younger brother, the Duke of Kent. William was concerned that, if Victoria were under 18 at the time of her accession, her domineering German mother could wield influence as regent. He was determined to live long enough – as he put it, very publicly, in August 1836 at a banquet marking his 72nd birthday – to spare the country a woman 'incompetent to act with propriety'. The old King managed it: Victoria turned 18 on 24th May 1837 and William IV died a month later, his duty done.

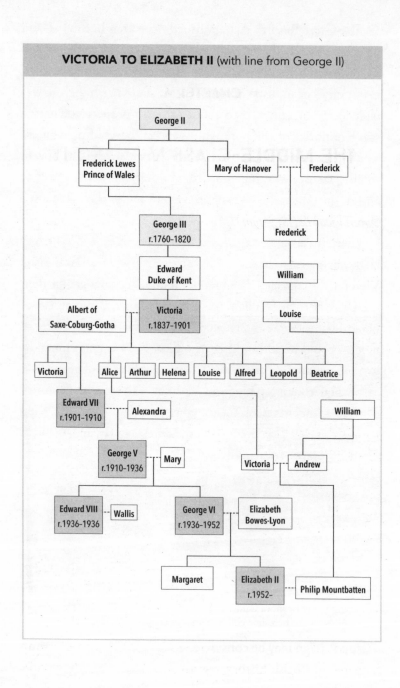

VICTORIA TO ELIZABETH II (with line from George II)

George II

Frederick Lewes Prince of Wales

Mary of Hanover -------- Frederick

George III r.1760–1820

Frederick

Edward Duke of Kent

William

Albert of Saxe-Coburg-Gotha

Victoria r.1837–1901

Louise

Victoria | Alice | Arthur | Helena | Louise | Alfred | Leopold | Beatrice

Edward VII r.1901–1910 ------- Alexandra

William

George V r.1910–1936 — Mary

Victoria — Andrew

Edward VIII r.1936–1936 --- Wallis

George VI r.1936–1952 — Elizabeth Bowes-Lyon

Margaret | Elizabeth II r.1952– ----- Philip Mountbatten

CHAPTER 6

THE MIDDLE-CLASS MONARCHY

Queen Victoria (1837–1901)

> I will be good.
>
> Princess Victoria, aged 10

Photographer Leonora Caldesini took this 1857 portrait of Victoria and Albert with their nine children on the terrace at Osborne House

Victoria's reign may be considered the most momentous of any monarch in British history, covering as it did a lengthy period of social and economic change. The Queen herself did little to change the institution – whatever happened to it came about largely despite rather than because of her interventions, certainly in the second half of her reign. Victoria brought her subjects to the edge of the 20th century by playing a central role on its ritual and ceremonial stage, and by adapting and ceding power, if not always gracefully.

The greatest adaptation, adopted perhaps unconsciously, was the creation of a *respectable* monarchy: one that seemingly mirrored the values of its middle-class citizens. Victoria's monarchy wore the same clothes, had the same (resolutely unintellectual) interests and seemed to have the same aspirations for the people as they had for themselves. Alongside the monarch, the Royal Family became part of the enterprise: their faces known and their useful good works – opening hospitals, inspecting troops, supporting charities, touring the country – publicised and appreciated. Like ordinary folk, but not quite: a sleight of hand that remains central to their continued popularity.

When, early on the morning of 20th June 1837, the diminutive teenager was woken in Kensington Palace by the Archbishop of Canterbury and the Lord Chamberlain, Lord Conyngham (husband of George IV's mistress), she already knew what they were going to tell her. The household had been warned the previous evening that the old King would not last the night. She confided to her journal on the 20th: 'Consequently *I* am queen.' Within hours she had met the Whig Prime Minister Lord Melbourne, and that morning presided over a formal meeting of the Privy Council – 'quite <u>ALONE</u>', she emphasised. She was proud to have undertaken these duties without the presence of her mother, the Duchess of Kent, and her grasping secretary Sir John Conroy, and well aware how much they wanted to control her. Those present at the Council noted her calmness and self-possession: immediately she appeared a more welcome proposition than the grumpy, rackety old kings who had preceded her.

Victoria was the youngest monarch for almost three centuries, since Edward VI, and none has been younger since. She certainly knew her own mind, even though during her 64 years on the throne – and despite battles, outbursts and obstructionism – she rarely got her own way against her ministers. Early in her reign, she was inevitably somewhat under the influence of Melbourne, who personally flattered, cajoled and advised her in the ways of constitutional monarchy, something her early education had lacked.

When Melbourne's government fell, the Tory leader Sir Robert Peel requested that Victoria reduce the number of Ladies of the Bedchamber. These were her closest companions, but also the approved choices of Melbourne and his Whigs. She refused to dismiss anyone, Peel refused to take office, and Melbourne soldiered on for a further two years, until the Tories decisively won a general election.

In time Victoria came to realise that she could not subvert or ignore a Parliamentary majority: she not only accepted Sir Robert Peel as her Prime Minister, but eventually came to trust and admire him. Though she was far from being a democrat, she expressed sympathy (not without a tinge of sentimentality and condescension) with the plight of the working classes:

> They are becoming so well-informed – are so intelligent and earn their bread and riches so deservedly that they cannot and ought not to be kept back – to be abused by the wretched, ignorant high-born beings who live only to kill time.
>
> Queen Victoria; Letter to Princess 'Vicky', December 1867

Well-informed, intelligent and deserving they may have been, but Victoria didn't think they should be in government. By keeping voting rights so limited, the Great Reform Act of 1832 contributed to the rise of the Chartists, a movement led by craftsmen and artisans. They developed the most coherent political reform programme of the period, marching to present petitions to Parliament, then quietly going home again. They did so several times, to successive Parliaments, presenting a charter of six main demands: all males over 21 to have the vote, secret ballots, annual elections, no property-ownership qualifications for MPs, payment for MPs and equal-sized constituencies.

Peaceful as they were, the Chartists were viewed and treated as extremists by the authorities, and when they gathered to deliver their petition in 1848, the Royal Family were sent to their new holiday home, Osborne House on the Isle of Wight, to escape the feared insurrection. Troops and special constables (including the future French Emperor Napoleon III, exiled in Britain at the time) were called up to defend the capital, but

Prince Albert took a great interest in photography, amassing a collection of daguerreotypes, including this one of the 1848 Chartists' rally

then stood by idle as the mass petition was delivered to Parliament by hansom cab, and subsequently ignored. The crowd, smaller than expected because of rain, dispersed peacefully. The Chartists' mass meeting on Kennington Common was probably the first ever news event recorded by daguerrotype, and it survives today – in the Royal Collection.

The Anti-Corn Law League, mobilised around the same time, was a middle-class employers' movement, focused solely on abolishing the hated legislation, and unlike the Chartists, its members achieved their goal in 1846. Victoria was terrified by the Chartists and wary of all legal and political reforms, but over time she was persuaded by her husband Prince Albert and Sir Robert Peel that the Corn Laws – which kept grain prices high to the benefit of the landowners and the detriment of the urban poor – had to go.

The Chartists had disbanded long before further parliamentary reforms came in 1867 and 1884, widening and increasing the electorate. The result was governments increasingly dependent on their majorities in the Commons – voted for by an expanding electorate – rather than on the Queen's approval. Victoria had a very poor relationship with both Liberal Prime Ministers, Palmerston and Gladstone, although they were her longest-serving premiers. But ultimately she had to accept them. Interestingly, she was never asked to create peerages in order to force one party's legislation through the House of Lords.

Victoria was partisan. She clearly favoured the Tories – the stiffly rectitudinous Peel, the sycophantic Disraeli and the patrician Lord Salisbury – consulting them even when they were out of office. She would occasionally oppose the appointment of ministers she disapproved of – radicals like Charles Dilke and Joseph Chamberlain – at least until they moderated their republican views. And in 1880, after the Liberals had won the election, she tried to persuade the party grandees, Lords Granville and Hartington, to become Prime Minister instead of the clear leader, Gladstone. They refused, pointing out that Gladstone was the people's choice (and as such, he would have declined to serve under either of them). Lord Salisbury was the last premier to be chosen from the peerage; from then on, queens, kings and nobles might obtain their positions by birth, but governments were chosen by voters.

Monarchy and Magic

Queen Victoria was a figurehead rather than a driving force in the country's government, and this wasn't lost on her subjects. In 1867, journalist Walter Bagehot noted provocatively in his book, *The English Constitution*, that Britain was a 'secret republic' whose ruler could no longer exercise power independently of ministers. His book remains the most clear-sighted summing-up of the modern, constitutional monarchy. The Queen had job security, ceremonial and dynastic authority, but barely any executive power. This was a kind of constitutional secret and, as Bagehot wrote, 'essential to the utility of English royalty as it now is. Above all things our royalty is to be reverenced and if you begin to poke about it, you cannot reverence it... We must not let daylight upon magic.'

According to Bagehot, the monarch had three rights: to be consulted by ministers, to encourage them, and to warn. The Queen had no veto: 'She must sign her own death warrant if the two Houses unanimously send it up to her.' It was therefore best not to have a sovereign who was imaginative or dynamic. No doubt Victoria would have been shocked if she ever read Bagehot's polemic, which was a worldwide bestseller that influenced many, including future US Presidents.

The bar on public intervention did not mean that the Queen was uninvolved, or stop her from making her views known. She was diligent in reading official documents and meeting her ministers – even the loathed Gladstone who, she said, had a way of addressing her as if she was a public meeting – and she generally kept a beady eye on proceedings, from the weighty to the most trivial, even conducting a correspondence with the First Lord of the Admiralty on the permitted size and shape of sailors' beards. Long after the 1871 Cardwell Reforms of the British Army – which, among other measures, abolished the purchasing of military ranks – she continued the tradition of personally signing every officer's military commission. Quick to spot when Government papers were missing or delayed, she kept abreast of all Parliamentary manoeuvrings.

There seems to be only one example of her intervening in legislation. This was the Public Worship Regulation Bill of 1874, introduced by the Archbishop of Canterbury, and aimed at removing 'Popish practices', such as ornaments, ritualism and wearing vestments, in the Church of England. The Queen publicly supported the measure as a defence of the Protestant constitutional order. (She was personally tolerant of individual Catholics, but did not think they should be in government, and nor indeed were they for many years.) This support was widely known, and Disraeli's cautious sympathy with the Archbishop of Canterbury's wider aims seems to have been nudged further by the Queen. The legislation misfired, resulting in five Anglican clergymen being jailed for using incense, and four being removed from their posts. Fortunately for Victoria, it was the issue of Parliament making rules for the Church that caused most outrage, rather than her own intervention.

Prince Albert: The Counsellor-Consort

Victoria's husband – her cousin, Prince Albert of Saxe-Coburg and Gotha – may be the most influential British royal family member of the past 200 years. Born a second son of the duke in a small German statelet, he was presented at the English court as a prospective husband for Victoria when both were teenagers, a match sponsored by their joint uncle, Leopold I, King of the Belgians. Victoria was smitten, writing that he was 'extremely handsome; his hair is about the same colour as mine; his eyes are large and blue, and he has a beautiful nose and a very sweet mouth with fine teeth; but the charm of his countenance is his expression, which is most delightful.' Once she was queen – and because she was queen – Victoria reversed the traditional order of things by being the one to propose marriage. From their wedding in 1840 to his death in 1861, Albert was Victoria's closest and most loyal adviser, acting unofficially as her private secretary, managing her occasional rages and even designing the family's holiday homes at Osborne on the Isle of Wight and Balmoral in the Scottish Highlands. He was paterfamilias – father of their nine children – while she was queen, and he managed the anomalous, subsidiary role of consort with discretion. As a foreigner, especially a supposedly penniless German princeling, Albert was viewed by many in England with suspicion. But after Victoria's dissolute and decadent Hanoverian uncles, his influence was key to restoring the Crown's reputation. The British middle classes treated the Royal Family as a template for how to live their own lives – they read about them in the press, purchased their portraits, copied them in their manners, attitudes and even their choice of holiday destinations. Albert was right to say that being sovereign was an 'immense moral responsibility.'

Ghémar Frères. Photographes du Roi. Bruxelles.

An enthusiastic pioneer of photography, Albert saw to it that royal portraits showed the family in their ordinary clothes, in relatively informal poses and settings. Not everyone approved: when the Prince of Wales's engagement photograph showed his bride Princess Alexandra touching his shoulder (rather as Charles and Diana's engagement photograph would, 120 years later) the *London Review* thundered: 'Can [anyone] possibly believe that the Prince and Princess allowed themselves to be shown after this fashion to the general gaze?' Despite the outrage, two million copies of the photograph were purchased. The Victorian Royal Family presented themselves – as have all subsequent generations of the family – as like us, but different.

Victoria was perhaps a naturally retiring soul. She had unhappy memories of the gruelling public tours to which she'd been subjected as a Princess, orchestrated by her mother with the aim of ensuring her daughter's accession. Prince Albert, however, encouraged the Queen to conduct a visible public life: they travelled Britain extensively, and visited places monarchs had never previously been, such as a Cornish tin mine and the industrial north.

Doubts about Prince Albert's loyalty were dispelled by the central role he played in organising the Great Exhibition of 1851. This spectacle in Hyde Park attracted global attention, celebrating British innovations alongside the glories of the Empire and the Industrial Revolution. Six million visitors came – equivalent to nearly a quarter of the population. Many were seeing London for the first time, thanks to cheap excursion trains; and for everyone the Exhibition provided the inaugural opportunity to 'spend a penny' in the all-new, coin-operated locks in the public toilets. Among the 13,000 exhibits were new labour-saving devices, an early prototype of the fax machine and the Koh-I-Noor diamond, recently acquired following the conquest of the Punjab.

Although the Queen would take advantage of the vast technological and economic changes of her long reign, she had little influence on their development. The biggest changes were already taking place when she came to the throne. Railways were spreading across the country – 250 miles of tracks in 1838, 5,000 12 years later – helping to increase the speed and safety of the movement of goods and people. The electrical telegraph, developed in the 1840s, revolutionised long-distance communication, as did the telephone, invented 30 years after that. Industrial development was spreading ever further, from the mill towns of the north to the metal-bashing factories of the Midlands and the craft workshops of London. The 1851 census was the first to show more people living in towns and cities than in the countryside – by then too, the population had doubled since the start of the century from 13 million to 26 million*. Living conditions for the poor and unskilled working classes in both towns and rural areas were often dreadful, but for skilled artisans and the middle and professional classes, prosperity was rising and a widening range of consumer goods was available. Britain transformed from a land of stage coaches, sailing ships and quill pens to one of typewriters and the popular press. By the time of Victoria's death, the first cars were kicking up the dusty roads and aeroplanes would soon be taking off.

The white heat of Victorian technology contributed to the changing perception of monarchy. The Queen's face appeared on mass-produced advertisements for everything from inks to metal polish, from Sydney to Alberta and Calcutta; her statue decorated the city squares of the expanding empire; her *Highland Journals* were best-sellers; and at the end of her reign, she even featured briefly and indistinctly in the moving images of the earliest newsreels. From the 1840s, the activities of the Royal Family fascinated the newspapers, and the coverage ranged from reverence to criticism, and sometimes raucous intrusiveness. The advances of this new age enabled monarchs to be seen more often, by more people, in more ways than ever before.

In the 1840s Europe was rocked by violent revolutions, but nothing similar occurred in Britain. Although there were several attempts to assassinate the Queen during this decade – three in 1842 alone – two of these were made by the same man, and only one – committed by the 17-year-old Arthur O'Connor with an unloaded pistol, apparently to secure the release

---

* It would be 38 million at the end of Victoria's reign in 1901.

1 **1840–10th June** Edward Oxford fires at the pregnant Queen as she departs for Hyde Park. He later claims the pistol had no bullets and the prosecution cannot prove otherwise. He is declared insane and spends 24 years in an asylum. On release he settles in Melbourne and writes a book about the city.

2 **1842–29th/30th May** Unemployed carpenter John Francis aims a gun at the Queen on Pall Mall, but it fails to fire. The next day he does fire, but misses. He is sentenced to be hanged, drawn and quartered but is sent to Australia instead, where he thrives in the building trade, dying a free man in Melbourne aged 62.

3 **1842–3rd July** John Bean fires a pistol loaded with tobacco and paper. Bean claims he meant no harm, merely to get himself transported to Australia. He receives 18 months for assault. On Prince Albert's suggestion, the subsequent Treason Act of 1842 recognises minor offences as treason without incurring the death penalty.

ATTEMPTS ON VICTORIA'S LIFE

Piccadilly

Pall Mall

Mall

5

2 **3**

Green Park

St James's Palace

St James's Park

1 **4**

Constitution Hill

Birdcage Walk

Buckingham Palace Garden

Buckingham Palace

6

4 **1849–10th June** Unemployed bricklayer William Hamilton fires at the Queen in Green Park, with a pistol borrowed from his landlord. He claims he wants to be in prison as he is tired of being out of work. Hamilton's landlord demands the gun back as collectors have offered him the huge sum of £40 for it. After five years on Gibraltar, Hamilton is transported to Australia.

5 **1850–27th June** Robert Pate strikes the Queen on her forehead with his cane as she leaves a house in Piccadilly. No explanation is offered for his attack nor does he plead insanity. After transportation to Australia, he marries a wealthy widow, returning to live in comfortable obscurity in London.

6 **1872–29th February** 17 year-old Arthur O'Connor hides in the grounds of Buckingham Palace until Victoria drives back in from her circuit of the park. A descendant of Irish revolutionaries, O'Connor claims to have had no wish to harm her, merely to get her to agree to release Irish prisoners. He receives a one-year sentence and 20 strokes with the birch. Victoria's disgust at the short sentence leads the authorities to offer him a 'deal' – less prison and no birch in return for transportation. O'Connor negotiates further – getting the court to pay twice for his travel and cover his expenses in Australia.

7 **1882 –2nd March** Roderick Maclean fires a shot at the Queen at Windsor railway station – a possible motive being that he'd sent some poems to her and received in reply a dismissive note from a lady-in-waiting. At the trial there is evidence as to his insanity – he believes people wear the colour blue to insult him. Found not guilty, but insane, he spends the rest of his life in Broadmoor. Subsequently, the Trial of Lunatics Act of 1883 permits juries to return a verdict of 'guilty, but insane'.

of jailed Irish rebels – had any kind of political motive. The attempts on the Queen's life were less a sign of revolutionary ferment than of what a very public figure she had become: an object of interest, reverence, worship, or for some, obsession.

Victoria's visibility would diminish considerably after Prince Albert's early death in December 1861. The official diagnosis was typhoid fever, but this seems unlikely: given his long-standing complaints of stomach pain, Crohn's Disease, kidney failure or even abdominal cancer are more probable causes. The Queen was devastated by Albert's death, and she retreated from her public duties for much of the rest of her reign.

In the weeks before his death, Albert had been highly stressed by the behaviour of his eldest son Edward, the Prince of Wales, nominally studying at Cambridge but spending more time with the Irish actress Nellie Clifden. It was after a hasty visit to Cambridge to remonstrate with his son that Albert's condition worsened. As a result, Victoria would blame the Prince of Wales for the loss of her beloved husband.

From then on she refused to trust her eldest son with anything other than routine public engagements. It was hardly surprising, then, that as a young man Edward ('Bertie', as he was known amongst the family) continued to keep questionable company and fritter his time away, or that his mother saw no reason to change her mind. On two occasions he even appeared as a witness in court – the first time a Prince of Wales had ever had to give evidence. The first was during the Mordaunt divorce case of 1870, where he had to deny improper familiarity with Lady Mordaunt. The second came in 1891 during a slander case, and concerned an allegation that a friend had cheated while playing baccarat – illegal at the time – during a weekend house party. The Prince's involvement in both matters may have been peripheral, but they scarcely showed him in a good light.

Edward partially made up for these lapses by promoting the monarchy in a new guise: as sponsors of charity and philanthropy. He could open hospitals, attend banquets and make speeches, the ceremonial events his mother found too fatiguing and at which he displayed great charm and skill. Gladstone recognised this, and encouraged Edward's public role, hoping to raise the moral tone of the monarchy and demonstrate its public usefulness: a design that continues today.

There was also an agenda behind Edward's 1862 tour of the Middle East – a destination sufficiently far-flung for the Queen to approve his going. The government saw it as soft diplomacy, hoping that Edward would charm the ruler of Egypt and thus curtail French designs on the Suez Canal. In 1875, he became the first royal to visit India: a successful trip, which contributed to Parliament making his mother Empress of India, as well as to Victoria taking a renewed interest in the jewel in her crown. Through the 20th century, Royal Family members would follow in Edward's footsteps, using the mystique of monarchy and personal charm to smooth the path of international relations.

Edward also provided the people with a substitute monarch at a crucial time. For if upheavals on the Continent in the 1840s had failed to ignite republican and revolutionary ideas in Britain, the Queen's disappearance in the 1860s did. Victoria's withdrawal into ostentatious mourning added fuel to an emerging scepticism about the institution she represented.

The historian George Otto Trevelyan issued a pamphlet on the subject of the Queen's spending, entitled *What Does She Do With It?* Criticism of her absence only made her less willing to show herself; by 1871, even Tories were pleading with her to show herself to her subjects. Lord Halifax wrote to the Queen's private secretary Sir Henry Ponsonby in 1871: 'The mass of the people expect a king or queen to look and play the part. They want to see a crown and sceptre and all that sort of thing. They want the gilding for their money.'

The Prince of Wales shared Halifax's view of the matter, writing to his mother: 'If you sometimes even came to London from Windsor – say for luncheon – and then drove for an hour in the park... the people would be overjoyed. We live in radical times and the more the people see the sovereign the better it is for the people and the country.'

In an era of mass-circulated news and images, royal visits, tours and ceremonies became national, even global events. Edward's visit to the Middle East was the first to be accompanied by an official photographer, and the tour album was published on his return, providing many people with their first true images of the pyramids of Giza, the temple of Karnac and the Dome of the Rock. When, on his return, Edward married Princess Alexandra of Denmark, the crowds waiting to see her arrival in London were so large that her carriage could barely squeeze through them, and seven people were killed in the crush.

The Prince of Wales (fourth camel from left) at Giza in Egypt, 1862

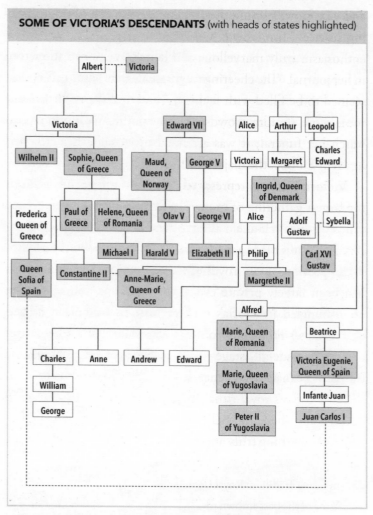

SOME OF VICTORIA'S DESCENDANTS (with heads of states highlighted)

Then in late 1871, the Prince fell gravely ill with typhoid. Once again, it became a public affair, even something of a publicity coup, with his recovery covered in sympathetic detail in the press and crowned with a service at St Paul's Cathedral. Republican mutterings all but died away, especially when, towards the end of her reign, Victoria finally emerged from seclusion.

In 1897, her Diamond Jubilee celebration was staged in sunshine with troops from all across the Empire parading past, and vast crowds lining the route to St Paul's for a thanksgiving service. 'The crowds were quite indescribable and their enthusiasm truly marvellous and deeply touching,' she wrote in her journal. 'The cheering was quite deafening and every face seemed to be filled with real joy.' Three years later, in January 1901, more sombre crowds turned out in huge numbers to watch her funeral; it was attended by most of the crowned heads of Europe, the majority of whom were related to her.

Victoria's funeral represented what is thought to have been the largest gathering of monarchs and rulers ever, attended by princes from as far afield as Egypt and Siam (Thailand). Victoria's death rites made a display for the whole world.

In previous eras, royal weddings and even coronations had been largely private events, witnessed by few and quite often bungled (Victoria's own coronation had been dogged by mishaps.) From now on, the pageantry would be choreographed in detail, stage-managed by courtiers, as carefully timed and exhaustively rehearsed as any West End musical. So slick are today's royal rituals that onlookers can hardly fail to become absorbed, and believe – wrongly – that they are witnessing something truly ancient.

Inventing Tradition: Royal Ceremonies

Many of the best-known royal ceremonies are either of modern origin or have been reinvented during the 20th century. The Knights of the Garter may date from the reign of Edward III in 1348, but the annual robed procession of the Queen and Prince of Wales and the 24 members of the Order through the grounds of Windsor Castle to St George's Chapel dates back no further than 1948. The Royal Maundy service, at which alms are handed out to pensioners on the Thursday before Easter, began in 1932, The ritualised state opening of Parliament, in which the royal representative Black Rod has the doors to the Commons slammed in his face, and has to knock and beg leave to enter, is a brilliant bit of theatre, summing up centuries of push and pull between monarchs and Parliaments. But although it relates directly to King Charles I's uninvited entry into the Commons Chamber in 1642, since when no monarch has crossed the threshold, the opening ceremony dates back only to the 1840s.

King Edward VII (1901–1910)

Edward VII openly enjoyed being king... His keenness for uniforms, decorations, and ceremonial caught one aspect of the public mood.

Oxford Dictionary of National Biography

After his mother's long reign, the accession of Bertie, aged nearly 60, instituted a change of style, if not of substance to the monarchy. He quickly announced that he would take his second name, and not, as Victoria had wished, his first, meaning he would be known as Edward VII, not Albert I. He would continue with his twelve-course dinners (he wasn't called *Tum Tum* for nothing, though never to his face), his dozen daily cigars and score of cigarettes. Also his game shooting on the Sandringham Estate in Norfolk, which he purchased for that purpose in the 1860s, his evening bridge parties, golf and horse racing jaunts and his annual round of holidays in Biarritz, Marienbad and sailing around the Mediterranean. And also with his mistresses, of whom the latest was society hostess Alice Keppel.*

---

* As it would turn out, great-grandmother of Camilla, Duchess of Cornwall, Prince Charles's second wife.

These were treated with discretion by the press and indulgence by the public, for Edward at least looked regal. Even when not sporting a crown, he cut an impressive figure, popularising the wearing of Homburg hats, Norfolk jackets and – mainly because of his 48 inch waistline – the leaving of the waistcoat's

Pictured here at Biarritz in 1907, many of Edward VII's 'style innovations' were adoptions: the Glenurquhart plaid spotted on Invernesshire gamekeepers during a shooting trip, became the Prince of Wales check, whilst his visits to the spa town of Marienbad left the King greatly enamoured of Homburg hats. His friendship with the Savile Row tailor Henry Poole also proved fertile, although less so for Poole, who died in debt in 1876, still owed money by the King.

bottom button undone. Although he seemed to embrace the new where fashion was concerned, he didn't welcome it from others. He is alleged to have given his Prime Minister, Lord Salisbury a lecture for mixing a Privy Councillor's tunic with inappropriate trousers – such punctiliousness was a trait he shared with his son George V and grandson George VI. In public, however, the King was generally charming. Horses from Edward VII's stable won three Derbies and a Grand National, and his was a more relaxed, popular and public reign than his mother's. It was under Edward that the centrepieces of the capital's royal pageantry, Admiralty Arch, the Mall, the Victoria Memorial and the frontage of Buckingham Palace were remodelled, though he did not live to see the work completed.

His lavish lifestyle was underpinned by a generous civil list of £470,000 (when Queen Elizabeth II was crowned fifty years later, her annual payment was only £5,000 more) and profitable investments engineered by his advisers. As a result, Edward VII was perhaps the first modern monarch to die in credit, leaving about £2m in modern values.

Edward VII still complained about having to pay income tax of about £18,000, and some of the costs of his staff. These included the Master of the Buckhounds and various hunt servants, prompting Edward to grouse that, in a country so devoted to sport, it was surprising that the king should have to pay for it. At the start of his reign, his successor George V would have the requirement to pay income tax rescinded as a quid pro quo for acquiescing to the Liberal government's reform of the House of Lords. After that, no monarch would pay the tax for eighty years, until Queen Elizabeth II agreed to do so in the early 1990s.

If Edward VII's lifestyle contributed to the golden glow of upper class society before World War One, it did not increase his authority as monarch. In 1903 he was at Balmoral when he learned that Arthur Balfour's Tory government was planning a reshuffle, and telegraphed to say that no changes should be made until he had been consulted. The reply informed him that the changes had not only been made, but announced. The

King objected, especially to the appointment of left-wing Hugh Arnold-Forster as Secretary of State for War. Now the monarch's right to appoint the Commander-in-Chief of the British Army, a royal prerogative ever since the 17th century, was being eroded. Balfour wanted a minister in charge, and was immovable, telling the King, bluntly: 'It is impossible for us to yield in a matter of this kind.'

Despite such rebuffs, Edward VII could claim a pivotal role in securing the Entente Cordiale alliance with France during a formal visit to Paris in 1903. The King spoke French and had visited the city many times as Prince, and his was the first state visit made to any country by a British monarch for more than 50 years. Despite the Government's reservations about what Bertie might promise or agree to, it was a great success, tying British and French diplomatic and military interests together in an alliance later joined by Russia. This was fortuitous, as Edward's relations with his nephew, Germany's Kaiser Wilhelm, were far less cordial, and they would worsen as Britain's foreign alliances threatened to encircle the German state.

In 1909, when Herbert Asquith's Liberal government needed royal help to secure the passage of its radical budget, Edward was placed in a dilemma which impinged directly on the monarchy's rights. The budget contained proposals to introduce a first state old-age pension (five shillings a week for those over 70 whose weekly income had been below ten shillings) as well as extra spending on Dreadnought battleships for the Navy, all funded via a super-tax on higher incomes and death duties. This provoked the inbuilt Conservative majority in the Lords to reject a money bill for the first time in 250 years. The Duke of Beaufort threatened to set his dogs on the Chancellor, Lloyd George and his radical colleague Winston Churchill, whilst Lord Anglesey, who had just bought himself a yacht, reduced his monthly subscription to the London Hospital from £5 to £3.

The government declined to back down and Asquith demanded that the King create sufficient new Liberal peers to swamp the Lords and force the measure through. Fearful of undermining the hereditary principle, Edward told the Prime Minister that he would agree to that only after a further general election. When that was held in January 1910, the Liberals lost their overall majority, but they retained power with the support of the first elected Labour Members and the Irish MPs, promising the latter that they would proceed with Home Rule for Ireland. The Lords subsequently passed the Finance Bill at the end of April 1910, without further peers being created, but the threat to form a Liberal majority in the upper house remained, since the government believed the King had conditionally agreed to it.

That Spring, the House adjourned for a ten-day recess, during which, on 6th May 1910, the King died, raddled with bronchitis and the effects of decades of over-indulgence. His last words were apparently uttered after he'd been told that one of his horses, Witch of Air, had just won the 4.15 at Kempton Park: 'I am glad of it.'

His funeral was one of the largest and last great Imperial ceremonies. Eight kings, an emperor and representatives of 70 other countries followed his coffin in procession through London, by train to Windsor and then through the town to St George's Chapel in the castle. Within a decade, many of those rulers had been deposed. But not the British Royal Family.

King George V (1910–1936)

George V was a shy, gruff man of plain and simple tastes

with an interest in shooting and stamp-collecting. His naval upbringing encouraged an excessive zeal for punctuality and routine.

Oxford Illustrated History of the British Monarchy

The new king was Edward's second son George V – his dim older brother Eddy, Duke of Clarence having fortuitously died of pneumonia aged 28 in 1892. George, whose chief interests ran to stamp collecting and shooting on his Sandringham estate, married his late brother's fiancée, Mary of Teck – it was the last arranged marriage for a member of the Royal Family, though by all accounts it was a happy one.

He reigned through some of the most turbulent times in British history: a constitutional crisis, the First World War, the Easter Rising and Irish independence, the General Strike, the first Labour government, the Great Depression and the formation of a National Government. Fortunately, through a mixture of dutifulness and constitutional propriety, he held on rather well.

George V, a deep-dyed Tory, was immediately confronted by the constitutional crisis – a legacy of his father promising a favour to the Liberals that had yet to be called in. George had little sympathy for the other side of the house, and little direct experience in dealing with politics. Edward VII's agreement to pack the House of Lords with Liberal peers had gone against his own Tory instincts and his belief in the hereditary principle, but he had died before he was called upon to do anything. After a discreet interval of a few weeks, the Liberal government introduced a Parliament Bill in a bid to prevent the Lords from vetoing future legislation, and called upon the new King to honour his late father's promise. George gave his confidential consent to the plan, led to believe that filling the Lords with Liberal peers was the only way to solve the current deadlock. He was misled, however, by his Liberal-leaning private secretary, Francis Knollys, who did not tell him the Tories were willing to form a government – and he wouldn't find out for another two years.

George was frugal in his habits, but he still complained of poverty. At the height of the 1931 economic crisis, he voluntarily reduced his £470,000 Civil List payment by £50,000 as a one-off gesture. He extended that – unilaterally – by reducing the Prince of Wales's annuity by £10,000 – news which the furious Prince received in a telephone call, whilst entertaining his mistress in a French nightclub.

A further election in December 1910 produced more deadlock. Rowdy Commons scenes ensued during the sweltering summer of 1911, especially when Asquith publicly told his Tory adversaries that the King was ready to appoint 249 Liberal peers. The Tories split between Hedgers – prepared to acquiesce – and Ditchers – determined to oppose to the end and die in the last ditch. The list of potential peers included Robert Baden-Powell, hero of Mafeking and founder of the Boy Scout movement, Thomas Hardy and J.M. Barrie, but finally they were not needed, as the controversial Parliament Bill was carried, by a mere 17 votes.

Westminster conflicts continued, though, with the Tories opposing Home Rule for Ireland, and coming close to inciting open insurrection amongst the British troops stationed there. Tensions rose as politics and longer-standing religious differences coalesced, and Ulster's Protestants armed themselves for a confrontation. Temporarily, however, affairs in Ireland were eclipsed by the bigger conflict in Europe. There, as well, it was about old promises being honoured: Britain fulfilling a long-standing commitment to Belgium's neutrality, and the alliance of Britain, France and Russia being invoked against Germany.

The King did his bit on the home front, wearing uniform throughout the war and constantly touring hospitals and factories. He also made regular visits to the Western Front to present medals (some 50,000 during the war), somewhat ostentatiously renounced alcohol and fine food for the duration, and his eldest sons served in the forces. The Prince of Wales was annoyed not to be allowed to serve in the front-line, but Albert, the second son (later George VI) served in the navy at the Battle of Jutland.

King George V knighting Major-General Manus W. O'Keefe at Bertangles château near Amiens, 12th August 1918

The conflict posed particular difficulties for George V and his family – their surname handed down from Prince Albert was Saxe-Coburg-Gotha, and they had scores of German relatives. In 1917, while British subjects with German surnames were being harassed, and even the Prime Minister Lloyd George mockingly referred to the King as 'my little German friend',

George V and his Private Secretary Lord Stamfordham decided to address the issue. They weighed up various alternatives, including Tudor, Stuart, York, Lancaster and Plantagenet, before settling on Windsor as the most patriotic. His cousin, the Kaiser, jeered that he was looking forward to a performance of 'The Merry Wives of Saxe-Coburg-Gotha', but in the climate of the time, it was a wise move for the monarchy.

Fresh dilemmas appeared that year as another cousin, Tsar Nicholas II, was deposed during the Russian Revolution. Initially George favoured giving the Romanov family sanctuary in Britain, provided that they could support themselves, but later, along with his government, he had second thoughts. The sight of the monarch offering welcome to a foreign autocrat was unlikely to be well received by the public, and with sympathy for the Bolshevik cause running strong in certain British cities and industries, it was feared that royal support for the Romanovs could turn that into something more determined. It also made no sense to lose Russia, even a newly-Bolshevik Russia, as an ally in the ongoing war. Preserving the British dynasty came first.

The long era of dynastic marriages between royal families was ending and in 1922, George's daughter Mary would marry a mere English aristocrat, Lord Lascelles. While monarchies crumbled all around Europe at the war's close, the British Royal Family endured, strengthened by a national sense of shared hardships, and the adroit deployment of the royal princes on official visits and royal tours. The charismatic Prince of Wales went across the empire to visit India, Australia and Canada, while his shy younger brother toured British factories.

Twice in the years after the war, the King was involved in advising on the choice of Prime Minister: decisions which did not override the consensus, or impose a choice which otherwise would not have been made, but pragmatically maintained the status quo. On the retirement of the mortally ill Tory, Bonar Law in 1923, there were two possible candidates: the aristocratic Lord Curzon and the stolidly middle-class, Worcestershire industrialist Stanley Baldwin. On his Private Secretary's advice, the King called for Baldwin – much to Curzon's chagrin – because the Prime Minister, by then, had to be in the Commons, and not be a peer.

A year later, the King summoned Ramsay MacDonald to form the first Labour government, and was mightily relieved when the new ministers arrived at the palace in morning suits, in accordance with tradition. They had been advised in advance that they could hire court dress from Moss Bros, 'a well-known and dependable firm.'

The King got on well with MacDonald and other members of the government, especially the Secretary of State for the Colonies, J.H. 'Jimmy' Thomas. In 1929, a risqué joke told by the Welsh former railwayman caused the King to laugh so hard that he burst the stitches in his chest from a recent operation. During the crisis following that year's Wall Street Crash, it was the King who personally cajoled MacDonald to stay on and lead the national coalition government with the Tories and Liberals, a decision which split the Labour Party.

As George's health declined in the 1930s, his public prestige was high. He was seen as unpretentious, and conspicuously conscientious in his duties. He appeared regularly in public, especially at sporting events – meeting test cricket teams at Lord's, presenting the F.A. Cup – visited factories and exhibitions and regularly featured in cinema newsreels. On Christmas Day 1932, he addressed the 'peoples of the Empire' on the radio, thus becoming the first monarch to be both widely seen *and* heard by his subjects, and inaugurating a seasonal tradition continued by his son and granddaughter. The initial broadcast was scripted by Rudyard Kipling, and the sheer wonder in the King's gruff and wheezy voice, as he pondered his words beaming to the remotest corners of the Empire – 'through one of the marvels of modern science' – was clearly authentic. At his Silver Jubilee in 1935, the summer before he died, he was surprised and touched by the size of the crowds cheering him in London: 'I am beginning to think they must like me for myself.'

The bronchitis he'd suffered for years led to severe breathing difficulties, and on 15th January 1935, he took to his bed at Sandringham, dying five days later. There may be no truth in the story that his parting words were 'Bugger Bognor!'; he'd spent time there in hope of alleviating his breathing problems with sea air, and his final royal deed was to grant the town its *Regis* ('of the king') suffix. His doctor Lord Dawson administered a cocktail of cocaine and morphine to him so that his heart would stop before midnight, and the sad news could be announced to the nation on the morning of 21st January by the respectable *Times*, rather than the less salubrious evening newspapers. A popular rhyme of the time went:

> *Greatest sorrow England ever had*
> *When death took away our dear Dad*
> *A king he was from head to sole*
> *Loved by his people one and all*

This familial imagery, the king as father to nation and Empire, would never have occurred to its citizens in earlier reigns, and must have been regarded with some detachment by the surviving five of his six children, to whom he seems to have been a notably stern parent.

King Edward VIII (January–December 1936)

> After I am dead, the boy will ruin himself within 12 months.
> George V, Letter to PM Stanley Baldwin, 1934

Just as George's father Edward VII had caused much anxiety to Prince Albert, the generational drama was repeated with the new heir to throne, known within the family by the last of his five forenames, David. He was not the first prince to rebel, nor was his father the first to doubt that his heir could do the job. But he was the first to abdicate.

Edward VIII was a popular, handsome, informal and raffish figure, still a bachelor in his early forties. He was the first monarch since Edward V, the Prince in the Tower, in 1483 to be proclaimed but not crowned. The public liked what they knew of the Prince of Wales, but it was not mutual; he'd complained to his mother back in 1925 that he was 'heartily sick of being cheered and yelled and shrieked at' by his subjects-to-be, echoing his father's dim view of himself by adding, 'I am quite the wrong person to be Prince of Wales.'

At the time he became King, he had been conducting an affair with an expatriate American divorcee named Wallis Simpson for the past two years, and she was now in the process of divorcing her compliant second husband. Edward had become besotted with her, showering her with expensive presents, taking her on a Mediterranean holiday and increasingly insistent on marriage. His publicly claimed concern for the poverty-stricken working class in the Depression – 'Something must be done,' he had said, visiting Welsh miners' homes in November 1936 – dissipated within days in the face of his infatuation.

Aware of the new King's personal shortcomings, and concerned about his forthright expression of views, Baldwin's government tried to end the relationship. At the time, Britain's press barons were deferential enough to keep the news from the British public, but the silence could not last. By the standards of the time, it was highly uncommon for anyone to be twice-divorced, let a potential Queen. And she was American: almost as outrageous, to some.

When, in December 1936, Britain finally read the news the rest of the world had known about for some time, Baldwin gave Edward a stark choice: leave Wallis or abdicate. To the government's private relief, he chose the latter, marrying the woman he loved, but remaining bitter ever afterwards that she'd been denied a royal title. Edward's defenestration happened so quickly and smoothly that his supporters, such as Winston Churchill, had no time to rally. The public received the news with shock and antipathy towards the King and his lover, which intensified the following year, when he and Wallis made an ill-advised, seemingly enthusiastic visit to Adolf Hitler. Edward

During his 12-day tour with Wallis in October 1937, the Duke of Windsor inspects SS troops at the elite training centre of Ordensburg–Krössinsee

spent most of the remaining 36 years of his life in idle but comfortable exile, mainly in Paris, after serving as governor of the Bahamas during the war.

This was the eve of World War Two, yet there was a whiff of bygone centuries about the affair: a king banished, effectively for going against the teachings of the Church – but with an elected government now wielding the power to bless or damn. Sir Ronald Lindsay, the British Ambassador to Washington, echoed the theme, in discussing the predicament of the next in line, Edward's brother George (aka 'Bertie'): 'He is like the medieval monarch who has a hated rival claimant living in exile.' He was bound to feel 'uneasiness as to what is coming next, sensitiveness, suspicion.'

King George VI (1936–1952)

George VI was a plain, straightforward, though sometimes in private, tempestuous man who was fortunate in his years of kingship, his life intimately intertwined with his subjects' experience of war and suffering. He did his duty without fuss, when national circumstances required his subjects to do the same.

ODNB

George was indeed uneasy: the shy, awkward, stammering younger brother of Edward was so unprepared for the duty suddenly thrust upon him that, when he learned the news of the abdication, he burst into tears.

Even so, George intended that his first royal act as King would be conferring the title of Duke of Windsor upon his brother: a conciliatory gesture which would allow him to be called 'Your Highness'. In the end, this would not take place until May 1937, relations between the brothers – and between

Edward and the rest of the family – having quickly soured over money and the new King's refusal to grant a royal title to Wallace. George was harassed by sometimes daily telephone calls from his brother, and at one point he was threatened with prosecution if he visited Edward's home at Balmoral Castle.

Edward's visit to Nazi Germany had done nothing to diminish his enthusiasm for the country and its leader: he was a supporter of appeasement and convinced that Hitler was a man of peace. In May 1939, he expressed these sentiments in a speech for American radio. With Europe plainly sliding towards another war, his words sounded like treachery to many, and the BBC refused to broadcast them. If George was embarrassed by his wayward brother, he was at least spared the knowledge that the Führer planned to install him as a puppet king if there should be a successful invasion.

The abdication did not ultimately shake the monarchy – it was over too quickly for that – but it shocked the Royal Family. It abjured everything their duty told them: a voluntary turning of the back on public service, on the dynasty and on the Church of England, a selfish dereliction of responsibility. On top of that, Edward knew how little his brother craved the limelight, making his abdication a fraternal betrayal as well as a constitutional one. But if Edward lost the affection of kin and nation, that only made George seem like the better man for the job.

Many in the court and government thought otherwise at first; some even wondered whether George was intellectually robust enough, though his shortcomings, such as a painful stammer, evoked public sympathy rather than censure. But at least he was happily married to a scion of the Scottish aristocracy and they had two daughters of their own – unlike his brother. An aura of ordinariness hung over him and his family, taking bike rides together through Windsor Great Park, with an obliging pause for the cameras. The same went for his pre-war youth camps, where working-class lads mingled with public schoolboys, whilst George self-consciously led renditions of 'Under the Spreading Chestnut Tree', complete with gestures.

The Royal Family stroll on the estate at Sandringham, in 1942

In 1938, when Prime Minister Neville Chamberlain returned from Munich with his ultimately meaningless assurances from Hitler, the King invited him to make a public appearance on the palace balcony. This was a clear breach of the monarchy's political neutrality, but even so, there was little condemnation; people either agreed with him, or felt his error was benign. Privately, the King favoured the appeasing Lord Halifax to succeed Chamberlain in 1940: 'I was disappointed as I thought (him) the obvious man,' he wrote, but he accepted advice, and sent for Winston Churchill when Halifax declined the post. Churchill had been one of Edward VIII's most vocal supporters in the abdication crisis – he had even been shouted down in the Commons – so George was bound to view him with caution. But the new Prime Minister responded with ostentatious loyalty to the Crown, allaying the King's fears.

The war gave the Royal Family a demonstrable sense of purpose, sharing in the people's struggle. The King and Churchill met weekly and came to appreciate each other's strengths: the monarch's stoicism and the politician's spirit. The King ensured that he and his family stayed visible to the people throughout the war, often making unannounced visits to boost morale immediately after bombing raids.

Buckingham Palace was itself bombed nine times, enabling the Queen famously to say, after the first occasion in September 1940, 'Now we can look the East End in the face' when visiting victims of the Blitz. When it was suggested they seek refuge in one of the dominions, the Queen replied stoutly, 'The children won't leave without me. I won't leave without the King. And the King will never leave.' *

This was a family affair, enlisting the Queen and Princesses – 'us four', in their father's words – in the war effort. Princess Elizabeth joined the ATS (Auxiliary Territorial Service) at 18; like her parents and sister, she carried a ration card and clothing coupons (though in recognition of their public roles, royals received rather more than others). The King's lugubrious and

---

* They did have the option of retreating to Windsor Castle when the bombing of the capital grew too intense, although according to the Princesses' nanny, Marion Crawford, sleeping in the 11th-century, bug-infested dungeons during air raids was far from comfortable. It has been speculated that the Castle was spared Luftwaffe bombs because Hitler had it in mind as a future residence; it was probably just chance.

halting radio broadcasts nurtured the image of national togetherness in the face of adversity: 'I wonder if we realise just how precious the spirit of friendliness and kindness is,' he mused to his nationwide audience.

George's shyness meant he struggled with the similarly taciturn Clement Attlee as post-war Prime Minister, and he was privately dismayed by the Labour Government's nationalisation programme, though he did not criticise it publicly. Attlee, for his part, never challenged the monarchy's constitutional status or sought to reduce its authority.

As the empire started to slip away, the King's focus was on creating the Commonwealth: India and Pakistan gained independence in 1947, Burma (Myanmar) and Ceylon (Sri Lanka) the next year, and in 1949 Ireland finally sloughed off its dominion status to become a republic. There were plans for more foreign tours post-war, but after one trip to South Africa in 1947, the King's declining health intervened.

George contracted lung cancer as a result of lifelong, heavy smoking. A secret operation to remove one of his lungs at Buckingham Palace in September 1951 failed to halt his decline and five months later, in February 1952, King George VI died in his sleep at Sandringham. A few days previously, he had waved his elder daughter Elizabeth off on a tour of Australia and New Zealand that he'd been scheduled to make himself.

The news of his death caught the British public by surprise: people had not been informed of the seriousness of the King's illness (nor had the King) and there was a widespread outbreak of grief, along with appreciation for a man who'd worn himself out through service to them during the war.

Queen Elizabeth II (1952–)

> The British monarchy doesn't depend entirely on glamour, as the long, long reign of Queen Elizabeth II continues to demonstrate. Her unflinching dutifulness and reliability have conferred something beyond charm upon the institution, associating it with stoicism and a certain integrity.
>
> Christopher Hitchens, *Slate*, 2011

Though unexpected, the accession of the young Princess – aged 25, already married to Prince Philip of Greece and with two young children – was immediately welcomed. It was a fresh spring breeze after wartime sacrifices and the grey hardship of the post-war years, and in the era of the baby boom, her status as a young mother of children struck a chord with many. Queen Elizabeth II was dutiful and serious like her father. On her 21st birthday in 1947, she had declared to her future subjects – in terms penned by her father's Private Secretary, 'Tommy' Lascelles (or, according to some sources, the journalist Dermot Morrah) – that her life, 'whether it be long or short shall be devoted to your service and the service of our great Imperial family to which we all belong.'

Lascelles, whom she inherited along with the throne, was sixty-five, her first Prime Minister was Winston Churchill, fast approaching his eightieth year. She was surrounded by old men and a drab court, hidebound by outmoded conventions. Debutantes – eligible young women of wealthy or aristocratic background – were still presented at court each summer and divorcees were excluded from the Royal Enclosure at Ascot. When Princess Margaret, the Queen's younger sister, wished to marry her father's former equerry, Group Captain Peter Townsend, she not only needed her sister's permission, but was also warned off her choice, partly because he was divorced. Faced with losing her royal title and allowance, she bowed to pressure, but the ending of the relationship caused her lasting unhappiness.

THE QUEEN IS CROWNED

In the early years of the reign, the main innovation was the decision to televise the Coronation, a step which had been fiercely contested by the elderly Churchill, although the broadcast proved a huge success and was shown all over the world. The service at Westminster Abbey was a strictly Anglican affair and the central part – the anointing with sacred oil – was not filmed, out of deference to its sanctity.

Initially, the Palace's media operation was all but nonexistent, and uncoincidentally, by the late 1950s, criticism of the royals' wealth and outdated ways, even of the Queen herself, was beginning to seep through the deference surrounding the institution. As changes in society were breaking down conventions and attitudes in the 1960s, the Royal Family conceded that more openness was needed to satisfy public curiosity. This was largely at the initiative of the Duke of Edinburgh, fulfilling a similar role to that of an earlier consort, Prince Albert, a century before: to blow away some cobwebs.

Two more sons appeared in 1960 and 1964. Princes Andrew and Edward were the first children born to a reigning British monarch for more than a century. Meanwhile their elder brother Charles rose to eligibility, and after his 20th birthday in 1969, he was invested as Prince of Wales at Caernarfon Castle, in a largely made-for-television ceremony. For the first time a Prince of Wales actually tried to speak Welsh. At Philip's initiative, the family also opened up to the public, albeit in a circumscribed and stilted way, via a one-off television documentary about their domestic lives, which was widely viewed at the time.

The success of the walkabout at events during the Silver Jubilee celebrations in 1977 led to its becoming an established practice: a way of creating, for the cheering crowds and the tv audience, the illusion of informal access to the Royal Family.

An informal mother-and-son moment following Prince Charles's investiture.

Far less successful, as it turned out, were the marriages of the Queen's children, particularly that of Prince Charles to Lady Diana Spencer in July 1981. Apart from producing the heir and a spare to ensure the succession, the fairy tale wedding degenerated into a sour soap opera, whose concluding story-lines involved sex tapes, tell-all television interviews, divorce and finally catastrophe, when Diana was killed in a car crash whilst being driven through Paris pursued by paparazzi in August 1997.

The intense and authentic outpouring of grief from a

shocked public briefly unnerved the Queen, whose adherence to stiff royal protocols (and grandmotherly sensitivities in staying at Balmoral to be with her teenaged grandsons) was not felt adequate to the occasion by a censorious tabloid media. As in Queen Victoria's reign, an absent monarch (even a grieving one) could swiftly be perceived as uncaring. The criticism was swiftly muted, however, by the Queen's live broadcast, publicly mourning the death of her estranged former daughter-in-law. It was not something her predecessors would ever have considered, even if the technology had been available.

Charles, Diana, Marriage and the Media

Princess Diana was much younger and less experienced than her husband, and she also, to his resentment, proved more charismatic, glamorous and artlessly charming than him. The claustrophobia and protocol of court life frustrated her, and although she was an able manipulator, the relentless intrusiveness of the modern media was destabilising.

Ultimately, though, the marriage foundered on a mixture of expectations and clashing personalities. Charles needed a wife, and Diana came from entirely suitable aristocratic stock. Unlike many couples of the 1980s, they only discovered how very different they were after marrying, and the myth of the Royal Fairytale made it hard to go back on their choices. That chimera had been promoted and fostered by the royals and their advisers, and hyped in the media. The whirlwind of scrutiny was inevitably reaped in disillusionment, divorce and the subsequent squalid death of the Princess.

Previous royals had experienced press fascination with their private affairs, but that had been largely controllable, with only national newspapers and compliant owners to square. The modern age offers an ever-widening range of worldwide media, fewer ties of loyalty, a total absence of hiding places and less deference. Even with their much-expanded media staff, modern royals have struggled to maintain the 'magic' that Walter Bagehot had said was so essential to their endurance.

When the time came for Charles and Diana's eldest son, Prince William to marry, there were no strategic reasons informing his choice. Catherine (Kate) Middleton came from a background that previous royals (and their advisers) would never have thought suitable. She is the daughter of a wealthy, middle-class Berkshire businessman and a former airline stewardess, with Northumbrian coal miners in her not-too distant ancestry. Unlike most of her predecessors, however, and in step with what much of the population now sees as the 'normal' life-path, she knew and had cohabited with her future husband at university, over a number of years. The pair had had sufficient experience of one another to know they were compatible; by contrast, Charles and Diana barely knew each other they married. William's younger brother Harry has also married a woman from outside the old circles: Meghan Markle is an American actress of mixed race heritage, daughter of a television lighting director and a social worker who, like Prince Harry's parents, divorced when their children were small. The couple could have served as a welcome shot in the arm for the royal brand, but their decision to withdraw to the USA has been an undeniable blow to the modern monarchy. They are currently making a career in the media, detouring occasionally to aim barbs at other royal family members, though not the Queen herself, in interviews and statements.

In November 1992, an accident of fate – a fire at Windsor

Castle – contributed to what the Queen described in a speech at the Guildhall as her *'annus horribilis'*, a year encompassing three Royal divorces. It also saw the end of the family's fiercely guarded exemption from income tax. The Palace maintained that the tax had been under discussion before the fire, but the timing of this announcement suggested otherwise. John Major's Tory government had just confirmed that the state – that is, its recession-hit tax-payers – would pay for repairs to the 100-odd rooms damaged in the Windsor fire. Public criticism had followed swiftly, and the monarch, as so often in the past, was obliged to cede privileges and make concessions. For centuries, our kings and queens have stood in an awkward relationship to their subjects: cloaked in ceremony and symbols of power, they are obliged to live a different, grander life to their subjects, who must pay for them to do so ('They want the gilding for their money,' as Walter Bagehot put it in 1867). As a result, they are vulnerable to resentment over their lifestyles and complaints that they don't do enough (or anything) for their money. This has been the case ever since the barons protested about King John.

The Royal Family can balance upon this tightrope, provided they are visible – and visibly fulfilling public duties – but crucially, not transgressing certain public proprieties. Any sense of entitlement is fatal. Prince Andrew, the Queen's once-popular second son, discovered this in 2019, when his association with the New York financier Jeffrey Epstein came fully to public attention after the latter's suicide in prison, while awaiting trial for sexual abuse and trafficking of teenaged girls.

The Prince, once considered a Falklands war hero by the press and public, had already acquired a new, less respectful tabloid title from 2001. That was when the former navy pilot began his new job as Special Representative for International Trade and Investment, in the course of which his taxpayer-funded globe-trotting, along with a penchant for taking private jets or helicopters when mere trains might suffice, earned him the nickname 'Airmiles Andy'. Ironically, it was when the Royal Family first attempted to prove their value for money – by publishing their annual expenses from 2002 onwards – that Prince Andrew's extravagance was revealed.

Andrew's friendship with Epstein was a prime cause of his downfall, but it was merely one in a long series of questionable associations, from dictators to soft porn stars. There was even a photograph, showing him with his arm around a teenaged girl who would later become one of Epstein's accusers. A public explanation was required and it was upon this, ultimately, that the Duke of York's ship foundered. In an interview on the BBC's 'Newsnight' programme, he came across as arrogant, out of touch and unapologetic. Days later, he stepped down from all public duties and severed his connection with many of the charities and institutions of which he'd been patron: the very abnegation of the royal role. But then, he had abnegated it already – since the reign of Aethelred, royals have accepted censure and performed acts of penance.

Early in her reign, the Queen had a tendency to defer to, and to be manipulated by her elderly Prime Ministers. Having resigned due to ill health in 1963, Harold Macmillan advised her – unconstitutionally, since he was no longer her minister – to appoint a Scottish aristocrat, the 14th Earl of Home, as his successor. The Earl, an earnest and pleasant throwback to a former age, who was most at home on his estate with his dogs, duly renounced his peerage, won election to the Commons as Sir Alec Douglas Home – and very nearly won the following year's general election.

In September 2019, it was different: Prime Minister Boris Johnson advised (or persuaded) the Queen to consent to an early and extended shutdown – or prorogation – of Parliament, in order to cut short MPs' scrutiny of the Brexit Bill. The Queen was required to accept his advice: a refusal would have embroiled the monarchy in partisan politics. As it was, Johnson's move backfired: the Supreme Court ruled that his advice had been illegal, and all blame landed on him.

Whatever her political leanings, the Queen's discretion over her views has scarcely wavered. When it has, those rare comments have focussed on an ancient trouble-spot for monarchs: the Union. In 1977, the year of both her Silver Jubilee and a heated public debate about Scottish independence, she said meaningfully: 'I cannot forget that I was crowned queen of the United Kingdom...' Under similar circumstances, shortly before the Scottish referendum in 2014, she advised that her subjects 'think very carefully about the future.' Both comments were opaque, and neither of them breached protocol, though her meaning was clear. If anything, they demonstrated how discreet she has always been on matters affecting the United Kingdom. The institution's strength over the last century has been its public passivity. As Bagehot wrote 150 years ago:

> The nation is divided into parties, but the Crown is of no party. Its apparent separation from business is that which removes it both from enmities and from desecration, which preserves its mystery, which enables it to combine the affection of conflicting parties – to be a visible symbol of unity to those still so imperfectly educated as to need a symbol... we have come to believe it is natural to have a virtuous sovereign.

The longer a monarch reigns, the more permanent they seem. As happened under George III and Victoria, respect for the Queen has grown as she has aged. Her Golden Jubilee in

2002 was celebrated with enthusiasm, tinged with sympathy, since it came a few weeks after the deaths of both her sister and her mother. Ten years later, the Queen and 90-year-old Prince Philip stood stoically through freezing temperatures in pouring rain, as a river pageant on the Thames marked her Diamond Jubilee.

In the summer of the same year, as part of the opening ceremonies of the London 2012 Olympics, she starred alongside James Bond actor Daniel Craig (and her corgis) in a sketch filmed inside Buckingham Palace, demanding that 'Mr Bond' fly her to the venue. An estimated billion people watched as a helicopter duly arrived over the packed arena and a pair of convincing body-doubles parachuted out; moments later, the real Queen made her entrance, to great applause. A modern spectacle, and yet time-honoured, too – monarchs have always known the importance of national pageantry and performance, and of their roles in it.

On 9th September 2015, Elizabeth II outlasted Queen Victoria's tenure to become the longest-reigning British monarch. Entering her nineties the following year, she still continued the practice of seven decades, attending to her daily delivery of 'red boxes' – official documents from the Government – every morning, meeting her Prime Minister each week (now on her 14th, four of the last five born during her reign) greeting ambassadors and attending some, though not all, investitures. The number of her official visits has been scaled back, increasingly handed over to her sons and grandson. Prince Philip formally retired from official engagements in 2017, but she soldiered on through the Covid-19 pandemic of 2020.

She bore with stoicism the loss of her beloved husband Prince Philip in April 2021, two months short of his hundredth birthday, and resumed her public duties that summer. Even at the age of 95, abdication was not contemplated so long as she remained in good health.

'We *are* amused': the Queen shares a giggle with Prince Philip during a review of the Grenadier Guards' Queen's Company at Windsor, in 2003.

The actions of her Uncle Edward VIII in 1936 amounted to a family trauma; ever since, 'abdication' has been something of a dirty word in royal circles. The Queen's sense of duty is inextricably linked to her faith. In a secular age, she is as devout as any of her predecessors and more so than many of them. For her, the pledge of service and the ritual anointing with oil at the coronation had a central, personal importance. They amounted, in her view, to a binding contract between herself and God.

Like almost all of her predecessors, the Queen has understood that she needed, in her own words, to be seen to be believed. Just as William the Conqueror lifted his helmet at Hastings, Queen Elizabeth I made stately progresses around the country and Edward VII opened hospitals, Elizabeth II has made ceaseless tours of Britain and the Commonwealth ever since acceding to the throne in 1952, and only began reducing her workload in her mid-nineties.

Monarchs who do *not* allow some daylight in on magic do not long survive. Or, as Queen Victoria's last Prime Minister Lord Salisbury asserted in a *Saturday Review* article 150 years ago: 'Seclusion is one of the few luxuries in which Royal Personages may not indulge... loyalty needs a life of almost unintermitted publicity to sustain it.' Uncomfortable and intrusive though this is, it is the price the monarchy has chosen to pay for its popularity and endurance. Some have understood that better than others; Prince Harry and his wife Meghan have yet to grasp that their celebrity and public utility is based largely upon his royal status.

In 1963, the former U.S. Secretary of State Dean Acheson famously said that Great Britain had lost an empire but not yet found a role. The British monarchy could be said to have lost an empire and then found a role – one it shows no signs of relinquishing.

EPILOGUE

While the Queen reigns, the British public have shown no sign of wishing for an alternative head of state. In a YouGov Poll in 2020, only 22% of respondents expressed a preference for a republic. The Interregnum, just over a decade of the 17th century, remains the only period in 1,500 years without a monarch.

Even in the 21st century, the British monarchy is the best-known in the world. This is partly because of Queen Elizabeth II's global significance: Head of State of 15 independent countries and head of the 54 countries of the Commonwealth; she stands in some symbolic relationship to about a third of the world's population. Remarkably, even in countries with no connection to the monarchy, there is a keen interest. Modern media has converted the British Royal Family into global celebrities.

Most monarchies have shrivelled, borne down by extravagance, autocratic and authoritarian style, an inability to adapt to change, to defeats or to natural or economic catastrophes. In the West, several European countries retain their monarchies, but they play a less prominent role in their citizens' lives.

The key to success was adaptation, acceptance of change. Monarchy has survived in Britain because it has evolved pragmatically and, not always or willingly, reached compromise with those forces challenging it, from the Vikings, the Church and the regional barons in the 10th and 11th centuries, to the press barons and the public in the 20th and 21st.

The process began in the 13th century, with the enforcement of a legal code applicable to all, including the monarch, and the calling of Parliaments. In the 16th century, a close and symbiotic relationship developed between the Crown and the national religion and the next century saw monarchs accepting limits on their power and the ending of divine right. In the 19th and 20th centuries, Parliament and ministers took over the running of the state, and an ever-widening proportion of the population was given the right to choose them in free elections.

Over the centuries, monarchs have played their part, (some) with tact, reserve, caution and pragmatism. However they have done it, they have passed the power that was once theirs in one principal direction: towards Parliament. For it was this institution which came to replace the regional barons and the Church as the principal power-sharer, pragmatically absorbing merchants, aldermen and lawyers, and latterly university lecturers, trades unionists, political advisers and even journalists into the political establishment.

There was a built-in tension from the start, since the first Parliaments in a modern sense were imposed upon kings. At the same time, those monarchs who could manage them were able to raise taxes to fund their needs and ambitions.

As they passed power to elected governments, monarchs lost control over the purse-strings. They had to account for their expenditure and justify their military campaigns; their extravagance was kept, more or less, in check.

This also meant the royal court could never become a rival to the government or Parliament. From the 18th century onwards, Britain's monarchs were usually unable to choose their Prime Ministers or Ministers, or to amend or rescind the laws they passed.

All these changes came alongside the growth of an increasingly ubiquitous, curious and sometimes outspoken media, informing, influencing and inflaming public opinion. The media have given monarchs new ways to be seen and heard, not just by their subjects, but by the whole world. This has enhanced the visibility and status of successive monarchs, but it carries a heavy price. Their families are part of the package, subject to the same obligations and expectations, and to the same condemnation if they get things wrong. Private ceremonies have become global news events, and monarchs have had to learn further rules for speaking and appearing publicly. Private lives have become public property. And how much magic is left, in the full glare of the studio lights?

Queen Elizabeth II has been the long-running exception: dutiful, serious-minded, discreet and non-partisan. Her executive scope is limited; she has accepted it as such, and made further concessions. Meanwhile, she has fulfilled the first duty recognised by all her predecessors since the Dark Ages: the succession of her heirs and the preservation of the dynasty. That is the contract.

So far, it works. Whilst accepting monarchs from Denmark, France, Wales, Scotland, Germany and Holland, the British have only once tried another way and never seriously considered it again since 1660. Nor has there been an alternative leader suitably charismatic and with sufficient unifying appeal to take the monarchy's place. At her Platinum Jubilee celebrations in June 2022 the Queen, now 96, appeared on the Buckingham Palace balcony to acknowledge the cheers of the vast crowd in the Mall with her three potential successors: her son, who will one day become Charles III, his son the future William V and his son, eventually George VII. If they are similarly long lived and the monarchy remains popular – according to opinion polls, somewhere between two thirds and three quarters of the population still support the institution – the House of Windsor should be secure into the 22nd century. But only time will tell.

Onwards and upwards: three generations of Windsors watch the RAF flypast from the Palace balcony in June 2022

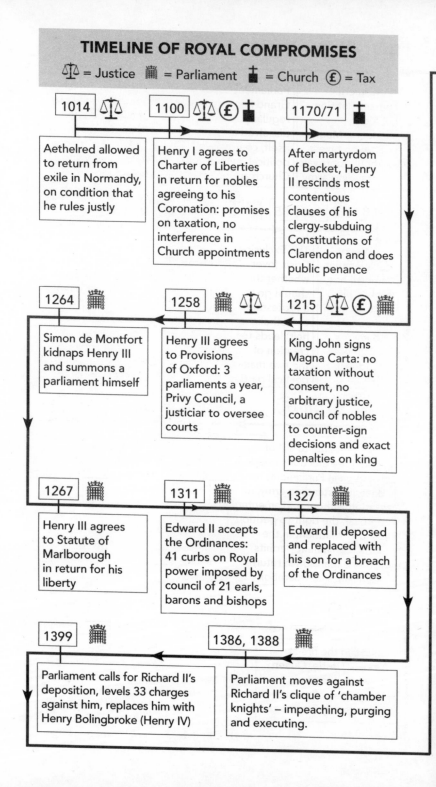

TIMELINE OF ROYAL COMPROMISES

⚖ = Justice   🏛 = Parliament   ✝ = Church   (£) = Tax

1014 ⚖

Aethelred allowed to return from exile in Normandy, on condition that he rules justly

1100 ⚖ (£) ✝

Henry I agrees to Charter of Liberties in return for nobles agreeing to his Coronation: promises on taxation, no interference in Church appointments

1170/71 ✝

After martyrdom of Becket, Henry II rescinds most contentious clauses of his clergy-subduing Constitutions of Clarendon and does public penance

1264 🏛

Simon de Montfort kidnaps Henry III and summons a parliament himself

1258 🏛 ⚖

Henry III agrees to Provisions of Oxford: 3 parliaments a year, Privy Council, a justiciar to oversee courts

1215 ⚖ (£) 🏛

King John signs Magna Carta: no taxation without consent, no arbitrary justice, council of nobles to counter-sign decisions and exact penalties on king

1267 🏛

Henry III agrees to Statute of Marlborough in return for his liberty

1311 🏛

Edward II accepts the Ordinances: 41 curbs on Royal power imposed by council of 21 earls, barons and bishops

1327 🏛

Edward II deposed and replaced with his son for a breach of the Ordinances

1399 🏛

Parliament calls for Richard II's deposition, levels 33 charges against him, replaces him with Henry Bolingbroke (Henry IV)

1386, 1388 🏛

Parliament moves against Richard II's clique of 'chamber knights' – impeaching, purging and executing.

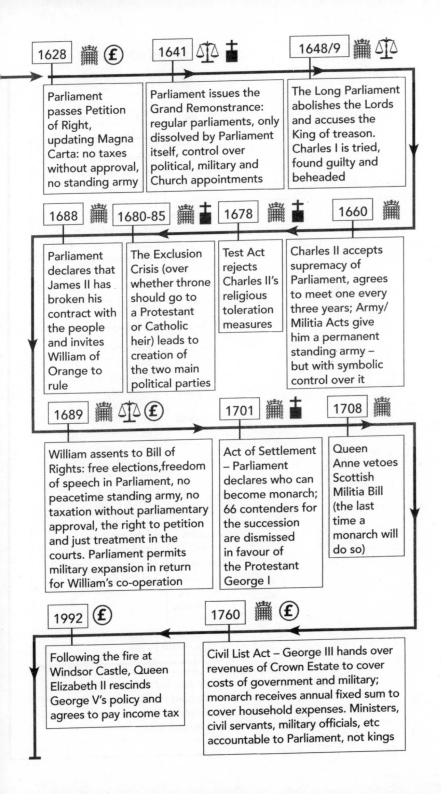

1628 — Parliament passes Petition of Right, updating Magna Carta: no taxes without approval, no standing army

1641 — Parliament issues the Grand Remonstrance: regular parliaments, only dissolved by Parliament itself, control over political, military and Church appointments

1648/9 — The Long Parliament abolishes the Lords and accuses the King of treason. Charles I is tried, found guilty and beheaded

1688 — Parliament declares that James II has broken his contract with the people and invites William of Orange to rule

1680-85 — The Exclusion Crisis (over whether throne should go to a Protestant or Catholic heir) leads to creation of the two main political parties

1678 — Test Act rejects Charles II's religious toleration measures

1660 — Charles II accepts supremacy of Parliament, agrees to meet one every three years; Army/Militia Acts give him a permanent standing army – but with symbolic control over it

1689 — William assents to Bill of Rights: free elections, freedom of speech in Parliament, no peacetime standing army, no taxation without parliamentary approval, the right to petition and just treatment in the courts. Parliament permits military expansion in return for William's co-operation

1701 — Act of Settlement – Parliament declares who can become monarch; 66 contenders for the succession are dismissed in favour of the Protestant George I

1708 — Queen Anne vetoes Scottish Militia Bill (the last time a monarch will do so)

1992 — Following the fire at Windsor Castle, Queen Elizabeth II rescinds George V's policy and agrees to pay income tax

1760 — Civil List Act – George III hands over revenues of Crown Estate to cover costs of government and military; monarch receives annual fixed sum to cover household expenses. Ministers, civil servants, military officials, etc accountable to Parliament, not kings

Image Credits

Introduction
Jubilympics mug, 2012, private collection
Queen Anne curing the young Samuel Johnson by touch. *Cassell's Illustrated History of England*, Vol. IV. 1865 (www.archive.org)

Chapter One
Sutton Hoo helmet, on display at the British Museum. Wiki Commons, own work, user: Geni, 2015
King Alfred burns the cakes. *Pictures of English History*, Joseph Martin Kronheim, 1868
King Athelstan presents a bible to St Cuthbert. Frontispiece from ca. 930 edition of Bede's *Life of St Cuthbert*, ca. 699-705. ©Alamy.
Portrait of King Aethelred 'the Unready', from the *Chronicle of Abingdon*, ca. 1220
Canute rebukes his courtiers, in *Famous Men of the Middle Ages*, by John Henry Haaren, 1904. ©Alamy
'Hic est Wilhelm Dux' (Here is Duke William), panel 55 of the Bayeux Tapestry. Wiki Commons, own work, user: Myrabella, 2007
'Dieu et mon droit', motto first used by Richard I in 1198. Public Domain

Chapter Two
Queen Elizabeth I visits Lord Hunsdon in 1600(?), engraving by George Vertue, 1742. Wellcome Images/Wellcome Trust, http://catalogue.wellcomelibrary.org/record=b1570462
The Exchequer Cloth in use in Ireland in *A Calendar of the Contents of the Red Book of the Irish Exchequer*, by James Frederick Ferguson, 1854. www.archive.org
Beckett pilgrim badge. ©Alamy
Enamel effigy on the tomb of Geoffrey of Anjou, ca. 1151, originally at Le Mans cathedral. Photograph, uploaded to Wiki Commons 2006
Death of Simon de Montfort at Evesham, from British Library Cotton MS Nero D ii, f. 177, Chronicle of Rochester Cathedral Priory (late 13th century)
Battle of Crécy, illustration from Jean Froissart's *Chronicles*, Chapter 129, 15th century. Bibliothèque Nationale de France, FR2643, f.165v
Edward III's effigy at Westminster Abbey. ©Alamy
Death of Wat Tyler, from 1881 facsimile of Froissart's *Chronicles*, www.archive.org
The Princes in the tower, illustration in *The Story of the Greatest Nations*, by E.S. Ellis and C.F. Horne, 1913. www.archive.org
Richard III, engraving by John Chapman, 1799. Welsh Portrait Collection/National Library of Wales, Public Domain
Crest of Henry VII, inc. the dragon of Cadwalladr, from whom Henry claimed descent, and the greyhound of Richmond, heraldic symbol of his father. Public Domain

Chapter Three
Depiction of Catherine of Aragon as Mary Magdalene, by Robert Sittow, late 15th/early 16th c. Detroit Institute of Arts, Public Domain

Portrait of Henry III by Hans Holbein the Younger, 1536-7. Walker Art Gallery WAG 1350/Google Arts & Culture asset ID eAHC0d0WiemXSA.

Illustration of unknown date depicting Mother Shipton and the downfall of Wolsey, reproduced as the frontispiece in *Mother Shipton Investigated: the result of critical examination in the British Museum library of the literature relating to the Yorkshire sibyl* by William Henry Harrison, 1881. www.archive.org

'Devise for the succession', written by Edward VI himself (probably in January 1553, then revised in June or July of that year). In Petyt MS 538 Vol. 4, f.317, a collection of State letters and papers in the Inner Temple Library

Detail from the burning of Thomas Cranmer 'in the diche at Oxford'; Cranmer thrusts his right hand into the flames because it had earlier been used to a sign a statement recanting his Protestant beliefs. Engraving by Wenceslaus Hollar in *Foxe's Book of Martyrs*, 1563. Atla Digital Library

The Ditchley Portrait of Queen Elizabeth I, painted by Marcus Gheeraerts the Younger, 1592; commissioned by Sir Henry Lee to mark the Queen's visit to his house at Ditchley, in Oxfordshire. ©Alamy

Queen Elizabeth's Guest Chamber, 44 High Street, Canterbury. (Listed Building number 1260873) Wiki Commons, own work, user: Whn64, 2013

Detail from the Marian Hangings, created by Mary, Queen of Scots and Bess of Hardwick, 1569-1584

The Defeat of the Armada, line engraving by Willem van de Passe in *A Thankfull Remembrance of God's Mercy*, by George Carleton, 1624. www.archive.org

Chapter Four

Apotheosis of James I, engraving by Simon Gribelin II, after Peter Paul Rubens. Met Museum, New York City: The Elisha Whittelsey Collection, The Elisha Whittelsey Fund, 1951. Accession Number: 51.501.7615. Public Domain

Charles I in three positions, by Anthony van Dyck, 1635-1636. Royal Collection/Google Arts & Culture asset ID: BQHR9te2WWtyOA.

Contemporary German woodcut depicting the execution of Charles I, 1649. Wiki Commons via British Library, General Reference Collection Crach.1.Tab.4.c.1.(18.) UIN: BLL01000009485

The Devils Patriarck, anti-Catholic pamphlet by Titus Oates, published in London in 1683. www.archive.org

'Welcome to London', broadside ballad,1688. Bodleian Library Ballads online: Pepys Ballads II: 255

Chapter Five

The South Sea Scheme, engraving by William Hogarth, 1721. Met Museum of Art/www.archive.org

'Bonnie' Prince Charles Edward Stuart (aged 45), painted by Hugh Douglas Hamilton ca. 1785. Wiki Commons via National Galleries of Scotland Accession No. PG622, ID 3855

'Temperance enjoying a frugal meal', cartoon by James Gillray in *The Works of James Gillray from the Original Plates, with the addition of many subjects not before collected*, 1851. National Library of India/www.archive.org

Still photograph from the 1993 production of Alan Bennett's stageplay 'The Madness of George III' at the National Theatre. ©Donald Cooper/Photostage/Alamy

'Royalty in a rage or Family quarrels', cartoon by Robert Cruickshank (see 'I.R.C. fecit' signature in bottom left corner) published in London in 1820. Wiki Commons via US Library of Congress: British Cartoon Prints Collection

A sovereign of William IV, 1832, engraver William Whyon.WikiCommons/ Newman Numismatic Portal

Chapter Six

Family portrait of Queen Victoria, Prince Albert and their nine children at Osborne House, 1857. Photographer: Leonora Caldesini. ©Alamy/Granger Historical Picture Archive

The first photograph of a news event: a daguerreotype of the Great Chartists' Rally, Kennington Common, 10th April 1848. Photographer: William Edward Kilburn. ©Pictorial Press/Alamy

Engagement photograph of Albert Edward, the Prince of Wales and Princess Alexandra of Denmark, 1862. ©Heritage Image Partnership/Alamy

Attempt on the life of the Queen by Roderick Maclean, 2nd March 1882. 'From a sketch supplied by Mr Burnside, Photographer'. *Illustrated London News*, Saturday 11th March 1882. Issue No. 2236, Vol LXXX www.archive.org

The Prince of Wales and entourage at Giza in 1862. Photographer: Francis Bedford. ©Archive Farms Inc/Alamy

King Edward VII at Biarritz in 1907. ©Granger Historical Picture Archive/Alamy

George V knighting Major-General Manus O'Keeffe at Bertangles château, France, 12th August 1918. Photographer: David McLellan for the Ministry of Information First World War Official Collection. Item Q9840 of the Imperial War Museum Collection. Public Domain.

The Duke of Windsor inspects SS troops in Germany, October 1937. German Federal Archive Accession No. 102-17964. Public Domain.

A Royal family stroll on the Windsor estate, 30th September 1942 ©PA/Alamy

The Queen is crowned at Westminster Abbey, 2nd June 1953 ©Chronicle/Alamy

HRH Prince Charles with his mother Queen Elizabeth II at his investiture as Prince Wales, Caernarfon Castle, 1st July 1969 ©Keystone Pictures USA/Alamy

Queen Elizabeth II and Prince Philip at The Queens Company Review at Windsor Castle, 15th April 2003. Photographer: Chris Young. ©PA/Alamy.

Epilogue

Stamp celebrating Queen Elizabeth II's 60th birthday in 1986 (21st April), showing images of her aged two in 1928, aged 16 in 1942, and 26 in 1952. Designed by Jeffrey Matthews. ©Alamy

The Queen, along with members of the Royal Family, watches a flypast by the Royal Air Force from Buckingham Palace balcony following the Trooping the Colour parade, as a part of her Platinum Jubilee celebrations, in London, 2nd June 2022 ©Paul Grover/Pool via REUTERS/Alamy